Hiding In Plain Sight

Sight

The False Doctrines of Seventh-day Adventism

Volume I

Elce-Junior Lauriston

Contact Address: elcelauriston@gmail.com

Facebook Handle: E J Thunder Lauriston

YouTube Channel Handle: E J "Thunder" Lauriston

Unless otherwise indicated, all Scripture quotations are from The ESV (The Holy Bible, English Standard Version®), copyright ©2001 by Crossway, a publishing ministry of Good News Publishers. Used by permission. All rights reserved.

Cover design: Zion McGregor

Editor: William Hohmann

Published by Elce-Junior Lauriston
Montego Bay, Jamaica, W.I.
1-876-352-2644

Table of Contents

About the Author (4)

Dedications (6)

Acknowledgements (7)

What Others Think About Volume I (8)

Preface (15)

Foreword (17)

Introduction (19)

Part I

Chapter One: A Brief History of the Roots of Seventh-day Adventism and Its Theological Framework **(22)**

Chapter Two: Ellen G. White: The Adventist Prophetess and Her Role in Their Doctrines and Denominational Life **(33)**

Part II

Chapter Three: The Investigative Judgement: Salvational Uncertainty, Biblical Heresy **(57)**

Chapter Four: The Biblical Gospel vs. the Investigative Judgement **(67)**

Chapter Five: Let's Move God's Throne! **(74)**

Chapter Six: Is God Investigating Every Name to Determine Who is Worthy of Salvation? **(77)**

Chapter Seven: God Has Forgiven and Blotted Out Our Sins **(82)**

Chapter Eight: Can Believers Know That They Are Saved Right Now? **(90)**

Part III

Chapter Nine: Eleven Faulty Hermeneutical Principles and Assumptions of Seventh-day Adventists and How to Refute Them **(96)**

Part IV

Chapter Ten: Michael the Archangel: Is He Jesus Christ or Just An Archangel? **(214)**

Chapter Eleven: Michael the Archangel is Jesus Christ in Adventism: The Implications for Jesus' Deity **(226)**

Chapter Twelve: Jesus is not Michael the Archangel: A Biblical Survey **(240)**

Chapter Thirteen: Dem Goats: Who Is Our Scapegoat, Satan or Jesus? **(253)**

Part V

Chapter Fourteen: Will The Sinlessly Perfect Seventh-day Adventist Please

Stand Up! **(273)**

Chapter Fifteen: A Refutation of the Adventist Myth of Sinless Perfectionism **(284)**

Part VI

Chapter Sixteen: What is the Adventist Health Message All About? **(292)**

Chapter Seventeen: A Biblical Survey of the Levitical Dietary Laws and Refutations of the Adventist Assumptions and Arguments **(303)**

Conclusion (332)

About the Author

Elce-Junior Lauriston was born on Isle de la Tortue (Turtle Island), Haiti. He grew up in Grand Bahama, the Bahamas, and currently resides in Jamaica, along with his wife Kahmal Williams-Lauriston, son Kah-El, and daughter Kah-Liyah. He was a prominent Seventh-day Adventist evangelist in Jamaica and the Cayman Islands, and also a theology student, training to become an ordained pastor in the SDA Church.

In his 3rd academic year of studies (September 2015) in the School of Religion and Theology at Northern Caribbean University (NCU), the Seventh-day Adventist flagship institution in Jamaica, he began to discover fatal flaws in the Adventist belief system and its core tenets as a result of his study of Biblical Hermeneutics and New Testament Greek. Lauriston discovered that these beliefs could not withstand intensive biblical and historical scrutiny.

Additionally, he discovered that SDA Church leaders and the professors at the university could not provide credible answers to his penetrating questions. This situation made it increasingly difficult for him to continue to believe in and teach the Church's doctrines, and therefore within six months of these discoveries, he withdrew from NCU and from Adventism altogether, along with his wife.

He is now an anti-Sabbatarian/anti-SDA apologist, a Christian apologist, Bible teacher, and sought-after speaker. He has been the main Bible teacher and facilitator for Oasis ministry from August

2016. He is the author of *All Foods Are Clean and Every Day is the Sabbath* (2017); co-author of *Lying for God: What Adventists Knew and When They Knew It*; *Freedom in Jesus, Freedom from Legalism: A Contextual and Exegetical Exposition of Colossians 2* (2017); and *The Sabbath: What You Need To Know: 16 Propositions Against Mandatory and Salvational Sabbath-Keeping* (2019). He is a member of the Hampden United Church, in Hampden, Trelawny, Jamaica. He holds a Bachelor of Theology degree from the Bethel Bible College of the Caribbean- Jamaica (2020).

Dedications

These volumes are dedicated to the Urban Apologetics community (UA). You saw the need for a work of this calibre and requested that I write it. It is a pleasure for me to have been considered qualified for this job. May it serve its purpose in the Urban Apologetics community and in the wider Body of Christ.

I also want to specially dedicate these volumes to Questioning and Former Adventists. I know very well the pain and agony, the anger, betrayal and frustration that initially come with finding out that you have been brainwashed, lied to, manipulated, and made to believe so many erroneous things that are simply biblically indefensible. I know the feeling of binge reading and watching endless resources trying to figure everything out. I know the feeling of wondering "now what" after discovering the lies and unorthodox theology and doctrines of Adventism. These volumes were written with you in mind. I hope that they will be handy resources that reveal the erroneous and unbiblical doctrines of Adventism, and the assumptions and argumentations they use so often to push their false views. But more importantly, you will appreciate the Christian responses and refutations that I have provided for them. Make good use of these volumes because they will arm you with the biblical and historical facts that will affirm your position in questioning and eventually leaving the false doctrines of Adventism.

To my fellow Former Adventists, your leaving Adventism for Christ and the Gospel is superbly commendable. Many of you have lost jobs, families, friends, social networks, pensions, a close-knit culture and community, and so much more. You have taken the hard road to sacrifice all of those things for the sake of the Gospel. I commend you. Continue to do what you can to let your voice be heard. Continue to expose the errors of a system that robs Adventists of so many spiritual and social blessings, and seeks to suck unsuspecting Christians into stifling legalism and unorthodoxy. You endure slander, disrespect, calumny, attacks, and countless other things from Adventists because you dare to expose and challenge the false narratives and doctrines that once held you bound. May God continue to strengthen you in this struggle to get the facts out there to warn unsuspecting Christians, and also to help Adventists see the light of the Gospel and biblical

Christianity. Your efforts, endurance, and contributions are not in vain. Keep up the good work: God will reward you greatly.

Acknowledgements

When I embarked on the journey of writing this book, I initially had in mind to write a short exposé on the false doctrines of Seventh-day Adventism. As I solicited feedback and input about what SDA doctrines to write about, in communications with Marc Brianvil, he constantly insisted that I write a thick, definitive work. I hesitated to be persuaded because a voluminous work would mean countless gruelling hours of researching, reading, documenting, and writing. I was not up to that initially. But as we communicated more and I began the project, the information got to be so much that I had to give in to the idea. I am glad I did. Thank you Marc.

As the single book got too long, I became concerned about the readers and the wisdom of having a single volume packed with so much information. The average person would have found it daunting, but thanks to the wise counsel and guidance of Zion McGregor, one book has turned into three, easily readable volumes. In addition to this, Zion has selflessly helped make these volumes a reality by liaising, managing, and directing in so many aspects, not to mention the beautiful covers he has designed. God bless you brother. I appreciate you.

Without the selflessness, keenness, and proficient editorial skills of William Hohmann, these volumes would not be what they are. Thank you Bill. Special thanks to Rev. Tyran Laws, Sheryle Hughes, and Enid Prasad for their engagement with the first draft of this manuscript and the critical comments, editorial suggestions, and the encouragement they gave. Pastors Colin Bailey and Karim Williams are great friends of mine and Former SDAs, who are anti-Sabbatarian/anti-SDA apologists as well. They were among the first set of persons to read the rough draft manuscript and gave me critical feedback. Thank you brothers.

A special thank you to my Oasis ministry family: Joan Hutcheson, Sam Brown, Helen Richards, Gwen Sumlin, Elaine Darity, Madeline and Warren Sanders, Vonyia Hutcheson, et. al., for their encouragement and support throughout this project.

When I began this project, my wife and children knew that they would have to bear with me as I put in the necessary work and hours to put these volumes together. For the ten months that I was producing them, they were very supportive, understanding, helpful, and caring despite the fact that sometimes they would be deprived of my time and attention, because I was so enrapt with the intricacies of writing. Thank you for being my rock and so understanding. I love you all.

What Others Think About Volume I

"It is with incredible respect for this scrupulous work and the brilliant theologizing and apologetics of the author that I highly recommend **Hiding in Plain Sight: The False Doctrines of Seventh-day Adventism Vol. I** to absolutely every believer! It is high time that the global Christian community become aware of the true nature and teachings of Seventh-day Adventism and its prophetess Ellen G. White, and to finally recognize, as many Christian leaders and apologists have been so reluctant to do in the past, that this movement is indeed a cult, a bastion of heresy and heterodoxy, disguised as a Christian denomination.

Elce-Junior Lauriston, in a very perspicuous manner, has presented one of the hardest hitting and most devastating apologetic blows to SDA theology than any non-formal text currently available. His contrasts of SDA theology with the biblical Gospel not only equip believers to soundly refute the many false doctrines of SDAs, but they also help to deepen the believer's understanding and appreciation for the finished work of Christ on the Cross and the assurance that we have of eternal life through faith in Jesus the Messiah. You'll walk away with a profound thankfulness for the grace of God and knowledge of New Testament theology, along with an ex-insider's expertise of what Seventh-day Adventists actually believe! May God use this insightful book to lead millions of SDAs into the knowledge of the truth, gospel clarity, and salvation!"- **Damon Richardson, PhD candidate, founder of *UrbanLogia Ministries*, Georgia, USA; author of "The Nation of Islam" in *Urban Apologetics: Restoring Black Dignity With The Gospel* (2021).**

"One who learns a foreign language via classes in school or by watching video presentations may become familiar with the words spoken by a certain people group, perhaps even fluently, but if they do not learn the cultural nuances, mores, and mindset which make that culture unique, all the learning is limited; something gets lost in translation! In **Hiding in Plain Sight**, E.-J. "Thunder" Lauriston pulls back the curtain and gives us a well-researched, no-holds-barred look at key Seventh-day Adventist doctrines and faithfully translates them for the proverbial "foreigners" in the larger Christian community, revealing vital information the Body needs to know. Highly recommended reading for anyone wanting to clearly understand Seventh-day Adventism and compare the organizational tenets against the Gospel of Jesus Christ." - **Colin Bailey, Assoc. Pastor,** *Faith Life Church*, **Dayton, Ohio, USA.**

"A superbly written book fulfilling its cover title **Hiding In Plain Sight: The False Doctrines of Seventh-day Adventism**. Pastor Elce-Junior "Thunder" Lauriston effectively exposes exceptional specifics of Adventism, which would normally be overlooked. This book is very elaborately written yet comprehensible to any casual reader. Citing various credible sources and references, together with this volume being a well-written and informative read, Pastor Elce equips the reader with a plethora of details and proper exegesis that eliminates confusion concerning the substance of numerous Adventist doctrinal statements and views, and the deceptive manner in which they are portrayed. I highly recommend this gem of a book to every objective person seeking actuality and clarity."- **Enid Prasad,** *Former Seventh-day Adventist*, **Fiji.**

"For centuries there has been an ongoing battle for preaching the one true gospel that we've been given. Paul in his letter to Galatia wrote that if anyone preaches another Gospel; let him be anathema. Cursed to the highest degree possible. Galatianism, or as some call it "the Galatian heresy," is what Paul was refuting: Obeying Mosaic laws as a means to be right with God. The Seventh-day Adventist Church is nothing more than a resurfacing of the same errors of law-keeping. Even more dangerous, Satan's participation in man's justification in their theology.

As one who was a leading evangelist and apologist in the organization, Elce, through the power of the Gospel, carefully surveys the history of the Seventh-day Adventist Church. From the baseless interpretations of Scripture from their inception, to how God's character and identity have been distorted, Elce covers every area of their false doctrines with gloveless punches of Gospel truths with the intent that readers will see the value and power of the Gospel. If the letter to the Galatians included a three-volume set— volume one is in your hand. As the angel in Rev. 10:9 told John, so I tell you, "Take it and eat it; it will make your stomach bitter, but in your mouth, it will be sweet as honey.""- **Greg Johnson, Music Director,** *Northview Christian Church***, Dothan, Alabama, USA.**

"There are times in history when God, in His divine wisdom, allows persons to ascend to the height of that which is false to make them a champion of deconstructing those errors with truth. The work of Elce- Junior Lauriston, culminating in his latest book, **Hiding in Plain Sight: The False Doctrines of Seventh-day Adventism,** is such! The author, in incredible, meticulous, God-gifted skill, walks us through the cunning shadows of Adventist errors into the light of biblical truth. This is a must read and resource for every believer!"- **Bishop-Elect Eugene J. Bell,** *The Master's Table Christian Fellowship***, Elizabeth, New Jersey, USA.**

"This is a great, eye-opening read! Elce-Junior "Thunder" Lauriston has written a comprehensive, thoroughly sourced volume that takes an honest look at the history, heterodoxy, cultic doctrines, and culture of the Seventh-day Adventist Church, along with its prophetess Ellen G. White. This volume should be required reading for all who are trapped in the intricate web of Adventism, those who are looking for real answers to their cognitive dissonance, and those desiring true rest and freedom in Our Lord Jesus."- **Stephen Baxter,** *Former Seventh-day Adventist***, Virginia, USA.**

"Elce-Junior "Thunder" Lauriston has dug deep to provide us with a detailed investigation into the true nature of Seventh-day Adventist doctrines, along with their genesis and histories. He also proves, without a doubt, that Ellen White is a critical figure in all that Adventists believe. She cannot be separated from their ideologies and dogmas. In this volume, he has turned his piercing, analytical lens upon many of the critical and foundational doctrines of this denomination, giving those within Adventism an opportunity to examine them fully and clearly, and those outside of Adventism answers when faced with questions and challenges posed by SDA members. As with his previous written and spoken works, Mr. Lauriston does not disappoint, but continues to edify Christianity by living up to the mandate of Titus 1:9."- **Sheryle Hughes, BSN, MABC, Director of *Hearts Restored Ministries*, Biblical Counsellor, Great Granddaughter of SDA Pastor William Edward Atkin, who was on the Voice of Prophecy alongside H.M.S. Richards, Sr.**

"**Hiding in Plain Sight** is a scathing, well-researched polemic on Seventh-day Adventism. Thunder leaves no room for doubt that the SDA religion is biblically unsound and stands on the dangerously faulty foundation of Ellen White and her teachings. Prepare to be shocked, engrossed, and most importantly, well-equipped to help rescue those in bondage to this great deception. A most necessary apologetics resource."- **Richelle Bryan, M.A. in Christian Apologetics (Biola University), *Apologetics in the City*, NYC, USA.**

"Good theology matters! The importance of this book cannot be overstated. Thunder has done a tremendous job highlighting troublesome doctrines of the Seventh-day Adventist Church. For me, none is more troubling than the Investigative Judgment. This is the doctrine that caused me to leave Adventism and to fully embrace the Gospel of Jesus Christ. Volume I is a treasure for those seeking a better understanding of the theological and doctrinal ins and outs of the Adventist Church. I'm grateful to call the author my brother, and this is another resource that he has produced to help aid believers through their murky doctrines."- **Minister Karim Williams, Assoc. Pastor, *Gilcrease Hills Baptist Church*, Tulsa, Ok, USA.**

"This book is an awesome tool for evangelism in the arena of Adventism. With a local Seventh-day Adventist Church only a short distance away from my home, it was always presented to me as an orthodox Christian church that just took their dietary habits a little more seriously than the average Christian. However, reading just a few pages of this book shattered many of my misconceptions of this religious sect. E.-J. does an outstanding job at highlighting the errors in the ideology of Ellen White and the Seventh-day Adventist Church. Most importantly, he unmasks the doctrines that are in direct opposition to the gospel of Jesus Christ. This book is a game changer!"- **Miss Tytus, YouTuber and Urban Apologist,** *Miss Tytus2*, **USA.**

"In some way, shape, or form all heresies demote Jesus from His eternal kingship and dilute His glory. They just vary on how they do it. Another commonality in non-historical, unbiblical perspectives that attempt to operate under the banner of Christianity is their attempt to place some prophet or founder at their helm, which further diminishes the divinity and uniqueness of Christ. Seventh-day Adventism is no different. With pointed clarity and through exhaustive research, E.-J. Lauriston successfully outlines the glaring discrepancies, inconsistencies, and heretical statements rife in the teachings and writings of Ellen G. White, with whom Adventism refuses to part ways. This book ensures that the falsehoods in SDA doctrines can no longer hide in plain sight." - **Pastor Alex McElroy, M.A. in Apologetics,** *Proof For The Truth Ministries*, **Chicago, IL, USA.**

"**Hiding in Plain Sight** is a riveting reminder of our need for sound biblical instruction in order to dismantle heretical teaching and false doctrine. With surgical-like precision, Elce-Junior Lauriston utilizes Holy Scripture to present a sound apologetic defense against the false doctrines of Seventh-day Adventism. After reading this initial volume, the reader will walk away with a clear understanding of how blindly following cultish leaders leads to establishing a denomination that is built on deceptions that are hiding in plain sight. Congratulations to this Man of God for his unwavering courage to confront the denominational doctrines he once faithfully supported, in an effort to bring truth to light. We pray that God will allow this volume to find its way into the hands of those who have been blindly following the teachings of SDA, only to be awakened to the opportunity for a brand new start." - **Bishop Kevin L. Betton Sr., DMin, PhD,** *Cathedral of Praise Church Ministry, Inc.*, **Hinesville, Georgia, USA.**

"The SDA movement is an often misunderstood and overlooked threat to the propagation of the true gospel of Jesus Christ. E.-J. Lauriston has written a much needed work that not only exposes the ugly historical realities of how the movement initially emerged and developed, but also brings clarity to its glaring theological missteps. From page to page I found myself immersed in this accessible yet rigorous critique of a movement that is leading millions astray. This book is a game changer!"- **Adam Coleman, founder of *Tru-ID Apologetics Ministries*, Richmond, VA, USA; author of "Black Atheism" in *Urban Apologetics: Restoring Black Dignity With The Gospel* (2021).**

"Hiding in Plain Sight: The False Doctrines of Seventh-day Adventism Vol. I is a phenomenal defense of the Christian faith against the teachings of the Seventh-day Adventist Church's doctrines. This is the first book that I've read on this subject that provides this level of historical information, the theological framework, and the specific doctrinal details that are problematic in the SDA movement. As a former member of the SDA Church, Elce-Junior Lauriston provides a unique inside look into the intricacies of the movement. Lauriston leaves no stone unturned as he provides the history of the movement, its growth and development, and details about its co-founder Ellen G. White.

I gained a tremendous amount of information and knowledge from this book. Chapters 3-8 were absolutely mind-blowing, as Lauriston dealt with how the doctrine of the Investigative Judgement developed and why it is a serious biblical heresy. The uncertainty of salvation and fear that the Investigative Judgement generates should be enough to cause SDA supporters to question this movement. It is unthinkable to believe that there are believers who will ultimately be rejected after this investigation by Christ. Thank God that Lauriston articulates clearly what the true biblical gospel is in refutation of this erroneous teaching. Chapters 10-12 amazingly deal with the SDA belief that Jesus Christ is Michael the Archangel, and what the implications of those teachings are for the deity of Christ. You definitely want to read these chapters thoroughly. This book is a complete work in the true essence of the word.

Additionally, Lauriston doesn't just expose us to the false teachings of the SDA movement, he also provides very detailed biblical methods on how these false doctrines should be refuted. He shares sound biblical hermeneutics that will help the reader refute the SDA doctrines, arguments, and assumptions. His expositions will also assist in the spiritual development of believers as well, as we value approaching the Scriptures properly and in their contexts. This book needs to be a part of every believer's library. Before learning of Elce-Junior Lauriston, I personally did not understand the dangerous nature of the SDA teachings. The title of this book is spot on, as the SDA adherents can easily go undetected if we have not been exposed to the details and implications of their doctrines. I truly thank God for Lauriston and his commitment to truth, and his desire to allow God to use him to rescue others from the heretical SDA movement."- **Elder Michael Holloway, founder of *Your Urban Church Apologetic Ministries*, Detroit, MI, USA.**

Preface

The months of August to October 2020 were eventful times for the Urban Apologetics community. One who was very loved, admired, and respected was discovered to be a Seventh-day Adventist. Her social media pseudonym is Neffer Nitty. She was a powerhouse apologist against Hebrew Israelites, the Hoteps, and the Conscious Community. When it was discovered that she was an SDA, having skilfully hidden this information for years, that did not sit well with the fellow apologists of the UA. Several of the leaders spoke with her, Dr Eric Mason, Pastor Damon Richardson, Adam Coleman, et. al., and sought to show her the errors of SDA theology and views, but she was not to be persuaded. She obstinately declined to be held accountable and challenged by presenting her views before a panel of the UA and subsequently be questioned or shown the doctrinal errors.

Eventually, I was brought in to respond to her written responses to specific questions that were asked to her. After a few weeks of vain attempts at having formal dialogue, her rejecting the biblical Gospel, accusing us of not understanding what SDAs believe and teach, and refusing to be held accountable to anyone, the UA had no choice but to officially part ways with her. We did a formal video where I presented several key issues and differences between Neffer's SDA faith with the Gospel and historical Christianity.

Even before cutting ties with her, as she began to see where everything was leading, she began to be very public with her prior well-hidden SDA faith in publishing memes and making Facebook posts that revealed that she is a staunch, fanatical SDA. She also began to make video presentations with popular, very conservative, and staunch SDA pastor Ivor Myers, Evangelist Dwayne Lemon, and several others. I did a few video responses to them. But Neffer Nitty still continued with her dismissive attitude, intransigence, and accusations that me and Pastor Colin Bailey (who also was drawn into the fray) do not know SDA doctrine and cannot be trusted to accurately express what they believe because we are ex Adventists. Despite her attitude and accusations, the more videos she and her cohorts produced, the more they were showing that we did accurately represent SDA doctrines and that they are indeed unorthodox and some flatly heretical.

About a week after my video responses to Pastor Ivor Myers, Dwayne Lemon, and Neffer Nitty, a few persons from the UA suggested that the videos be archived for future use or that I write a brief book on the false doctrines of Adventism. After getting some ideas of what specifics they would want me to cover, I began writing. I had thought to produce a small volume on the false doctrines of Adventism, but as I studied, researched, acquired resources, and dug deeper into the doctrines, arguments, and assumptions, I realized that a small volume would not suffice. What was supposed to have been a very small volume has turned out to be three volumes.

In these volumes, I cover all the major false doctrines, arguments, assumptions, proof-texts, and theological views of Seventh-day Adventism. These volumes are written in such a way that scholars and academics, pastors and leaders, Christian apologists, Questioning and Former SDAs, the wider Body of Christ, and any inquisitive researcher will benefit greatly from them. SDA lingo, subconscious views, doublespeak, and alternate definitions of biblical terms are explained, their popular proof-texts to support their doctrines are highlighted and contextually examined, and statements and quotes expressing what they believe are sourced from some of the most authoritative sources among them. After reading these volumes, it is my hope that you would have gotten a thorough grasp, if necessary, of SDA theology, but more importantly that you would have been sufficiently equipped to reject and refute them.

Foreword

About a year ago, information was disclosed to the Urban Apologetic community (UA) about one of its, now former members, which shocked us to the core. One of the UA's most prominent and stalwart apologists was confirmed to be a member of the Seventh-day Adventist community. Admittedly, this was, initially, more confusing than alarming, due in part to the general ignorance of the UA community to the intricacies of SDA doctrines. For most of us (not all), our "critique" of the SDA community had been superficial, relegating their beliefs about the Sabbath and dietary laws to something analogous to "Christian preference," much like how many Christians view worship styles. And perhaps it is our former ignorance of the intricacies of SDA beliefs and the former UA member who holds them that demonstrate a quintessential example of the author's thesis "**Hiding in Plain Sight**." If this type of "infiltration" could occur among the emerging authorities of the Black church community, then the average layperson would undoubtedly be vulnerable to its delusion, which raises a question, "Why didn't we see it before?"

The short answer is, you don't see what you don't know. For example, one's lack of knowledge about Renaissance artists' proclivity to insert "hidden" details in their work (often their names) might make it difficult to look for Rembrandt's name and year ensigned at the top of the wall (in the painting) and the capital R (for Rembrandt) painted to look like a belly button in his work "The Anatomy Lesson of Dr. Nicholaes Tulp." Similarly, one would not know to look for the "hidden" doctrines of a religion, if there is no knowledge that such doctrines exist in the first place.

Still, a more precise answer to "why we didn't see it before" is the lack of recognizing a key hermeneutic of cults and cult-like groups, which is to focus on content (i.e., interpretation of scripture), while obfuscating the system in which they understand that content. In this way, they often use similar language, similar texts, and similar interpretive principles as we do to make their points. However, the points that they make are integral to a system of thought that is foreign and often antithetical to the system of Christian orthodoxy. Thus, they can speak of "obedience to Christ," which all Christians affirm, but unbeknownst to us link that "obedience to Christ" to a larger system, (i.e., the Investigative Judgment), which is, at its core, a work-based orientation of salvation. It is precisely in this vein that groups like the SDAs "hide in plain sight."

Therefore, we need resources that can not only address specific content-oriented questions but disclose the methodological strategies that these groups are using. Thus, on the one hand, we need a resource that can exegetically defend why the king "looking over" the dinner guest in the Parable of the Wedding Feast (Matt 22:1–14), or God coming down "to see" in Gen. 18 is not legitimation of the SDA's doctrine of the "Investigative Judgement," lest their interpretations win out by default. On the other hand, we need a resource that arms the reader against the methodology and the "endgame" of the SDAs, especially given the fact that a major part of their doctrines are eschatological, in the sense that one needs to understand SDA's "true" beliefs from the vantage point of their eschatology. Thankfully, Elce-Junior Lauriston has provided such a resource for the church in his massive and extensive three-volume work.

I am not only drawn to this book as a pastor and urban apologetics author, but as an academic. Elce-Junior "Thunder" Lauriston, only holds a Bachelors in Theology but shows a lot of promise as an emerging thinker. Some of his treatment on Sabbath issues, I have found to be noteworthy challenges to presumptions held by even some scholars. There is no doubt in my mind that a decade from now the author will have solidified his standing in academic circles so that no scholarly treatment of the SDA will be considered complete without first engaging Lauriston as a formidable interlocutor.

If you decide to keep reading, your experience as a reader will be comparable to the audience member to whom the secrets of the magician's greatest tricks were shown: it is an eye-opener. Get your highlighter ready and your pencil or pen in hand as you prepare to see what was "**Hiding in Plain Sight**."
Rev. Tyran T. Laws, PhD candidate (Wheaton College); co-

author of an urban apologetics book, *The Round Table: A Christians Conversation With Marginal Beliefs Affecting the Black Church Experience* (2016).

Introduction

The Seventh-day Adventist Church is a well-known denomination with respected organizations, universities, schools, hospitals, charities, parachurch and independent ministries all over the world. It boasts a worldwide membership of roughly 18-20 million adherents. In countries around the world, Adventists are in almost every sector of society. Some have even risen to key and top leadership positions ranging from presidents, governor-generals, prime ministers, and other stately and prestigious offices. They have TV and radio stations, social media pages, websites, and other high-tech electronic mass communication channels.

Adventists generally blend in well with the wider public wherever they live. They don't have any overtly weird and crazy practices and rituals as other groups may have. They are generally law-abiding citizens, business owners, teachers, lawyers, and anything else they want to be or what they can afford to do. They are typically known for their church-going on Saturday in most parts of the world and their abstinence from pork, shellfish, alcohol, and wearing jewelry.

But is this all there is to Seventh-day Adventism? In some parts of the world, some Adventists present themselves to be very ecumenical. But do they really believe the same things that most Christians generally believe about the Bible, Jesus Christ, salvation, justification, the Christian church, and other Christian doctrines and themes? Underneath all of the Evangelical verbiage and texts, what do Adventists really believe about Jesus, salvation, the Sabbath, the dietary laws, jewelry and cosmetics, Sunday worship, the Bible, the atonement, Protestant Christians, Roman Catholicism, themselves, the nature of man, and a host of other Christian themes and issues?

If you want to go deeper and truly know what they believe about these issues and themes, you have the right resource in your hands. In these volumes, **Hiding in Plain Sight: The False Doctrines of Seventh-day Adventism**, you will be shocked to discover that Adventists are not regular, Evangelical Christians as they appear to be. Seventh-day Adventism is a perfectly disguised cult with a lot of false doctrines that diminish Jesus Christ, Scripture, the atonement, New Covenant faith, God's grace, and the Gospel, while it elevates Satan, Ellen White, works for salvation, and salvational uncertainty. It also legalistically makes a lot of things salvational that Scripture teaches are not salvific. You will come to understand why Adventists speak of Roman Catholicism and Protestant Christianity the way they do, and why they are inimical to the wider Christian church. You will get to understand why they are so averse to Sunday worship, generally have no assurance of salvation, and why so many of their doctrines and interpretations of Scripture are so unorthodox.

Having been an SDA for 10 years, a leading conference evangelist, and a top theology student before my departure from Adventism in 2016, and having debated, discussed, and reasoned with Adventists from probably every spectrum of Adventism, and of course being thoroughly versed in their literature, I am more than proficient in the doctrines, beliefs, assumptions, and views of Adventists to write about them. It is my hope that you will find these volumes good, go-to resources on Seventh-day Adventism. May they be a blessing to you, not only to prevent you from being sucked into their false doctrines but also to equip you to refute them when they confront you.

Seventh-day Adventism constantly challenges the Christian faith, established from the 1st century A.D., and seeks to supplant it with its newly-devised 1844 faith. Therefore, I take the exhortation of Jude 3 very seriously in these volumes as I expose and refute their false doctrines, and also defend the historical Christian faith. Jude exhorts, "Beloved, although I was very eager to write to you about our common salvation, I found it necessary to write appealing to you to contend for the faith that was once for all delivered to the saints." I must contend for the faith: I must equip you to contend for it.

To the Glory of God,
Elce-Junior Lauriston, B.Th.
Montego Bay, Jamaica, W.I.
August 2021

Part I

SDA History

SDA Authority

Ellen G. White

Theological Framework

Chapter One

A Brief History Of The Roots Of Seventh-day Adventism And Its Theological Framework

"Seventh-day Adventism was born out of widespread fanaticism, biblical illiteracy, bitter disappointments, questionable visions, and stubborn irrationality."

The genesis of Seventh-day Adventism

Seventh-day Adventism was born in 19th century North America at a time known as the Second Great Awakening. This period in North American history was marked with much religious fervour and fanaticism, the rise of many cult groups, and a general expectation of the "end of the world" and life as they knew it. There were prophets of every description and ilk, each one trying to 'out-prophet' the other. There are several notable North American groups and churches that arose during this same time period, and several of them were within a 200 mile radius. The Church of Jesus Christ of Latter-Day Saints (Mormons), Jehovah's Witnesses, the Advent Christian Church, Church of Christ (Scientist), among others, saw their genesis from this time period.[1]

These churches are often referred to as Restorationist Movements because they are all of the view that Christianity had been in full or

---

[1] Arthur and Teresa Beem, *It's Okay Not To Be A Seventh-day Adventist* (North Charleston, SC: BookSurge Publishing, 2008), p. 21-29.

partial apostasy from the death of the apostles of Jesus Christ up to the 1800s, when their specific sect was born. They believe that God specifically raised up their church to be the "end time" church to "restore" Christianity. Because of this, they all have an exclusivist mindset and eschatology, and view their individual churches as being the "true church" for the Last Days. So, Mormons see themselves as the "latter-day saints"; Adventists think they are the "remnant church of Bible prophecy"; Jehovah's Witnesses believe that they are the "true religion"; while Christian Science sees itself as existing to "reinstate primitive Christianity and its lost element of healing."[2] The Seventh-day Adventist Church finds its beginning within this milieu. Seventh-day Adventism was born out of widespread fanaticism, biblical illiteracy, bitter disappointments, questionable visions, and stubborn irrationality.

It all started with a Baptist preacher named William Miller. After reading Daniel 8:14 that said, "Unto two thousand three hundred days, then shall the sanctuary be cleansed" (KJV) and using the popular and spurious "one day for a year" interpretation of Bible prophecy, William Miller was convinced that Jesus Christ was returning in the year 1843. He calculated it to be that date because it was believed that 457 B.C. was the time when Darius' decree to restore and rebuild Jerusalem was issued (Dan. 9:25). Miller would go on to invent fifteen bizarre proofs of prophetic interpretation that all supposedly led to the culmination of that 2,300 days prophecy in 1843.[3] Miller believed that the "cleansing of the sanctuary" meant that the earth would be destroyed by fire at the Second Coming of Jesus Christ.

Miller's preaching gained traction and many people began to follow him in anticipation of the imminent Second Coming of Jesus. Many people left their churches to join the Millerite Movement.

---

[2] Mary Baker Eddy, *Manual of the Mother Church* (Boston: The First Church of Christ, Scientist, 1908), p. 17.

[3] Robert K. Sanders, *William Miller and his 15 Proofs*, http://www.truthorfables.com/Miller's_Time%2520_Proved_15_Ways.htm (Accessed Nov. 2, 2020).

Ministers who pointed out to Miller and his followers that their date-setting was wrong according to Matthew 24:36 were accused of not loving Jesus and the Second Coming and basically lacked faith. The original timeframe that Miller and his followers had set for the Second Coming was March 21, 1843 to March 21, 1844. March 1843 came and went and Jesus did not return. Miller and his followers realized that they had forgotten to not count the "zero year" when they transitioned from B.C. to A.D., so they recalculated and this time Jesus was coming in the Spring of 1844—for sure this time.

Spring passed and Jesus still did not return. Disillusioned and disappointed for the second time, they went back to the drawing board and based on calculations for the Jewish Day of Atonement of that year that occurs on the tenth day of the seventh month, Samuel S. Snow worked out October 22, 1844 as the antitypical fulfilment of the Day of Atonement and the Second Coming. The Millerites were absolutely sure that Jesus would come on October 22, 1844. They stressed the Day of Atonement and seventh month so much so that they were called "the seventh month movement." Whereas before they only had a specific timeframe for Jesus to come, now they had worked out the Second Coming to the specific day.

The Great Disappointment and Advent pandemonium

As the Millerites anticipated to be ushered into Glory within months and knowing the specific day, countless of them neglected their fields. Some did not plant anything because they would be in heaven before they could have harvested anything. Many sold their homes, farms, and possessions because they would no longer need those things. Crops that were ripe for harvesting were left to rot in the fields, as the time for Jesus to return drew near. Some quit their jobs and others rejected job offers.[4] Of course they were warned, jeered, and ridiculed but these kinds of behaviours often strengthen people in their fanaticism rather than serve to awaken their common sense and rationality. Many well-intentioned Christian ministers refuted Miller's date-setting and wisely admonished their members not to get sucked into the fervour, but most of these ministers were accused of

---

[4] Beem, *It's Okay Not To Be A Seventh-day Adventist*, p. 36-37.

being indifferent, of being false shepherds who did not love Jesus nor wanted Him to return, and their warnings were ignored.[5] Some had to even expel some members from their congregations for disorderly conduct, insubordination, and fanaticism. Ellen G. Harmon (later White) and her family suffered such a fate.[6]

October 21, 1844 was an intense day for the Millerites. Their long-awaited Jesus was one day away. He would return to earth in a matter of hours and rescue them from this earth, cleanse it, and vindicate their faith and preaching. Many of them had made "ascension robes" for themselves and their little ones to be ushered into the presence of Jesus. Adventists continue to vehemently deny that their predecessors made and wore ascension robes,[7] but the historical facts confirm that they did. *Academy Apologia* has a video presentation on YouTube titled "Defeating Adventism #20 – Seventh-day Adventists and Ascension Robes" in which the presenter provides many historical records and newspaper articles from Massachusetts, Maine, Maryland, Pennsylvania, New York, Louisiana, Vermont, Kentucky, Alabama, and Michigan that confirm that they made and wore ascension robes in anticipation of Jesus' return.[8] Many had climbed up high rocks, mountains, rooftops, and higher grounds looking up for Jesus to burst the eastern sky and rapture His children. But October 22, 1844 came and nothing happened in the morning hours. As the day drew to a close, still nothing happened in the night hours. When the clock struck 12 am October 23, 1844, the Millerites were devastated. They were greatly "disappointed" for the third time, but more devastatingly this time.

Seventh-day Adventists still celebrate October 22 every year in commemoration of "The Great Disappointment." The Millerites were humbled in the dust. Their hopes were shattered and their lives destroyed. Many were reduced to instant poverty. Confusion and gut-wrenching despair were covering almost every face. Their enemies, looking on, jeered them even more. It was disastrous. Some

---

[5] Ellen G. White, *Early Writings* (Washington, DC: Ellen G. White Estate, Inc., 2008), p. 233.

[6] Ibid, p. 13.

[7] https://m.egwwritings.org/en/book/1443.2 (Date accessed Nov. 2, 2020).

[8] Academia Apology, "Defeating Adventism #20 – Seventh-day Adventists and Ascension Robes," https://www.youtube.com/watch?v=-nYGK9SOMy8&t=49s (Date accessed Nov. 2, 2020).

husbands killed their wives and children, then committed suicide. Some mothers killed their children, then committed suicide also. Young men and women alike were attempting suicide, and some even succeeded in committing suicide.[9] Many became impoverished, having sold their lands, houses, not having sown their fields, and some for leaving their harvest crops to rot. It was complete chaos for the Millerites. Many of the Millerites disbanded and went back to their former churches. Many Millerites became insane at that time, and many more years after the Great Disappointment. So many people had lost their minds that the insane asylums were filled with Millerites. Millerite insanity was considered to be "more of a public health threat than yellow fever and cholera"[10] in the states where they were most populated.

Face-saving visions and blaming God

Whereas most of the Millerites recanted Millerism and went back to their churches, some rationalized that something did happen but that they simply had the wrong event. The major group that came out of Millerism, that doggedly held that something did happen, later became the Seventh-day Adventist Church. On October 23, 1844, a Millerite Adventist by the name of Hiram Edson claimed to have had a vision in a cornfield as he and a few friends were walking through it. He reported that he saw heaven opened and Jesus, instead of returning to the earth to cleanse it by fire, actually moved from the Holy Place of the heavenly sanctuary to the Most Holy Place to begin a work of "investigative judgement" or "cleansing" of the sins of believers. He claimed that it is after that work would be finished, then Jesus would return to earth and cleanse it. This supposed "vision" by Hiram Edson would give these otherwise hopeless Millerites new hope and impetus to forge ahead with the belief that something did happen and that all of their experiences were right and that they were led by God.[11]

Ellen White would later confirm this "vision" of Hiram Edson

---

[9] Beem, *It's Okay Not To Be A Seventh-day Adventist*, p. 43-44.

[10] Ibid, p. 45.

[11] *Advent Pioneers Biographical Sketches and Pictures* (Washington, DC: Ellen G. White Estate, Inc., 2020), p. 10-11.

when prophetess status was conferred on her by those who refused to accept their disillusionment. She would later assert that Miller's failed prophecy and proof-text of Daniel 8:14 was the foundation of Adventism. She said, "The scripture which above all others had been both the foundation and the central pillar of the advent faith was the declaration: "Unto two thousand and three hundred days; then shall the sanctuary be cleansed." Daniel 8:14."[12]

Ellen White would go even further to say that God had directed Miller's false date settings and speculative chart, and claimed that He purposefully hid a number in their calculations and thus effectuated the bitter and ghastly disappointment experienced by the Millerite Adventists. She wrote, "I have seen that the 1843 chart was directed by the hand of the Lord, and that it should not be altered; that the figures were as He wanted them; that His hand was over and hid a mistake in some of the figures, so that none could see it, until His hand was removed."[13]

Despite these new interpretations and theories concocted by the Millerites, William Miller apologized to the public and renounced his date-setting and errors. He also rejected the subsequent movements, groups, and theories that arose out of the Advent Movement and the Great Disappointment. He said:

> I have no confidence in any of the new theories that grew out of that movement, namely, that Christ then came as the Bridegroom, that the door of mercy was closed, that there is no salvation for sinners, that the seventh trumpet then sounded, or that it was a fulfilment of prophecy in any sense. The spirit of fanaticism which resulted from it, in some places leading to extravagance and excess, I regard as of the same nature as that which retarded the Reformation in Germany, and the same as have been connected with every religious movement since the first advent. The truth is not responsible for such devices of Satan to destroy it.[14]

---

[12] White, *The Great Controversy*, p. 409.

[13] White, *Early Writings*, p. 74.

[14] Sylvester Bliss, *Memoirs of William Miller* (Boston: Joshua V. Himes, 1853), p. 334.

In December 1844, two months after the Great Disappointment, Ellen White claimed to have had her first vision.[15]

Interestingly, this vision was not published until 1846. Even more interesting is the fact that the Mormon prophet Joseph Smith had died six months prior to Ellen White's first vision (Smith died on June 27, 1844). Ellen White's first vision bears striking similarities with his. Ellen White was very close to Joseph Smith. Mormonism was growing rapidly where she grew up. Pastor Dale Ratzlaff documents that one of Ellen White's second cousins had married Joseph Smith. He said:

> Many of Ellen White's relatives had Mormon connections, and Mormonism was flourishing in the area where Ellen lived in the early years of her life. In 1842, Ellen Harmon's second cousin, Agnes Moulton Coolbrith Smith, widow of Don Carlos Smith, became a wife of Mormon prophet Joseph Smith at Nauvoo, IL.[16]

Ratzlaff then compared Joseph's first vision with hers and the similarities are ineluctable. This Mormon connection, influence, and apparent borrowing of themes, views, and concepts becomes very glaring when one studies and compares some of the doctrines and practices of both denominations.

Bad Theological And Doctrinal Fruits From A Bad Tree

From this Great Disappointment fiasco and the visionary experiences of Ellen White that propelled her to prominence among the Advent group, they would continue to set new dates for the Parousia of Jesus just about every subsequent year. In 1851 Ellen White said, "Now time is almost finished, and what we have been 6 years in learning [from 1844] they will have to learn in months."[17] This Advent group would be plunged into further false doctrines and

---

[15] White, *Early Writings*, p. 13.

[16] Dale Ratzlaff, *The Mormon Connection: Did Ellen White Copy from Joseph Smith?* http://www.lifeassuranceministries.org/proclamation/2015/2/themormonconnect.html (Accessed Nov. 11, 2020).

[17] White, *Experience and Views*, p. 55.

teachings such as:

The "Shut Door" doctrine

Arianism and Semi-Arianism

Rejection of the Christian Trinity

Death-grip loyalty to the writings and unorthodox teachings of Ellen G. White

The Investigative Judgement

A Ten Commandment-centred Great Controversy between Christ and Satan that undermines the sovereignty of God

Mandatory and salvational Sabbath-keeping in which the Sabbath is the "seal of God," the seal of salvation

That Sunday is a wrong, pagan, and sinful day to worship God on

That Sunday will soon become the dreaded "mark of the beast"

That the Roman Catholic Church is the antichrist of Daniel 7 and the harlot of Revelation 17 and 18

That Protestant churches are all "apostate and fallen" daughters of the whore of Babylon (Roman Catholicism)

Mandatory and salvational adherence to the Levitical dietary laws and vegetarianism

A purely physical and materialistic view of humans

Soul sleep

Annihilationism

That Seventh-day Adventism is the "true church" tasked with a special "Three Angels' Messages" of Revelation 14:6-12 to give to a lost and dying world that will save humanity, including those who are already Christians.

That mainstream Christians will be the eschatological evil people who will unite with secular governments and enforce universal Sunday laws that will bring about persecution and death to Adventists for worshiping on Saturday and for refusing to worship God on Sunday.

On May 21, 1863, the Seventh-day Adventist Church was

officially founded and organized in Battle Creek, Michigan, USA.

How the doctrines were crafted and cemented

What is of utmost importance to note in this historical survey is that in the early days and doctrinal development of Adventism, Ellen White expressed that she could not understand the Bible nor make sense of it for several years. While her compatriots would be reading and studying the Bible, she would be in a corner, clueless. When they got stuck on various points, she would break off into vision and it is in those visionary experiences that everything was made clear to her. After her visions, she would explain everything to them and they would accept her explanations and they would become cemented as Adventist doctrines. She says:

> Again and again these brethren came together to study the Bible, in order that they might know its meaning, and be prepared to teach it with power. When they came to the point in their study where they said, "We can do nothing more," the Spirit of the Lord would come upon me, I would be taken off in vision, and a clear explanation of the passages we had been studying would be given me, with instruction as to how we were to labor and teach effectively. Thus light was given that helped us to understand the scriptures in regard to Christ, His mission, and His priesthood. A line of truth extending from that time to the time when we shall enter the city of God, was made plain to me, and I gave to others the instruction that the Lord had given me. During this whole time I could not understand the reasoning of the brethren. My mind was locked, as it were, and I could not comprehend the meaning of the scriptures we were studying. This was one of the greatest sorrows of my life. I was in this condition of mind until all the principal points of our faith were made clear to our minds, in harmony with the Word of God. The brethren knew that when not in vision, I could not understand these matters, and they accepted

as light direct from heaven the revelations given. For two or three years my mind continued to be locked to an understanding of the Scriptures.[18]

What this admission clearly reveals is the visionary and phenomenological nature and dependency of Adventist doctrines, as concocted by the early Adventist pioneers and Ellen White. As their prophetess, she was biblically illiterate and inept. She was a blockhead who was incapable of contextual exegesis of Scripture. She relied on questionable, ecstatic, visionary experiences to help craft, explain, or confirm the doctrines of the Seventh-day Adventist Church. What is interesting about this is that these visionary experiences that would enable these prophets to "understand Scripture" or to craft doctrines and beliefs was a commonality in the 19th century. Ellen White was no exception.

Ironically, Colossians 2:18 discourages building doctrinal truths and practices on visionary experiences that have no solid biblical foundation and backing. Yet this is exactly how Adventist doctrines were crafted, explained, and confirmed. It is no wonder that they contradict the Word of God so much and are unorthodox, heterodox, and some heretical. Fifty years later, Ellen White penned that no amount of Scripture should change these very same Adventist doctrines. She said if the application of "a mass of Scripture" contradicts the doctrines of the Adventist Church, those applications should be rejected and the Adventist doctrines should stand untouchable. She says:

> We are not to receive the words of those who come with a message that contradicts the special points of our faith. They gather together a mass of Scripture, and pile it as proof around their asserted theories. This has been done over and over again during the past fifty years. And while the Scriptures are God's word, and are to be respected, the application of them, if such application moves one pillar from the foundation that God has

---

[18] White, *Selected Messages, Book I*, p. 206-207.

sustained these fifty years, is a great mistake. He who makes such an application knows not the wonderful demonstration of the Holy Spirit that gave power and force to the past messages that have come to the people of God.[19]

As a result of this "prophetic" injunction, from Dudley M. Canright, who was a personal friend and close associate of Ellen White, to Dr Desmond Ford, Robert Brinsmead, Dr Russell Earl Kelly, Dr Jerry Gladson, Dr Clinton Baldwin, Dr Andre Hill, Pastor Mark Martin, Dr Richard Fredericks, Dr Steve Daily, Pastor Dale Ratzlaff, Pastor Michael Pursley, Colleen Tinker, Nikki Stevenson, Margie Littel, Dr Brian S. Neumann, Daniel Dulcich, Stephen Baxter, Kerry Wynne, William Hohmann, Pastor Colin Bailey, Kevin and Sheryle Hughes, Bill Fritz, Anthony Andreola, Dr Esmie and Pastor Arthur Branner, Pastor Bryan Reid, Prof. John Rosier, to myself and scores of others today, no matter how many times we prove that some of the doctrines of the Seventh-day Adventist Church are biblically wrong, untenable, and heretical, they have not budged one bit to renounce and change them. They remain the same as they were from Ellen White's time. With some, they have merely added Evangelical language to them. This really proves that Scripture is not the final authority for the Seventh-day Adventist Church on biblical and theological matters. Its final authority is Ellen White. The standard by which they test a doctrine or belief for its veracity is not Scripture contextually exegeted, but by the Adventist doctrines as affirmed, explained, and taught by Ellen White.

---

[19] White, *Selected Messages, Book I*, p. 161, par. 2.

Chapter Two

Ellen G. White: The Adventist Prophetess And Her Role In Their Doctrines And Denominational Life

"Adventists constantly decry Roman Catholicism for their belief that the Pope is infallible, yet they officially view Ellen White as being infallible just like the Catholics view the Pope. Ellen White is their female pope."

Seventh-day Adventism cannot exist without Ellen White

Ellen G. White[20] was born November 26, 1827 and died July 16,

---

[20] This chapter on Ellen G. White is not intended to deal with every issue concerning her. The aim of this chapter is to highlight her role as their authoritative prophetess, her writings as the foundation of their doctrines, beliefs, assumptions, interpretations, and views, and her continuous role in their denominational life and structure. Recommended resources that extensively deal with Ellen White and her issues are: Sydney Cleveland, *White Washed: Uncovering the Myths of Ellen G. White* Second Edition (Casa Grande, AZ: LAM Publications, LLC, 2011); Dirk Anderson, *White Out: An Investigation of Ellen G. White* (Glendale, AZ: Life Assurance Ministries, 1999, 2001); D. M. Canright, *Life of Mrs. E. G. White Seventh-day Adventist Prophet: Her False Claims Refuted* (Salt Lake City, UT: Grant Shurtliff Publisher, Sterling Press, 1998); Terrie Dopp Aamodt, Gary Land, and Ronald L. Numbers, eds., *Ellen Harmon White: American Prophet* (New York, NY: Oxford University

1915. She was a young Millerite who had anticipated the Second Coming of Christ in 1843-1844. She said that she had her first vision in December 1844, at the age of 17.[21] From that point on, she became a unifying figure among the small band of Millerites who would later form the Seventh-day Adventist Church. For the next 70 years of her life, up until her death, she functioned as the SDA Church's prophetess. To this day her role remains the same as it was from the very beginning of Adventism. Seventh-day Adventism cannot exist without Ellen G. White in the same way that Jehovah's Witnesses cannot exist without Charles T. Russell, Mormons without Joseph Smith, Muslims without Mohammed, Christian Scientists without Mary Baker Eddy, and Theosophists without Helena P. Blavatsky. Ellen G. White is the centre around which Adventism revolves.

Adventists believe that she is God's end time prophet for the last day church (themselves). In theory they deny that her writings are on par with Scripture, but subconsciously, in practice, and in reality they see her writings as being on par with Scripture, even superior to it. Her writings are a main source of spirituality and the spiritual nurturing of the SDA Church. They use her writings in sermons, Sabbath School Study Guides, Bible classes, lectures, university courses and classes, church guidelines and practices, etc., alongside Scripture. They preach and study from her books and writings in the same way that Christians do with Scripture. Her writings are constantly used to clarify, interpret, buttress, fill in missing details, or to further strengthen anything in their official 28 Fundamental Beliefs, Church Manual, and in Scripture. Sometimes she is used to end a debate or discussion on a particular biblical issue or interpretation.

Ellen White claimed for herself direct inspiration from God, and Adventists believe and affirm this about her as well. The majority of

Press, 2014); Brian S. Neumann, *The White Elephant in Seventh-day Adventism* (Mustang, OK: Tate Publishing & Enterprises, LLC, 2016); Ronald L. Numbers, *Prophetess of Health: A Study of Ellen G. White* (New York, Hagerstown, San Francisco, London: Harper and Row Publishers, 1976); Steve Daily, *Ellen G. White: A Psychobiography* (Conneaut, PA: Page Publishing, Inc., 2020).

[21] White, *Life Sketches of Ellen G. White*, p. 64, par. 1.

their doctrines, views, beliefs, interpretations of Scripture, and practices are based on her writings. Her writings are at the heart of Adventist church life, culture, diet, practices, theology, organisation, church disciplinary actions and procedures, evangelism, and overall existence. From the very beginning of their movement, this position of Ellen G. White in Adventism was cemented. She stated:

> After the passing of the time in 1844 we searched for the truth as for hidden treasure. I met with the brethren, and we studied and prayed earnestly....When they came to the point in their study where they said, "We can do nothing more," the Spirit of the Lord would come upon me. I would be taken off in vision, and a clear explanation of the passages we had been studying would be given me, with instruction as to how we were to labor and teach effectively. Thus light was given that helped us to understand the scriptures in regard to Christ, his mission, and his priesthood. A line of truth extending from that time to the time when we shall enter the city of God, was made plain to me, and I gave to others the instruction that the Lord had given me.[22]

What this statement reveals is that Ellen White had the final say in their doctrinal formation and beliefs. It was her "visions" and "clear explanations" of passages that helped them "understand the scriptures" and solidify their doctrinal positions. This statement also reveals the cosmic scope with which she conceptualized her views, interpretations, visions, explanations, and instructions. She said that they extend from her time until the very end "when we shall enter the city of God," which is heaven itself, at the Second Coming of Christ.

This position of Ellen G. White writings and their significance to Adventists must be clearly understood if one is to properly understand the underlying theology, views, and interpretations of Adventists on Scripture and on any biblical subject. The unique

---

[22] White, *Review and Herald*, May 25, 1905.

teachings and doctrinal views of Adventists cannot be established from Scripture alone, contextually exegeted, nor on actual Christian church history. Her writings are the lens through which Scripture and Church history are filtered, interpreted, and understood by Adventists.

Before persons are baptized into the SDA Church, there is a set of 13 vows, in the form of questions, that they must affirm and pledge to submit to before they can become members. Vow number 8 asks, "Do you believe the Biblical teaching of spiritual gifts, and do you believe that the gift of prophecy is one of the identifying marks of the remnant church?"[23] The "gift of prophecy" is Ellen White and her writings. The official Fundamental Belief of Adventists on Ellen White says:

> The Scriptures testify that one of the gifts of the Holy Spirit is prophecy. This gift is an identifying mark of the remnant church and we believe it was manifested in the ministry of Ellen G. White. Her writings speak with prophetic authority and provide comfort, guidance, instruction, and correction to the church. They also make clear that the Bible is the standard by which all teaching and experience must be tested. (Num. 12:6; 2 Chron. 20:20; Amos 3:7; Joel 2:28, 29; Acts 2:14-21; 2 Tim. 3:16, 17; Heb. 1:1-3; Rev. 12:17; 19:10; 22:8, 9.)[24]

This Fundamental Belief of Adventists makes them have two authoritative sources for doctrine and practice. Ellen White's writings "speak with prophetic authority," and so does the Bible. The Bible speaks with "prophetic authority," therefore it logically means that Ellen White and Scripture speak with the same authority for SDAs, and as will be shown later on, Ellen White's writings are held

---

[23] The Secretariat, General Conference of Seventh-day Adventists, *Seventh-day Adventist Church Manual* (Doral, FL: Inter-American Division Publishing Association, 2005, 2007), p. 32.

[24] https://www.adventist.org/beliefs/fundamental-beliefs/church/the-gift-of-prophecy/ (Date accessed March 27, 2021).

in higher authority than Scripture because for them her writings are the divine interpreter of Scripture. The previous wording of this Fundamental Belief says, "Her writings are a continuing and authoritative source of truth…."[25] The Word of God is "a continuing and authoritative source of truth" too. I suppose this wording got too controversial for them and revealed their overt multiplicity of sources of doctrinal authority, so they attempted to sanitize it in order to deceive the masses by using "prophetic authority" but that still does not change anything. It was certainly a good attempt at masking their belief though.

The Fundamental Belief statement also says that her writings "provide comfort, guidance, instruction, and correction to the church." This is an echo of what Scripture does for the Christian church. Scripture provides comfort, guidance, instruction, and correction to the church. 2 Timothy 3:16-17 says, "All Scripture is breathed out by God and profitable for teaching, for reproof, for correction, and for training in righteousness, that the man of God may be complete, equipped for every good work." Their statement about what Ellen White's writings does for them is a direct echo and rephrasing of this text. They tried to sanitize their view again in attempts to make themselves seem to believe in the Bible alone by ending the statement with "They also make clear that the Bible is the standard by which all teaching and experience must be tested." But why exactly do we need Ellen White's writings to tell us this about Scripture for this to be true about Scripture? Christians hold Scripture in that esteem already. This is nothing but an attempted sleight of hand because, as we will see, for Adventists her writings are the divine interpreter of Scripture that "correct inaccurate interpretations of it derived from tradition, human reason, personal experience, and modern culture."

At the 2015 SDA General Conference Session, the delegates reaffirmed their faith in Ellen White's writings in a "Statement of Confidence." Part of it says:

---

[25] Ministerial Association, General Conference of Seventh-day Adventists, *Seventh-day Adventists Believe,* 2nd Edition (Boise, ID: Pacific Press Publishing Association, 2005), p. 247.

We reaffirm our conviction that her writings are divinely inspired, truly Christ-centred, and Bible-based. Rather than replacing the Bible, they uplift the normative character of Scripture and correct inaccurate interpretations of it derived from tradition, human reason, personal experience, and modern culture.[26]

If Ellen White's writings "correct inaccurate interpretations" of Scripture, and she is "divinely inspired," that means that she is the infallible interpreter of Scripture. If she is the infallible interpreter of Scripture, that makes her above Scripture. Adventists constantly decry Roman Catholicism for their belief that the Pope is infallible, yet they officially view Ellen White as being infallible just like the Catholics view the Pope. Ellen White is their female pope. Of course they will deny this but simply ask them to name one biblical, doctrinal, theological, or interpretational thing that she got wrong, and the silence will be deafening. This is so because they believe that she got nothing wrong! And if she got nothing wrong, what does that make her?

Infallible!

Adventists generally affirm that whatever is true of the Bible is also true of Ellen White's writings. They hold them to the same standard. For example, the 1978 Teacher's edition of the SDA Sabbath School- Quarterly Study Guide, said, "The Bible and the writings of Ellen White are inerrant."[27] Dr Ron Graybill, former Assistant Secretary of the Ellen G. White Estate, once stated, "We believe the revelation and inspiration of both the Bible and Ellen White's writings to be of equal quality. The superintendence of the Holy Spirit was just as careful and thorough in one case as in the other."[28]

---

[26]https://www.adventist.org/articles/statement-of-confidence-in-the-writings-of-ellen-g-white/?fbclid=IwAR2qu7nRPtBZLrJ-S6rN6B_xHooj9CrrsnjW4U8W-eVTyNsXlaVdtmJUvVY (Date accessed March 27, 2021).

[27] Teacher's edition of the SDA Sabbath School-Quarterly Study Guide, p. 112, Feb. 11, 1978.

[28] Dr Ron Graybill, "Ellen White's Role in Doctrine Formation," in *Ministry Magazine,* October 1981, https://www.ministrymagazine.org/archive/1981/10/ellen-whites-role-in-doctrine-formation (Date accessed March 27, 2021).

Adventists want Christians to believe that they get all of their teachings and beliefs from the "Bible alone," but this is not so at all. The peculiar doctrines, interpretations, and views of Adventists cannot be sustained from the Bible alone. They are derived from and grounded in the writings and unorthodox views of Ellen White. Ellen White shaped the doctrines and denominational structure of their church. Dr. Alberto Timm, Associate Director of the Ellen G. White Estate, in Silver Spring, Maryland, admitted:

> The Seventh-day Adventist Church has been largely shaped by Ellen White's prophetic guidance. In the formation of its message, she helped the church to build a solid doctrinal-lifestyle biblical platform; to develop a major theological framework based on the Great Cosmic Controversy motif; to study the Scriptures from an exegetical-systematic perspective; and to uncover a concentric concept of theological centre.[29]

In an article about Ellen White, the *Encyclopedia Britannica* pointedly noted:

> Throughout the work of organization and the establishment of an Adventist orthodoxy, Ellen White's visions were a guiding force. The scriptural interpretations that came to her were promptly accepted. Much of the church program thus revealed was published in her Testimonies for the Church, which eventually grew from 16 pages in its 1855 edition to fill nine volumes. Her views on health, especially her opposition to the use of coffee, tea, meat, and drugs, were incorporated into Seventh-day Adventist practice.[30]

---

[29] Dr. Alberto R. Timm, *The Ecclesiological Role of Ellen G. White*, January 1, 2013, https://www.perspectivedigest.org/archive/18-1/the-ecclesiological-role-of-ellen-g-white (Date accessed March 27, 2021).

[30] Encyclopedia Britannica, *Ellen Gould Harmon White: American religious leader*, https://www.britannica.com/biography/Ellen-Gould-Harmon-White (Date accessed March 27, 2021).

At the General Conference Session of SDAs, held in Utrecht, the Netherlands, June 30, 1995, the delegates voted on a "Statement of Confidence" in the writings of Ellen White in which they said, "We consider the biblical canon closed. However, we also believe, as did Ellen G. White's contemporaries, that her writings carry divine authority, both for godly living and for doctrine."[31] This statement could not have been more forthright. Ellen White's writings is another Bible for Adventists, despite that they constantly double-speak and try to publicly deny it all the time.[32] This statement is an official SDA World Church statement and belief, irrespective of the fact that it was made almost 3 decades ago. They have not changed their views about Ellen White's writings. They only occasionally sanitize the language to deceive the wider public, but their beliefs have not changed. This statement was clear that her writings carry "divine authority," and that they are for "godly living and for doctrine." Again, Scripture carries "divine authority" and it is definitely for "godly living and for doctrine." For Adventists, the writings of Ellen White are another Bible and they are of the same authority as Scripture. They do the same things that Scripture does for Christians.

---

[31] https://secc.adventistfaith.org/visitors-statements-spirit-of-prophecy (Date accessed Jan. 8, 2021).

[32] In 1982, in response to Walter Rea's book *The White Lie* that showed many problems with the writings of Ellen White and that she was a plagiarist, the General Conference of SDAs put together an ad hoc committee to study and make a statement on Ellen White's writings. They concluded that study with 10 affirmations and also 10 denials regarding Ellen White's writings. Not only are these affirmations and denials full of confusion and contradictions, but they also show how convoluted and double-speaking SDAs are regarding Scripture and Ellen White. Denial number 4 says, "We do not believe that the writings of Ellen White may be used as the basis of doctrine." But 13 years later (June 1995), at the General Conference Session of SDAs, which is the highest level of authority in the SDA Church, they affirmed the very opposite! They said, "We consider the biblical canon closed. However, we also believe, as did Ellen G. White's contemporaries, that her writings carry divine authority, both for godly living and for doctrine." Adventists constantly double-speak to purposefully mislead the public about their beliefs while they incessantly hold onto those beliefs they try so hard to deny. This is exactly how cults operate. One can read the contradictory "affirmations and denials" here: https://www.ministrymagazine.org/archive/1982/08/the-inspiration-and-authority-of-the-ellen-g.-white-writings.

Statements like these made by the General Conference of SDAs are not mere whimsical suggestions that can be shrugged off. These statements are the most authoritative among them. Ellen White made it absolutely clear that when the General Conference of SDAs is in session, it is "the voice of God," it is God's "highest authority" on earth, and every SDA must heed the resolutions of that governing body. She said, "The voice of the General Conference has been represented as an authority to be heeded as the voice of the Holy Spirit."[33] If Adventists despise General Conference decisions and views, they are despising God's voice: "God has invested His church with special authority and power which no one can be justified in disregarding and despising, for in so doing he despises the voice of God."[34] God's voice through the General Conference must be respected: "God has bestowed the highest power under heaven upon His church. It is the voice of God in His united people in church capacity which is to be respected."[35] The highest authority for Adventists is the General Conference: "The highest authority under God among Seventh-day Adventists is found in the will of the body of that people, as expressed in the decisions of the General Conference, when acting within its proper jurisdiction."[36] Ellen White instructed Adventists that when the General Conference makes a resolution, their private views and positions must be surrendered and they must obey and embrace what the General Conference says. She said:

> I have been shown that no man's judgment should be surrendered to the judgment of any one man. But when the judgment of the General Conference, which is the highest authority that God has upon the earth, is exercised, private independence and private judgment must not be maintained, but surrendered.[37]

---

[33] White, *Manuscript Releases*, vol. 14, p. 278, par. 3.

[34] White, *Testimonies for the Church*, Vol. 3, p. 417 (1875).

[35] White, *Testimonies for the Church*, Vol. 3, p. 451 (1875).

[36] White, quoted in *Action Of General Conference*, 1877 Yearbook, 1914, p. 255. Also quoted in *The Paulson Collection of Ellen G. White Letters*, p. 422, par. 1.

At the 2003 *Faith and Science Conference II*, held at Glacier View, Colorado, Cindy Tutsch, Associate Director of the Ellen G. White Estate, in a presentation pointed out that Adventism's peculiar doctrinal views and interpretations owe their "continuing veracity" to Ellen White's writings and her Great Controversy worldview. She said, "Ellen White's biblically predicated Great Controversy model, then, is authoritative in determining the continuing veracity of such pivotal doctrines as salvation, the Sabbath, the mystery of death, the parousia, and the sanctuary."[38] Her writings are used to establish, defend, and propagate their doctrines. Without Ellen White, the peculiar doctrines and interpretations of Adventists cannot stand under scrutiny. Seventh-day Adventism cannot exist without the writings of Ellen White. Her husband James White recognized this and said:

> Our position on the Testimonies [Ellen White's writings] is like the keystone to the arch. Take that out and there is no logical stopping place till all the special truths of the message are gone. Nothing is surer than this, that this message and the visions [of Ellen White] belong together.[39]

It is because Adventism cannot exist without Ellen White that despite the insurmountable evidence presented by persons such as Dudley M. Canright, Walter Rea, Dr Ronald L. Numbers, Dr Desmond Ford, Dr Fred Veltmann, Dr Clinton Baldwin, Pastor Dale Ratzlaff, Colleen Tinker, Nikki Stevenson, Pastor J. Mark Martin, Dr Jerry Gladson, Dr Andre Hill, Stephen Baxter, Kismarr Givans, Keswick Johnson, Pastor Colin Bailey, Kerry Wynne, Larry Dean, myself, and countless of others about her plagiarism, absurd beliefs, theological errors, unbiblical teachings, historical gaffes, hypocrisies, and heretical statements, Adventists continue to reject all the evidence. They try very hard to explain them away. Some ignore

---

[37] White, *Testimonies For The Church*, Vol. 3, p. 492 (1875).

[38] Cindy Tutsch, *Interpreting Ellen G. White's Earth History Comments*, Aug. 13-21, 2003, https://whiteestate.org/legacy/issues-genesis-html/ (Date accessed March 27, 2021).

[39] James White, *Review and Herald Supplement*, August 14, 1883.

them. They make ridiculous excuses and play semantic games to exonerate her. They make personal attacks on the characters of her critics in attempts to discredit them. Some go in outright denial mode, while others defend Ellen White as being justified in everything she said and did. They do these things because of their subconscious and overt views about her and her writings.

Exalted claims Ellen White made for herself and her writings

Adventists love to play the denial and obfuscation game when it comes to matters relating to Ellen White, especially regarding her prophetic role and writings. They constantly speak with a forked-tongue. They like to claim that she never claimed to be a prophet, but this claim is ridiculous. Even if she never claimed to be a prophet, they have embraced her as a prophet. They have invested her with prophetic status and authority in the same way as the biblical prophets. So whether or not she made the claim is immaterial because the reality is she is their authoritative prophet. However, their denial that she did not claim to be a prophet is a lie that is used to deceive the unsuspecting public.

Ellen White did claim to be a prophet, and in some cases she claimed to be more than a prophet. She said:

> Early in my youth I was asked several times, Are you a prophet? I have ever responded, I am the Lord's messenger. I know that many have called me a prophet, but I have made no claim to this title. My Saviour declared me to be his messenger...my work includes much more than the word 'prophet' signifies.[40]

Ellen White tried to obfuscate the terms 'messenger' and 'prophet' to deny that she claimed to be a prophet, but when referring to persons who God called to be His mouthpiece, a messenger and a prophet were biblically the same thing. They were interchangeable titles for prophets (2 Chron. 36:15-16; Isa. 42:18-21; Hag. 1:13; Mal. 3:1; Matt. 11:7-10). She claimed to have made no

---

[40] White, *Selected Messages*, Book 1, p. 32, par. 4.

claim to the title "prophet" but she further claimed that her work goes beyond that of a *mere* prophet. This means that she is a prophet and much more than that. This is exactly what she said a few paragraphs down, "My commission embraces the work of a prophet, but it does not end there."[41] All of the Adventist arguments and denials about Ellen White not claiming to be a prophet are farcical because she did claim to be a prophet and even much more than that. And if they really believe that she never claimed to be a prophet, then why do they believe that she was a true prophet? Why do they embrace her as a prophet who is no different from the biblical prophets? It is very odd that they would try to deny her prophetic status, but at the same time give her the same prophetic status as biblical prophets.

Adventists treat Ellen White's writings the way they do because Ellen White set the precedence for how they should understand and treat her writings. She made astounding and otherworldly claims for herself and her writings. Ellen White believed that both the Scriptures and her writings were authored by the Holy Spirit: "The Holy Ghost is the Author of the Scriptures and of the Spirit of Prophecy."[42] She claimed verbal inspiration for her writings when she said, "The Spirit of God works upon my mind and gives me appropriate words with which to express the truth."[43] And also, "When writing these precious books, if I hesitated, the very word I wanted to express the idea was given me."[44]

What is shocking about these claims to verbal inspiration on her part is that she affirmed it for herself but denied it for the Bible writers! Ellen White said:

> It is not the words of the Bible that are inspired, but the men that were inspired. Inspiration acts not on the man's words or his expressions but on the man himself, who, under the influence of the Holy Ghost, is imbued with

---

[41] Ibid, p. 36, par. 2.

[42] White, *Selected Messages*, Book 3, p. 30, par. 3.

[43] Ibid, p. 51, par. 5.

[44] Ibid, p. 51, par. 7.

thoughts. But the words receive the impress of the individual mind.[45]

In this statement, Ellen White unequivocally rejected and denied the verbal inspiration of Scripture. But at the same time she affirmed verbal inspiration for herself and her books. What this logically means is that Ellen White subconsciously conceptualized her writings to have been inspired to a higher degree than Scripture itself! That is blasphemous. There is no way that intelligent people cannot understand what these statements are saying, nor can they possibly be "taken out of context" as Adventists incessantly assert whenever any statement of Ellen White that shows her unorthodox or heretical teaching is being discussed.

God's definitive voice: is it Jesus or is it Ellen White?

Ellen White went so far as to seem to replace Jesus as being the definitive means by which God speaks to us. She said:

> In ancient times God spoke to men by the mouth of prophets and apostles. In these days he speaks to them by the testimonies of his Spirit [Ellen White's writings]. There was never a time when God more earnestly instructed his people concerning his will, and the course that he would have them pursue, than now. But will they profit by his teachings? will [sic] they receive his reproofs and heed the warnings? God will accept of no [sic] partial obedience; he will sanction no compromise with self.[46]

There are so many unmistakably clear, but arrogant, claims in this statement. Firstly, Ellen White rephrases Hebrews 1:1-2 and replaces Jesus with herself and her writings. Hebrews 1:1-2 says, "Long ago, at many times and in many ways, God spoke to our fathers by the prophets, [2] but in these last days he has spoken to us by his Son...." The author of Hebrews was drawing a contrast between

---

[45] White, *Selected Messages*, Book 1, p. 21, par. 2.

[46] White, *Review and Herald*, June 9, 1885, par. 10.

how God spoke to the fathers, and the means He used, with how God speaks since Jesus brought in the eschaton—the last days. In the last days, God speaks definitively through His Son Jesus Christ. Ellen White read this statement and expunged Jesus and inserted herself as that definitive voice through whom God speaks in the last days by saying, "In ancient times God spoke to men by the mouth of prophets and apostles. In these days he speaks to them by the testimonies of his Spirit." This is arrogant and blasphemous. Ellen White is taking the place of Jesus as God's most definitive and authoritative voice for the last days.

Secondly, Ellen White throws a lot of shade on how God spoke before her time and exalted her speaking for God as the most clear when she said, "There was never a time when God more earnestly instructed his people concerning his will, and the course that he would have them pursue, than now." This is very ridiculous. The Old and New Testaments are replete with God's definitive will and instructions for His people. But Ellen White believes that those times were inefficient and it is through her that God clearly communicates His will to His people.

Thirdly, Ellen White made it clear that what she was communicating was God's "will," "teachings," "reproofs," and "warnings." This was made clear in her statement: "But will they profit by his teachings? will [sic] they receive his reproofs and heed the warnings? God will accept of no [sic] partial obedience; he will sanction no compromise with self." And lastly, she strongly asserted that God requires full obedience to her writings and instructions.

The importance, functions, and purpose of her writings

Ellen White understood her writings to have been a necessary fence around the Bible. She stated that Adventists need her writings because they have neglected the Bible. God gave them her writings to simplify things for them, and they ought to be acquainted with her writings in the same way that they should be with the Bible. She stated:

> I took the precious Bible, and surrounded it with the several "Testimonies for the Church," given for the people of God. "Here," said I, "the cases of nearly all

are met. The sins they are to shun are pointed out. The counsel that they desire can be found here, given for other cases situated similarly to themselves. God has been pleased to give you line upon line and precept upon precept. But there are not many of you that really know what is contained in the Testimonies. You are not familiar with the Scriptures. If you had made God's word your study, with a desire to reach the Bible standard and attain to Christian perfection, you would not have needed the Testimonies. It is because you have neglected to acquaint yourselves with God's inspired book that He has sought to reach you by simple, direct testimonies, calling your attention to the words of inspiration which you had neglected to obey, and urging you to fashion your lives in accordance with its pure and elevated teachings.[47]

The irony in this statement is that it shows how ignorant Adventists are about Scripture, despite their claim to be "people of the Book." Because of their biblically illiteracy, they need Ellen White's writings. If they would just read their Bibles alone, they'd have no need for her writings. The flip side to this, though, is that they live in cognitive dissonance. When they use this statement or when persons like myself point it out to them, they argue that they need her writings, even if they know their Bibles, because she is their inspired prophet. When Former Adventists affirm that we are satisfied with Scripture alone and that we do not need her writings as any sort of biblical and spiritual guide, we are often chided for not subscribing to her writings. It is extremely difficult to help SDAs understand Scripture and the Gospel because of their chameleon approach and dissonant mentality.

Ellen White denied claims to infallibility when she said, "I do not claim infallibility."[48] Adventists deny this about her and her writings as well. But this is not true at all, as was already seen. She claimed

---

[47] White, *Life Sketches of Ellen G. White*, p. 198, par. 1.

[48] White, *Daughters of God*, p. 272, par. 6.

infallibility in various ways and they also claim it for her in various ways also. She said, "These books contain clear, straight, unalterable truth and they should certainly be appreciated. The instruction they contain is not of human production."[49] This statement is a claim to infallibility. That which is "unalterable truth" is infallible. That which is of divine production, as she claimed here, is infallible. There is no way that Ellen White and SDAs can claim that the Holy Spirit authored Ellen White's books, just as He authored Scripture, and then claim that they are fallible. The very fact that the Holy Spirit is claimed for the authorship of her books, as He is of Scripture, automatically makes her books infallible just as Scripture is infallible. There is no way that her books can contain "unalterable truth" from God but at the same time those unchangeable truths be fallible. But it is not surprising that Ellen White and Adventists double-speak on this issue as they do on countless other things. Ellen White's belief in her infallibility is further affirmed and strongly asserted in this statement:

> In my books, the truth is stated, barricaded by a "Thus saith the Lord." The Holy Spirit traced these truths upon my heart and mind as indelibly as the law was traced by the finger of God, upon the tables of stone, which are now in the ark, to be brought forth in that great day when sentence will be pronounced against every evil, seducing science produced by the father of lies.[50] [Italics mine]

This statement is so strong, with Ellen White arrogating so much divine authority and infallibility for her writings, that it needs no elaboration.

Not only did Ellen White think that her books were divinely inspired, but she also thought this for letters that she wrote to people and congregations as well. She said:

When I went to Colorado, I was so burdened for you,

---

[49] White, *Letter H-339*, Dec. 26, 1904.
[50] White, *Colporteur Ministry*, p. 126.

that, in my weakness. I wrote many pages to be read at your camp-meeting. Weak and trembling, I arose at three o'clock in the morning, to write to you. God was speaking through clay. But the document was entirely forgotten; the camp-meeting passed, and it was not read until the General Conference. You might say that it was only a letter. Yes, it was a letter, but prompted by the Spirit of God, to bring before your minds things that had been shown me. In these letters which I write, in the testimonies I bear, I am presenting to you that which the Lord has presented to me. I do not write one article in the paper expressing merely my own ideas. They are what God has opened before me in vision-- the precious rays of light shining from the throne.[51]

Ellen White was very conscious of the words she chose to communicate to Adventists. She said that her letters were testimonies from the Spirit of God. They were things that God had presented to her in vision and they were not merely her own opinions nor ideas. Her letters and testimonies are "precious rays of light shining from the [God's] throne." Ellen White did not mince her words. She had an exalted, infallibly truthful, and divine-origination conceptualization of her writings. And it was because of this understanding that she got so offended that her letter was not read at the camp-meeting, where she intended it to be read.

Ellen White considered it an insult to the Holy Spirit when some Adventists thought that her writings and letters were "merely the opinion of Sister White." She said:

Yet now when I send you a testimony of warning and reproof, many of you declare it to be merely the opinion of Sister White. You have thereby insulted the Spirit of God. You know how the Lord has manifested Himself through the Spirit of prophecy.[52] Past, present,

---

[51] White, *Pamphlet 117*, p. 49, par. 1.

[52] The phrase "Spirit of Prophecy" ("SOP" abbreviation by SDAs), as is used here by Ellen

and future have passed before me. I have been shown faces that I had never seen, and years afterward I knew them when I saw them. I have been aroused from my sleep with a vivid sense of subjects previously presented to my mind and I have written, at midnight, letters that have gone across the continent, and arriving at a crisis, have saved great disaster to the cause of God. This has been my work for many years. A power has impelled me to reprove and rebuke wrongs that I had not thought of. Is this work of the last thirty-six years from above or from beneath?[53]

Ellen White considered disagreements and contentions with her writings and views to be disagreements and contentions with God Himself. And again, she thinks this to be the case because of her belief about the heavenly origin and infallibility of her writings and views:

> Those who resist the messages of God through his humble servant, think they are at variance with Sister White, because her ideas are not in harmony with theirs; but this variance is not with sister White, but with the Lord, who has given her her work to do.[54]

Where Ellen White is concerned, any opposition to her writings and ideas is opposition to God. This view that she had of her writings and messages is no different from that which the biblical authors and prophets had about their writings and messages. Ellen White really believed that she was on par with the biblical prophets and Adventists have repeatedly argued this for her.

To lose faith in her writings is the precursor to losing faith in God altogether

---

White, is a reference solely to Ellen White and her writings. They have extracted this from Rev. 19:10 and believe that it is referring exclusively to her.

[53] White, *Selected Messages*, Book I, p. 27, par. 1.

[54] White, *Review and Herald*, Tuesday, Aug. 26, 1890.

Ellen White believed her writings to be so essential to the faith of SDAs that she said Satan will make special efforts to reduce their effectiveness and that this attack from Satan will be "the very last deception."

> The very last deception of Satan will be to make of none effect the testimony of the Spirit of God. 'Where there is no vision, the people perish' (Prov. 29:18). Satan will work ingeniously, in different ways and through different agencies, to unsettle the confidence of God's remnant people [Seventh-day Adventists] in the true testimony.[55]

She believed her writings to be so indispensable to faith that she gave a prediction of a downward spiral from faith to total destruction, and this end begins with doubting her writings. She asserted:

> It is Satan's plan to weaken the faith of God's people in the Testimonies. Next follows skepticism in regard to the vital points of our faith, the pillars of our position, then doubt as to the Holy Scriptures, and then the downward march to perdition. When the Testimonies, which were once believed, are doubted and given up, Satan knows the deceived ones will not stop at this; and he redoubles his efforts till he launches them into open rebellion, which becomes incurable and ends in destruction.[56]

According to this statement, in conjunction with the previous one, "the very last deception" of Satan will be to weaken faith in Ellen White's writings and to render them of "none effect." After Satan does this then persons will become sceptical about SDA doctrines. Ellen White is inadvertently admitting that SDA doctrines and interpretations are grounded in her writings because in giving up her writings, their doctrines would be automatically affected thereafter and

---

[55] White, *Selected Messages*, Book I, p. 48.

[56] White, *Testimonies for the Church*, Vol. 4, p. 211.

be discarded. If Adventist doctrines and interpretations were not grounded in her writings, why would they be affected and discarded once one stops reading them? Ellen White further declares that when SDA doctrines are questioned and given up, then persons will begin to doubt the Bible itself. And after the Bible is given up, then it is a natural "march to perdition."

Ellen White gave special attention to her writings and believed that they are the key to preserving faith. Giving up her writings will inevitably lead to 'incurable rebellion' that will end in destruction. Ellen White was so stoked and megalomaniacal about her writings and self-importance that she placed them before Scripture as the precursor to losing faith in Scripture and in God altogether. Before one is capable of losing faith in Scripture and head to destruction, one must first lose faith in Ellen White and the SDA doctrines. These statements are very strong, clear, unmistakeable, and downright cultic. Ellen White placed her writings above Scripture, as the fence surrounding Scripture, and as that which is essential to understanding Scripture.

The Seventh-day Adventist Church is very clear that she is "divinely inspired" and that her writings "correct inaccurate interpretations" of Scripture. How much clearer can it be dear reader? What more statements do I need to produce from Ellen White herself, top-tier Adventists, and official denominational statements to prove exactly what Ellen White's writings are to SDAs?

Does the Greater Light need a "lesser light"?

Just in case you need a little more to be convinced, Ellen White considered her writings to be a "lesser light" that points people to the "greater light," the Bible. She said, "Little heed is given to the Bible, and the Lord has given a lesser light to lead men and women to the greater light."[57] To this day, Adventists still call Ellen White and her writings "the Lesser Light." As innocuous as this self-styled title appears, it is ridiculous and is very problematic. Jesus is very clear

---

[57] White, *The Colporteur Evangelist*, p. 37 (1902).

that He is the light of the world (John 8:12; 9:5). And all believers in Him are the light of the world also (Matt. 5:14). But we are not "the light of the world" in the sense that our books and writings are "divinely inspired" and authoritative books on which doctrine is to be built, nor that our writings should "correct inaccurate interpretations" of Scripture as SDAs use it for Ellen White. We are the light of the world in a moral sense. Jesus Himself explained that in Matthew 5:16 by saying, "In the same way, let your light shine before others, so that they may see your good works and give glory to your Father who is in heaven." Paul referred to believers as lights of the world in this moral sense also when he said, "Do all things without grumbling or disputing, that you may be blameless and innocent, children of God without blemish in the midst of a crooked and twisted generation, among whom you shine as lights in the world" (Phil. 2:14-15).

Believers are never referred to as "lesser lights" whose writings and prophetic authority are needed to point to Jesus or to the Word of God as the "Greater Light." The Word of God does not need help in shining brightly. It shines brightly on its own already (2 Pet. 1:19). Jesus does not need help to shine brightly. As Jesus and God's Word shine brightly, they can draw people to themselves without any writings of extra-biblical prophets (John 12:32). The concept of Ellen White being a necessary "lesser light" pointing to the "greater light" of Scripture is absurd and shows that Adventists must be in a pitch black theological cave to even need a lesser light. A lesser light is only needed and useful if one is in obscure darkness. A lesser light is not needed nor useful in blazing sunlight. A flashlight has absolutely no use on a sunny day. One would look downright silly to be outside on a sunny day with a flashlight turned on pointing one to the sun. The effulgent glory of the sun will drown out the meagre light of the flashlight and render it useless. This is exactly what it is with Scripture and Ellen White's writings. Scripture is like an effulgent sun, shining gloriously and believers are outside on a sunny day, basking in its glory and have no need for a flashlight to point us to the sun.

As a matter of fact, contrary to what Ellen White and Adventists claim for her writings in pointing to Scripture and making them clear, they actually make Scripture very confusing, cryptic, and perplexing. Reading Scripture through the lens of Ellen White is a maze of confusion for SDAs. That is why so many false doctrines and legalism are rife in their doctrinal statements and religious experiences. Ellen White is bad news when it comes to biblical understanding and interpretation. It is when Adventists put down her writings and contextually read Scripture that illumination comes. As Scripture enlightens them, they see glaring contradictions between her writings and Scripture, and eventually have no choice but to stop reading Ellen White or to leave Adventism altogether. A noted former SDA professor, pastor, and theologian Dr Jerry Gladson evinced my point when he said:

> When I read her writings even before Rea, particularly her extensive interpretations of biblical texts, they often seemed to miss the essential spirit of Scripture. Intuitively, I sensed she was moving in an entirely different theological direction than Scripture, toward a sectarian vindication of Adventism rather than toward a broader, more ecumenical understanding. She seemed to bend or exploit Scripture toward her own ends, which is understandable, given her theological orientation. This intuition about Ellen White is difficult to put into words, but I felt it keenly the more I studied the Bible in depth during my graduate work. Eventually, the conflict I saw between the biblical text and what Ellen White had to say about it became so great that I had to stop reading her, at least in the area of biblical interpretation.[58]

Those Adventists who do see the glaring issues with Ellen White and Scripture and stay in Adventism usually live in a maze of cognitive dissonance, internal conflict, unorthodox and heretical doctrines, and an abashed reluctance and inability to defend their doctrines and bizarre interpretations.

---

[58] Dr Jerry Gladson, *A Theologian's Journey From Seventh-day Adventism to Mainstream Christianity* (Glendale, AZ: Life Assurance Ministries, 2000), p. 162.

Because of what I presented in this chapter, Ellen White's writings will be used extensively throughout these volumes as I deal with the false doctrines of SDAs. Ellen White is Adventism. Adventism is Ellen White. There is no way around this. One cannot know nor truly understand what they believe and teach, nor their subconscious and underlying assumptions without Ellen White's writings. Any Ellen White statement on any Adventist matter or doctrine is the default Adventist belief, position, interpretation, and view. This is so because of what they have said and what they *officially* believe and teach about her writings. And of course, that is the pinnacle on which she set her writings for Adventists.

Additionally, this is a fair approach because the Seventh-day Adventist Church has never officially rescinded *any* view, interpretation, doctrine, teaching, book, nor any other material that Ellen White has produced, directly or indirectly. They continue to proverbially bend over backwards to hide the embarrassing materials, to reinterpret, to defend, and to explain them away. But they have never rescinded anything from her nor have they ever disassociated themselves from anything regarding Ellen White and her writings.

Conclusively, the Seventh-day Adventist Church has two sources of authority–the Bible and Ellen White's writings. Despite this, they place the greater weight of authority on Ellen White's writings for doctrines, denominational policy, and practices. The SDA Church and the writings of Ellen White are mutually dependent upon each other. Knock down one, the whole of Adventism will dissolve. Her writings must be obeyed by conscientious Adventists. She stated:

> We must follow the directions given through the spirit of prophecy. We must love and obey the truth for this time. This will save us from accepting strong delusions. God has spoken to us through His word. He has spoken to us through the testimonies to the church and through the books that have helped to make plain our present duty and the position that we should now occupy. The warnings that have been given, line upon line, precept upon precept, should be heeded. If we disregard them, what excuse can we offer?[59]

Ellen White leaves Adventists no choice about her conviction and position. She stated that God speaks through the Bible and her writings and books with equal authority. Adventists must get in line with and obey what Ellen White says. If they presume to disregard her writings, she asked, what excuse can they offer to God? Their souls will surely be in jeopardy. This is what Ellen White taught. This is what Adventists believe. On the basis of the evidence presented, Adventists do not believe in the Bible alone as the foundation for faith, doctrine, and practice. They have two sources of authority–Ellen White and the Bible, with Ellen White having the greater authoritative edge over the Bible. And given the fact that she is the authority that interprets the Bible for them, this places the Bible under her authority, thus making Ellen White their singular, actual authority. They simply use the Bible to validate her authority. This is a clear rejection of the Protestant declaration of Sola Scriptura and automatically puts Adventism in the cult realm.

Part II

---

[59] White, *Testimonies for the Church*, Vol. 8, p. 298, par. 1.

Investigative Judgement

Salvational Uncertainty

The Biblical Gospel

Forgiveness of Sin

Assurance of Salvation

No Condemnation

Chapter Three

**The Investigative Judgement:
Salvational Uncertainty, Biblical Heresy**

"The Investigative Judgment generally drives a lot of fear,

terror, and salvific uncertainty in Adventists."

A unique doctrine, a nagging liability

The Great Disappointment of October 22, 1844 had left Millerite Adventists devastated. The following day, Hiram Edson claimed that as he and two others were walking through a cornfield he was enrapt in a vision in which he saw Jesus moving from the Holy Place of the heavenly sanctuary into the Most Holy Place to begin a work of "investigative judgement" to cleanse the heavenly sanctuary of sins. Adventists have yet to explain how this heavenly sanctuary was defiled with sin to begin with, nevertheless this view would provide immediate comfort and renewed, fanatical zeal to the specific group of Millerite Adventists who later formed the Seventh-day Adventist Church. Despite the fact that it was Hiram Edson who had this "vision" and initially concocted the Investigative Judgement, the SDA Church never conferred prophet status on him. One wonders why this "vision" was not initially given to Ellen White. And, why did God abandon him thereafter when it came to "visions" and switched to Ellen White?

The Investigative Judgement, or the Sanctuary doctrine, is *Fundamental Belief #24* in the official beliefs of the Seventh-day Adventist Church.[60] Jews, who read the Old Testament in Hebrew, did not see this doctrine and still cannot see this doctrine in the Book of Daniel, where Adventists claim to extrapolate this doctrine. No Christian from the 1st century A.D. to the present day ever saw, believed in, and taught the/an Investigative Judgement. No Christian who reads the Bible alone sees such a doctrine. No Christian church nor theologian post-1844 sees this doctrine in Scripture. This doctrine is uniquely held by Adventists and can only be explained, justified, and defended with the writings of Ellen White.

Of course after the Adventist Millerite fanatics invented the Investigative Judgment, they tortured Scripture to make it conform to it. But naturally and contextually, Scripture does not teach the

---

[60] See *Seventh-day Adventists Believe*, "Christ's Ministry in the Heavenly Sanctuary," p. 347-370.

doctrine of the Investigative Judgment. This doctrine continues to be one of the most troublesome of the Seventh-day Adventist Church. Dissidents from the Adventist Church and critics alike usually name this doctrine as one of the major ones that they discovered to be problematic, unbiblical, and heretical. Some Adventist scholars have tried hard at defending this doctrine, while others will not touch it with a proverbial ten foot pole.

When Dr Desmond Ford discovered the errors with this doctrine in the 1980s and published his findings, he was fired from the Adventist Church. His discovery and writings influenced many other SDA pastors and members, who eventually left Adventism. Dr Desmond Ford wrote extensively on the sanctuary and the Investigative Judgement. Despite his efforts and showing the glaring errors with the doctrine, it remains unchanged because Adventists have an infallibility mentality and fixation regarding their distinctive doctrines. The only thing that has happened with it is that Adventist pastors do not talk and preach about it as much as they did in the past. They tend to shy away from it, but they believe it nonetheless. The other thing that has happened is that they have tried to reinterpret it to squeeze it into the Gospel. Many change the way it is presented but the doctrine itself remains intact. The doctrine is so anti-Gospel that it can't be revamped. It needs to be discarded altogether.

The Investigative Judgement is very confusing and complex. It is fraught with bad assumptions, arbitrary proof-texting, and historical revisionism, so I will not be taking a critical look at it, nor will I attempt to refute it point by point. A quick internet search of Dr Desmond Ford will show that he has done extensive work on it. Pastor Dale Ratzlaff has written an excellent point by point refutation of the Investigative Judgment.[61] In 2001-2002, a forward-thinking Adventist scholar by the name of Dr Raymond F. Cottrell wrote a thorough refutation of the Adventist assumptions and arguments for the sanctuary doctrine and presented his findings to various Adventist forums, hoping that they would see that it is a big liability

---

[61] Dale Ratzlaff, *Cultic Doctrines of Seventh-day Adventism: An Evangelical Wake-Up Call,* Second Revision (Glendale, AZ: LAM Publications, LLC, 2009).

that they need to discard. But almost two decades later, the doctrine remains unchanged. His paper is entitled *The Sanctuary Doctrine: Asset Or Liability?* and can be found online as a free PDF document.[62]

In January 2018, Winston McHarg published an article in *Adventist Today*, a progressive and independent journalism ministry for Seventh-day Adventists, entitled "*Why the Little Horn of Daniel 8 Must Be Antiochus Epiphanes*," in which he made a very good case that indeed Antiochus Epiphanes IV is the little horn of Daniel 8.[63] Two months later, Dr Clifford Goldstein, Editor of the Adult Bible Study Guide for the General Conference of Seventh-day Adventists, responded with "*The Little Horn of Daniel 8*" and sought to prove that Antiochus Epiphanes IV is not the little horn in order to defend the Adventist Investigative Judgment.[64] One week later, Dr Andre Reis responded to Dr Goldstein's article and thoroughly refuted all his points and assumptions, and showed how impossible it is to prove the 1844 Adventist Investigative Judgment from Daniel 8. To date, neither Dr Goldstein nor any other Adventist scholar or pastor has responded to Dr Reis' refutation. Dr Reis' article is aptly titled "*The Absolutely Final Comment on the Little Horn of Daniel 8*."[65] His refutation is truly absolute and final. However, his conclusions will not be accepted by the Adventist Church because any official declaration against the Investigative Judgement would mean refuting Ellen White's claim to divine inspiration and will have the potential of destroying Adventism altogether.

The Crux of the Investigative Judgement

---

[62] Dr Raymond F. Cottrell, *The Sanctuary Doctrine: Asset Or Liability?*, http://www.rethinkingadventism.com/support-files/cottrell_1844.pdf (Date accessed June 3, 2021).

[63] Winston McHarg, "Why the Little Horn of Daniel 8 Must Be Antiochus Epiphanes," *Adventist Today*, January 14, 2018, https://atoday.org/why-the-little-horn-of-daniel-8-must-be-antiochus-epiphanes/ (June 3, 2021).

[64] Dr Clifford Goldstein, "The Little Horn of Daniel 8," *Adventist Today*, March 12, 2018, https://atoday.org/the-little-horn-of-daniel-8/ (Date accessed June 3, 2021).

[65] Dr Andre Reis, "The Absolutely Final Comment on the Little Horn of Daniel 8," *Adventist Today*, March 16, 2018, https://atoday.org/36283-2/ (Date accessed June 3, 2021).

The Investigative Judgment generally drives a lot of fear, terror, and salvific uncertainty in Adventists. It is these points about the Investigative Judgment that I will focus on and show how horrendously wrong and anti-Gospel they are. Ellen White clearly explained what this Investigative Judgement is and when it started. Only the points that are most critical in respect to the Gospel will be dealt with and refuted. Ellen White:

> Attended by heavenly angels, our great High Priest enters the holy of holies, and there appears in the presence of God, to engage in the last acts of His ministration in behalf of man to perform the work of investigative judgment, and to make an atonement for all who are shown to be entitled to its benefits....So in the great day of final atonement and investigative judgment, the only cases considered are those of the professed people of God. The judgment of the wicked is a distinct and separate work, at a later period.[66]

According to this statement, on October 22, 1844, Jesus entered into the Most Holy Place of the heavenly sanctuary to appear in God's presence to engage in "the last acts of His ministration" for man, to investigate them. This "ministration" is "an atonement" that will reveal who all are "entitled to its benefits." This Investigative Judgement is a "final atonement" that is considering the cases of God's professed people. The wicked aren't being investigated in this Investigative Judgement, only alleged believers. The wicked will be investigated at a later (unknown) period. On page 483 of *The Great Controversy* Ellen White stated:

> As the books of record are opened in the judgment, the lives of all who have believed on Jesus come in review before God. Beginning with those who first lived upon the earth, our Advocate presents the cases of each successive generation, and closes with the living. Every name is mentioned, every case closely

---

[66] White, *The Great Controversy*, p. 480, par. 1.

investigated. Names are accepted, names rejected. When any have sins remaining upon the books of record, unrepented of and unforgiven, their names will be blotted out of the book of life, and the record of their good deeds will be erased from the book of God's remembrance.

According to this statement, Jesus is investigating the lives of all who believed in Him beginning with Adam's generation, moving to every successive generation, and then it will close with the living. The name of every believer will be mentioned and their lives "closely investigated." Some believers will be accepted for salvation and some will be rejected and be lost. Any unrepentant and unforgiven sin will have the names of believers blotted out of the book of life with all their good deeds erased. This criteria effectively blocks all from salvation, if you think about it. This also effectively prevents members from realizing how a new heart given to them by Christ resolves the problem. Being aware of the reasons behind a lot of Adventist teachings reveal how they reflect a demonic influence. Every sin is recorded with "terrible exactness" against believers:

> Opposite each name in the books of heaven is entered with terrible exactness every wrong word, every selfish act, every unfulfilled duty, and every secret sin, with every artful dissembling. Heaven-sent warnings or reproofs neglected, wasted moments, unimproved opportunities, the influence exerted for good or for evil, with its far-reaching results, all are chronicled by the recording angel.[67]

On page 486, Ellen White states that God will investigate believers with "searching scrutiny" to determine our fate:

> At the time appointed for the judgment –the close of the 2300 days, in 1844 – began the work of investigation and blotting out of sins. All who have ever taken upon themselves the name of Christ must pass its searching

---

[67] Ibid, p. 482, par. 1.

scrutiny. Both the living and the dead are judged "out of those things which were written in the books, according to their works.[68]

Interesting choice of language by Ellen White. It is saying, these are the people who appropriated the name of Christ, and that it was not Christ who chose them and took them for Himself. This reveals the man-centred, works-driven nature of the Investigative Judgement and many other SDA doctrines. And at the same time, the diminishing of the sovereignty of Christ and God. This statement also reveals that the Investigative Judgement began the process of "blotting out of sins." This means that the sins of believers are not blotted out and will not be blotted out until this process is over. In essence, believers' sins are still retained in heaven and charged against them. In order for their sins to be blotted out and for them to be saved, they "must pass its searching scrutiny."

This scrutiny that every believer must go through is so intense and meticulous that Ellen White said it will be as though there is no other being on earth:

> Though all nations are to pass in judgment before God, yet He will examine the cases of each individual with as close and searching scrutiny as if there were not another being upon the earth. Everyone must be tested, and found without spot or wrinkle or any such thing.[69]

In other words, every believer must be sinlessly perfect to qualify for salvation after they go through the Investigative Judgement. A single, forgotten, unrepented of sin is enough to condemn a believer in Ellen White's Investigative Judgement. She said, "Sins that have not been repented of and forsaken will not be pardoned and blotted out of the books of record, but will stand to witness against the sinner in the day of God."[70] Believers must have supercomputer memories to recount and repent of *every single sin* in order to have them be

---

[68] Ibid, p. 486, par. 1.

[69] Ibid, p. 489, par. 3.

[70] Ibid, p. 486, par. 2.

blotted out and to be pardoned. The purpose of the Investigative Judgement is to ensure believers have achieved sinless perfection to determine their fitness for heaven. Ellen White made this clear: "This work of examination of character, of determining who are prepared for the kingdom of God, is that of the investigative judgment."[71]

One of the most frightening things about the Adventist Investigative Judgement is that none of them know when God would have finished investigating the lives of dead saints and moved on to the living. In 1888 Ellen White said, "The judgment is now passing in the sanctuary above. For many years this work has been in progress. Soon–none know how soon–it will pass to the cases of the living."[72] Absolutely no one knows when their names will come up in the Investigative Judgement. One's name may come up and one is condemned but one continues with church-going and religious activities and will have no clue that one has already been rejected and condemned. When the Investigative Judgement is over, every believer's destiny would have been decided. And they would have no idea if they would be saved or lost. Ellen White said, "When the work of the investigative judgment closes, the destiny of all will have been decided for life or death."[73]

A believer will only know if they did enough to pass the Investigative Judgement and thus be saved when they shockingly wake up to the resurrection of life. If they did not do enough and did not confess every sin and be forgiven, then they will surprisingly wake up to the resurrection of damnation. The underlying crux of the Investigative Judgement is that no one is currently, truly saved. Present salvation is impossible. Not only does the Investigative Judgement contradict Scripture and the Gospel, but even worse it makes God appear to be an unstable, ignoramus, petty, draconian sadist who is just looking for the most minute sin, reason, and imperfection in order to condemn believers.

Some popular proof-texts Adventists use

---

[71] Ibid, p. 489.

[72] Ibid, p. 490, par. 1.

[73] Ibid, p. 490, par. 2.

Having established the framework and theology for their Investigative Judgement, Adventists then read those back into Scripture and force Scripture to teach the Investigative Judgement. For example, they believe that Genesis 18-19 teaches the Investigative Judgement because God came down with two angels "to see" if Sodom and Gomorrah had done according to their great outcry of their evil that came before God (Gen. 18:20-21). But this story is not an investigative judgement at all. This story is revealing God's justice upon the wicked and involving some of His righteous servants in the process. God was not investigating the sins of believers in Sodom and Gomorrah to determine their salvation, as the Investigative Judgement teaches. These were ungodly, unsaved people who God came to destroy and informed Abraham of the proceedings as an object lesson for Him and His children after him.

Many Adventists use the Parable of the Wedding Feast to justify the Investigative Judgement (Matt. 22:1-14). They believe that the king coming in to scope out those who were attired and then discovered a man not having the proper wedding attire is an instance of the Investigative Judgement. Not only is this bad, inconsistent hermeneutics but it also shows that they would grasp at every straw to justify their errors. Adventists vehemently reject the given meaning of parables in favor of their own interpretations that are Adventist friendly. They reject the literal rendering of the story of the Rich Man and Lazarus (Luke 16:19-31). They reject the immaterial spirit. They reject conscious existence and experiences immediately after death. That story teaches those things so they reject it, and do a lot of gymnastics to deny the obvious in what it teaches. They consistently claim it to be a parable that should not be understood or interpreted literally. Yet, they understand and interpret the Parable of the Wedding Feast literally to prop up the Investigative Judgement, despite the parable not teaching an investigative judgment. That parable is about the Jews. It is showing how some rejected Christ and the Gospel, so He called the Gentiles (vs. 1-10). It also teaches that anyone who does not have on Christ's appropriate robe of righteousness will be discovered and condemned, no matter how well hidden they are among His people (vs. 11-14). If it is teaching an Investigative Judgement as Adventists argue, then Luke 16:19-31 is a parable that is teaching consciousness after death and immediate rewards thereafter (the story is those things). Consistency demands this, but we cannot expect Adventists to be consistent.

In most places in the New Testament where Adventists see the word "judgement" or references to the "judgement seat of Christ/God," they read their Investigative Judgement into those texts. For example, Romans 14:10, which says, "...For we will all stand before the judgment seat of God" is seen as a proof-text for the Investigative Judgement. 2 Corinthians 5:10 is another major one. It says, "For we must all appear before the judgment seat of Christ, so that each one may receive what is due for what he has done in the body, whether good or evil." This for them is the Investigative Judgement which began in 1844. Another major Investigative Judgement proof-text is 1 Peter 4:17-18, which says, "For it is time for judgment to begin at the household of God; and if it begins with us, what will be the outcome for those who do not obey the gospel of God? [18]And "If the righteous is scarcely saved, what will become of the ungodly and the sinner?" One of their most pivotal proof-texts for the Investigative Judgement is Revelation 14:7, which says, "Fear God and give him glory, because the hour of his judgment has come...." Revelation 20:12 is another one. It says, "And I saw the dead, great and small, standing before the throne, and books were opened. Then another book was opened, which is the book of life. And the dead were judged by what was written in the books, according to what they had done" (cf. Dan. 7:10).

These are just a sample of the many proof-texts they use to squeeze the Investigative Judgement into and out of Scripture, but those Scriptures do not teach an Adventist Investigative Judgement neither as a prototype type nor as the actual thing that started on October 22, 1844. The issue here is not whether or not Scripture teaches judgement. Scripture certainly teaches about God judging people in the past (John 16:11), that God's judgment abides on some people even now (John 3:18-19), and that there is a judgement to come at the end of the world (Acts 17:31). Scripture is too replete with these for me to even expound on them. The issue here is, does Scripture teach the Adventist Investigative Judgement? Just by looking at the crux and purpose of the Investigative Judgement and the claim for when it supposedly began, it should be clear to any believer who is knowledgeable of Scripture and the Gospel that the Investigative Judgement is against Scripture and is very anti-Gospel, and that the Bible does not teach it.

Chapter Four

The Biblical Gospel Vs. The Investigative Judgement: When Did Jesus Enter the

Most Holy Place?

"The New Testament always speaks of Jesus as being at the "right hand of God," in the Most Holy Place."

At His ascension or on October 22, 1844?

Ellen White had made it clear that Jesus entered into the Most Holy Place of the heavenly sanctuary to perform "the closing work of atonement" before He is able to come again.[74] The Seventh-day Adventist Church has argued and maintained that Jesus went into the Most Holy Place ever since Ellen White and the Adventist pioneers concocted this view to save face, what with their Great Disappointment. What this view means is that Jesus was locked away from the Most Holy Place from His ascension in the 1st century A.D. until October 22, 1844, when God granted Him access to it so that He could begin the Investigative Judgement and final atonement. But contrary to what they contrive and teach, Jesus did not go to the Most Holy Place on October 22, 1844. He actually went to the Most Holy Place at His ascension in the 1st century A.D. The New Testament always speaks of Jesus as being at the "right hand of God," in the Most Holy Place.

When Stephen was making his defense to the Jewish leaders, Acts 7:55-56 says, "But he, full of the Holy Spirit, gazed into heaven and saw the glory of God, and Jesus standing at the right hand of God. [56]And he said, "Behold, I see the heavens opened, and the Son of Man standing at the right hand of God." After stating this, he was stoned to death (vs. 57-60). This passage is beyond clear about where Jesus went and was when He ascended. He went straight to the right hand of God, which was the Most Holy Place. In Ephesians 1:19-21, Paul extolled the position and power of Christ at God's right hand by saying:

> And what is the immeasurable greatness of his power
> toward us who believe, according to the working of his

---

[74] White, *The Great Controversy*, p. 481.

great might [20]that he worked in Christ when he raised him from the dead and seated him at his right hand in the heavenly places, [21]far above all rule and authority and power and dominion, and above every name that is named, not only in this age but also in the one to come.

Jesus was at the Father's right hand the moment He ascended to heaven. He is in a position of unlimited power, authority, and greatness.

In Colossians 3:1-4, Paul was very clear about where Christ was, our position in Him, and he used that to exhort believers to be heavenly-minded. He said:

If then you have been raised with Christ, seek the things that are above, where Christ is, seated at the right hand of God. [2]Set your minds on things that are above, not on things that are on earth. [3]For you have died, and your life is hidden with Christ in God. [4]When Christ who is your life appears, then you also will appear with him in glory.

This is amazing news for Christians. Paul says we have been raised with Christ and that He is seated at the right hand of God. Paul is making these statements in the 1st century A.D.! He is not speaking about 1844. Paul exhorted the Colossians to be heavenly-minded because their lives were "hidden with Christ in God." They were in the Most Holy Place in Jesus Christ and when He appears the second time, they all, along with every other believer, will appear with Him in glory. Our lives, salvation, and glory are secured in Jesus, by Jesus. It is not by our works and potentially passing the Investigative Judgement that will procure these for us as Ellen White teaches. We already have these things in Jesus.

The Apostle Peter was not confused about Jesus' location after His ascension as Adventists are. He stated clearly that He "...has gone into heaven and is at the right hand of God, with angels, authorities, and powers having been subjected to him" (1 Pet. 3:22). There is no New Testament author who anticipated that Jesus would enter the Most Holy Place and sit at God's right hand on October 22, 1844. Whenever they spoke of where Jesus was they constantly said it was at God's right hand.

Hebrews 1:3-4 affirms about Jesus:

> He is the radiance of the glory of God and the exact
> imprint of his nature, and he upholds the universe by the
> word of his power. After making purification for sins,
> he sat down at the right hand of the Majesty on high,
> [4]having become as much superior to angels as the name
> he has inherited is more excellent than theirs.

Whereas in the SDA Investigative Judgement Jesus begins the purification of sins in 1844, the author of Hebrews, writing around 68 A.D. states that Jesus *had already made* purification for sins, and after doing that He sat at God's right hand. His atonement was complete! Hebrews 6:19-20 states, "We have this as a sure and steadfast anchor of the soul, a hope that enters into the inner place behind the curtain, [20]where Jesus has gone as a forerunner on our behalf, having become a high priest forever after the order of Melchizedek." Texts like these are mangled by Adventists. They cannot afford to let these texts say what they say. This text pulverizes their 1844 Investigative Judgement. But despite their mangling, this text is crystal clear. It affirms the assurance and hope that we have in Jesus. It affirms that He entered into "the inner place behind the curtain," this is the Most Holy Place, as our Substitute.

We *know* that this is the Most Holy Place because it speaks of Him being a "high priest" forever after the order of Melchizedek. Regular priests did not minister in the Most Holy Place of the earthly sanctuary, only the high priest did. As a high priest, the "inner place behind the curtain," that Jesus has entered is the Most Holy Place. When one reads Adventist literature about the sanctuary and the Investigative Judgement, one will see that they completely locked Jesus out of the Most Holy Place and only granted Him access to it in 1844. They wreck every passage in the Book of Hebrews that affirms that Jesus did go into the Most Holy Place at His ascension. This passage suffers much violence at their hands, but the context clues are unconquerable. It only points to one location with regards to His heavenly ministry and what it meant, and that is the Most Holy

Place, at the right hand of God.

Similar to Hebrews 6, Hebrews 9:11-12 says:

> But when Christ appeared as a high priest of the good things that have come, then through the greater and more perfect tent (not made with hands, that is, not of this creation) [12]he entered once for all into the holy places, not by means of the blood of goats and calves but by means of his own blood, thus securing an eternal redemption.

Of course Adventists spin a lot of webs to keep Jesus away from the Most Holy Place in this passage. They argue that it is referring to the anterior Holy Place. But reader, don't you see the clues that dismiss their arguments? The very first clue is the reference to the "high priest." Any discussion about the high priest and the tabernacle is referring to the Most Holy Place. That is where the high priest ministered.

Despite the author using "holy places,"[75] referring to where Jesus "entered," it is the Most Holy Place because He entered "once for all" with His own blood and not with the blood of animals. This passage is talking about the yearly Day of Atonement when the high priest would enter the Most Holy Place with the blood of goats and calves to atone for the sins of the people and for the tabernacle (Lev.

---

[75] The author uses the Greek τὰ ἅγια (ta hagia) in reference to the Most Holy Place here. Adventists have tried to exclude the Most Holy Place from the definition of ta hagia because of the clear implications for their doctrine. They try to pin ta hagia to the entire sanctuary itself or to the Holy Place. They argue that if the author meant the Most Holy Place in this verse, he would have used hagia hagion as he did in 9:3. But this argument is very shallow and weak. The author of Hebrews uses ta hagia to refer to the entire sanctuary (8:2; 9:1), the Holy Place (9:2), and the Most Holy Place (9:12; 10:19). Identifying the specific compartment he is referring to when he uses ta hagia is determined by context and subject matter. In 9:12 we are absolutely sure that he is referring to the Most Holy Place because of the context and subject matter. He is contrasting the Old Covenant *high priest* and his ministry on the *Day of Atonement* with Jesus' high priestly and more efficient atoning ministry. The mention of Jesus as "high priest" and reference to Day of Atonement animal sacrifices already rules out every other meaning of ta hagia. It can only mean the Most Holy Place because *only the high priest* entered the Most Holy Place with those sacrifices once a year (9:7).

16:1-16). The author is contrasting Jesus' better and more efficient high priestly ministry with that of the Old Covenant system. As our high priest, Jesus entered into the Most Holy Place, in the 1st century A.D., with his own blood and through that He secured eternal redemption for us. Hebrews 10:11-14 continues with the contrast:

> And every priest stands daily at his service, offering repeatedly the same sacrifices, which can never take away sins. 12But when Christ had offered for all time a single sacrifice for sins, he sat down at the right hand of God, 13waiting from that time until his enemies should be made a footstool for his feet. 14For by a single offering he has perfected for all time those who are being sanctified.

The priests of the Old Covenant stood daily, constantly offering sacrifices that could not take away sins. Their standing indicated that their work was never complete. They had to always be on the move, ready to work, constantly, when they were on duty in the sanctuary. But Jesus made one perfect sacrifice and that is efficient for all time. That single sacrifice of Jesus truly cleanses sin. Notice the continuing contrast. The priests constantly stood at their service, but after Jesus made His single sacrifice He sat at the right hand of God. This indicated that His work was completed, finished, and perfectly satisfactory. He patiently sits in authority, power, and glory waiting until all His enemies are fully subjected to Him.

Verse 14 is potent and squashes the Investigative Judgement. The author says that His single sacrifice "has perfected for all time" believers who are being sanctified. This totally negates the Adventist Investigative Judgement. Despite the fact that we are growing in Christ and overcoming sins and imperfections daily, that's what being sanctified is, the author assures us that Christ has already perfected us for all time. Our salvation is superbly secured in Jesus. We are complete in Jesus (Col. 2:10). We are perfected for all time the moment we come to faith. Nevertheless, we continue to grapple with the flesh and experience victories (Gal. 5:16-26). We continue to be sanctified. But this sanctification is not for salvation as it is in

Adventism and the Investigative Judgement. Our sanctification as believers is to make us more like Christ and to demonstrate that we are truly saved and belong to God. In other words, our good works and sanctification are not to earn or gain salvation, they are to reveal that salvation has taken place. These are the good works that God had already prepared for us to walk in when we come to faith (Eph. 2:10). And irrespective of where a believer may be on the sanctification scale, he or she is still saved and stands perfectly righteous, justified, and complete in Jesus. This totally crushes the Investigative Judgement.

In verses 19-22 of Hebrews 10 the author confidently stated:

> Therefore, brothers, since we have confidence to enter the holy places by the blood of Jesus, [20]by the new and living way that he opened for us through the curtain, that is, through his flesh, [21]and since we have a great priest over the house of God, [22]let us draw near with a true heart in full assurance of faith, with our hearts sprinkled clean from an evil conscience and our bodies washed with pure water.

In the Old Covenant system only the high priest had access to the presence of God in the Most Holy Place. But the author is saying here that we can confidently enter into the Most Holy Place by the blood of Jesus. Jesus gives us direct access to God. Whereas the curtain of the Old Covenant sanctuary served to debar persons from the presence of God, the author says that Jesus' flesh is the new and living curtain that gives us full access to God in the Most Holy Place. Jesus is our great high priest, and therefore we can approach God with "full assurance of faith," with clean consciences, and purified bodies. The biblical Gospel is so beautiful. Reading and internalizing these truths of the Gospel is exciting and joy-inducing. In contrast, the Adventist Investigative Judgement is rife with doom, gloom, depression, despair, and anxiety.

Lastly, Hebrews 12:2 exhorts us as we run this Gospel race to keep "looking to Jesus, the founder and perfecter of our faith, who for the joy that was set before him endured the cross, despising the shame, and is seated at the right hand of the throne of God." This text further disproves the Investigative Judgement. It affirms that Jesus is the founder and perfecter of our faith. He initiates and establishes our faith. And He will perfect it to the very end. He looked forward to the joy of His success and vicariously died for us, enduring the Cross and ignoring the shame that came with it. After the completion of His mission, the author reiterates that He sat at the right hand of God in the Most Holy Place. All of these passages we investigated are undeniably clear about where Jesus went at His ascension and what that meant for Him and for believers. They pulverize the Adventist Investigative Judgement and the argument that Jesus went into the Most Holy Place on October 22, 1844.

Chapter Five

Let's Move God's Throne!

"Another heretical aspect of this "Moving Throne" theory of Adventists is that after Jesus and the Father left the throne in the Holy Place, Ellen White says Satan occupied it and started to work to keep God's people deceived."

Adventists try to reconcile the "right hand of God" statements of Scripture we looked into in the previous chapter with their 1844 movement to the Most Holy Place by merging Scripture with Ellen White's "moving throne" vision. In *Early Writings* she wrote:

> I saw the Father rise from the throne, and in a flaming chariot go into the holy of holies within the veil, and sit down.... Then a cloudy chariot, with wheels like flaming fire, surrounded by angels, came to where Jesus was. He stepped into the chariot and was borne to the holiest, where the Father sat. There I beheld Jesus, a great High Priest, standing before the Father. On the hem of His garment was a bell and a pomegranate, a bell and a pomegranate.[76]

According to this vision, both God the Father and Jesus were locked out of the Most Holy Place for 1800 years until October 22, 1844.[77] Based on what Ellen White wrote, we can conclude that God the Father has two thrones, one in the Holy Place and the other in the Most Holy Place.

Whereas Hebrews consistently presents Jesus as being a high priest after the order of Melchizedek, disqualified from being a Levitical priest, and superior to them, in this vision Ellen White sees Jesus as a Levitical priest in the way He is dressed and also in His posture! Bells and pomegranates were worn on the hems of the

---

[76] White, *Early Writings*, p. 55.

[77] The context of Ellen White's vision and statements about the "moving thrones" of the Father and Jesus is October 22, 1844. It is for this reason that I conclude that she had them "locked" out of the Most Holy Place until October 22, 1844. Adventist theology does not teach nor accept that Jesus entered the Most Holy Place at His ascension.

Levitical high priest to prevent them from dying when they appeared before God. Exodus 28:33-35 states:

> On its hem you shall make pomegranates of blue and purple and scarlet yarns, around its hem, with bells of gold between them, [34]a golden bell and a pomegranate, a golden bell and a pomegranate, around the hem of the robe. [35]And it shall be on Aaron when he ministers, and its sound shall be heard when he goes into the Holy Place before the LORD, and when he comes out, so that he does not die.

All of those passages we read in the Book of Hebrews and other places in Scripture in the previous chapter unanimously affirm that Jesus is *seated at the right hand of God*, a position He occupied from His ascension in the 1st century A.D. But in this vision, Ellen White sees Jesus not only dressed as a Levitical priest but also ministering like one also because she saw Him "standing before the Father." Dear reader, this is biblical contradiction, illiteracy, and heresy of catastrophic proportions! The Adventist "high priest Jesus" is a Levitical priest continuing Levitical priestly duties in heaven! This is biblically outrageous! This fanciful vision of Ellen White is woefully wrong. God could never have been the one who gave Ellen White this vision. It contradicts God's Word in glaring and egregious ways. Ellen White herself said, "Whatever contradicts God's word, we may be sure proceeds from Satan."[78] From her own admission, her visions proceeded from Satan, especially this one, because they contradict God's Word.

Scripture never presents God as having two thrones—one in the Holy Place and another in the Most Holy Place. Scripture always presents God as having *one* throne in the Most Holy Place. This throne was the Mercy Seat that was on top of the Ark of the Covenant (Exo. 25:17, 21-22). God's presence was manifested on the Mercy Seat by His Shekinah Glory. God did not have a throne in the Holy Place, at all. The Old Covenant sanctuary only had one throne

---

[78] White, *Patriarchs and Prophets*, p. 55.

and that was in the Most Holy Place. Another heretical aspect of this "Moving Throne" theory of Adventists is that after Jesus and the Father left the throne in the Holy Place, Ellen White says Satan occupied it and started to work to keep God's people deceived:

> I turned to look at the company who were still bowing before the throne; they did not know that Jesus had left it. Satan appeared to be by the throne, trying to carry on the work of God. I saw them look up to the throne, and pray, "Father, give us Thy Spirit." Satan would then breathe upon them an unholy influence; in it there was light and much power, but no sweet love, joy, and peace. Satan's object was to keep them deceived and to draw back and deceive God's children.[79]

Ellen White keeps piling up heresy upon heresy. Scripture does not teach that God and Jesus have thrones in the Holy Place, which they vacated in 1844, and moved to the ones in the Most Holy Place. Neither does Scripture ever teach that Satan has occupied God's throne nor can occupy it (although he desired it- Isa. 14:12-14). But in this vision, Ellen White has God the Father and Jesus abandoning the throne in the Holy Place and Satan occupying God's vacant throne, in God's sanctuary, and God's people praying to Satan and he responding to their prayers. The Bible never teaches this. This is barefaced heresy that should be rejected by all conscientious Christians.

Chapter Six

---

[79] White, *Early Writings*, p. 56.

Is God Investigating Every Name To Determine Who Is Worthy Of Salvation?

"He experienced the separation that we should have (Matt. 27:46), and now we experience the life, acceptance, and closeness to God that He always had. God is not subjecting us to an Investigative Judgement to potentially give us what we already have in Jesus."

Are you worthy?

Ellen White had made it clear in the Investigative Judgement about who is being investigated and for what purpose they are being investigated. In *The Great Controversy* p. 483, she wrote:

> As the books of record are opened in the judgment, the lives of all who have believed in Jesus come in review before God. Beginning with those who first lived upon the earth, our Advocate presents the cases of each successive generation, and closes with the living. Every name is mentioned, every case closely investigated. Names are accepted, names rejected.

It is ironic to note in this quote that Ellen White refers to Jesus as our "advocate," yet He is not functioning as our advocate. Instead, she has Him functioning as our prosecutor and judge. This is contradictory. Also, according to this statement, all the names of people who first lived upon the earth that believed in Jesus will kick start the Investigative Judgment to see if they are worthy and entitled to the benefits of His atonement. After they are "closely investigated" to determine their salvation, Jesus will begin the same process with the living. Some names will be accepted and deemed worthy to be saved, while others will be rejected and be lost. Again, no believer can be secured in Jesus nor can they be sure of their salvation in this Investigative Judgement. A lot of Adventists consider the doctrine of eternal security or having security of salvation to be a heresy. If we can have any form of security in Jesus as Scripture teaches, then their Investigative Judgement doctrine becomes moot. And they can't have that, so they bastardize a biblical doctrine in order to maintain their heretical doctrine.

Contrary to what Adventists believe and teach, Jesus is not performing a work of atonement in the Investigative Judgement nor is He making atonement to determine who are entitled to its benefits and thus can be saved. Jesus has done that already—on the Cross. Paul says in Romans 5:6-11:

> For while we were still weak, at the right time Christ died for the ungodly. [7]For one will scarcely die for a righteous person—though perhaps for a good person one would dare even to die—[8]but God shows his love for us in that while we were still sinners, Christ died for us. [9]Since, therefore, we have now been justified by his blood, much more shall we be saved by him from the wrath of God. [10]For if while we were enemies we were reconciled to God by the death of his Son, much more, now that we are reconciled, shall we be saved by his life. [11]More than that, we also rejoice in God through our Lord Jesus Christ, through whom we have now received reconciliation.

This is the beautiful, biblical Gospel! God is not going through our lives and scrutinizing us to determine if we are entitled to the benefits of Christ's atonement and therefore safe to save. We have been saved already. We have been enjoying the benefits of Christ's atonement made on the Cross. We have been reconciled to God and will not be "rejected" by Him.

Paul again affirms in 2 Corinthians 5:17-21:

> Therefore, if anyone is in Christ, he is a new creation. The old has passed away; behold, the new has come. [18]All this is from God, who through Christ reconciled us to himself and gave us the ministry of reconciliation; [19]that is, in Christ God was reconciling the world to himself, not counting their trespasses

against them, and entrusting to us the message of reconciliation. [20]Therefore, we are ambassadors for Christ, God making his appeal through us. We implore you on behalf of Christ, be reconciled to God. [21]For our sake he made him to be sin who knew no sin, so that in him we might become the righteousness of God.

How can Adventists read passages like these and still let the Investigative Judgement override them? It is unfathomable how they do it. Deception can truly warp our minds to the point that what is extremely clear in Scripture is rejected for that which is confusing and contrived. This passage is clear that we are new creations in Christ. We have been reconciled to God. God does not count our sins against us as Ellen White said He does in the Investigative Judgement. And not only are we reconciled, but also God has given us the ministry of reconciliation.

Lastly, Paul said that Jesus became sin for us so that we can become "the righteousness of God." As my friend Joan Hutcheson likes to say, "This is shouting stuff!" And indeed it is. Believers are not anticipating rejection and condemnation from God. We are already reconciled to God and are at peace with Him. We are not anticipating our sins to be thrown back at us as the reason we will be rejected because we are already the righteousness of God. Jesus took our sin and became sin for us. He experienced the separation that we should have (Matt. 27:46), and now we experience the life, acceptance, and closeness to God that He always had. God is not subjecting us to an Investigative Judgement to potentially give us what we already have in Jesus.

Were they worthy?

In Ellen White's statement above, no one before the start of the Investigative Judgement was saved, accepted by God, nor was worthy. It is only after they go through the Investigative Judgement that it would be determined if they were worthy or not. Of course Scripture does not teach this. But we must really ask, was anyone saved, worthy, and received eternal life before the Investigative

Judgement began on October 22, 1844? The answer is a resounding "yes!" Tons of believers were saved, commended, enjoyed the benefits of Christ's atonement, and were considered worthy long before Adventists *invented* the Investigative Judgement that sought to deprive them of such blessings.

Romans 5:14 calls Adam "…a type of the one who was to come." Adam is a type of Christ. According to 1 Corinthians 15:45-49, Jesus is the Second Adam. Hebrews 11:4 says of Abel, "By faith Abel offered to God a more acceptable sacrifice than Cain, through which he was commended as righteous, God commending him by accepting his gifts. And through his faith, though he died, he still speaks." God called Abel a righteous man. Although in Abel's time the atonement was future, it was still before 1844. God called him righteous. He enjoyed the benefits of the atonement before 1844. Will God have to process Abel through the 1844 Investigative Judgement to ensure that He did not make a mistake in calling him a righteous man? Ellen White said that Abel and his generation will have to go through the Investigative Judgement and be closely scrutinized to determine their fate. But Scripture affirms Abel as being righteous and commended by God. He was already destined for salvation, before the Investigative Judgement started in 1844.

Hebrews 11:5 says of Enoch, "By faith Enoch was taken up so that he should not see death, and he was not found, because God had taken him. Now before he was taken he was commended as having pleased God." Enoch was commended as pleasing God. Enoch did not die. He was translated. God took Him! No Investigative Judgement needed before! But according to Ellen White, even Enoch will be subject to the Investigative Judgement to determine his fate and worthiness. This is madness! Verse 7 calls Noah "an heir of the righteousness that comes by faith." Will he need to go through the newly invented Investigative Judgement to determine if that conclusion about him is true? Certainly not! Ellen White was grossly mistaken in her statements.

2 Kings 2:11 states that God took Elijah by a whirlwind to heaven. Elijah's salvation was secured. He had taken on the name of Christ before the Investigative Judgement started in 1844. Obviously, this has

to be revoked so that he can be processed through it. God must have made a mistake in translating Elijah and having him skip the Investigative Judgement. According to Matthew 17:1-4, Moses was with Elijah, in the spiritual abode of the righteous before 1844. God will have to reverse Moses' circumstance and drag him through the Investigative Judgement where he will undergo intense scrutiny to see if he is worthy to be saved. We can add the rest of the saints in Hebrews 11 that were determined worthy and saved, and missed out on the 1844 Investigative Judgement: Abraham, Sarah, Isaac, Jacob, Joseph, Moses, Rahab, Gideon, Barak, Sampson, Jephthae, David, Samuel, and the prophets. They were all saved and did not need to go through the Investigative Judgement to determine their status. They were saved and righteous before the invention of the Investigative Judgement. Will their status be revoked as they are processed through it, or possibly receive acceptance and salvation thereafter? Hebrews 12:22-23 says that their spirits are already in heaven! It says:

> But you have come to Mount Zion and to the city of the living God, the heavenly Jerusalem, and to innumerable angels in festal gathering, [23]and to the assembly of the firstborn who are enrolled in heaven, and to God, the judge of all, and to the spirits of the righteous made perfect.

The spirit of every righteous saint is currently in heaven with God! They all went to heaven before October 22, 1844. God declared them worthy. Why would God need to begin an investigation of their lives in 1844 to either accept or reject them? Ellen White was a psychological wreck who painted God in her own delusional, scary image. Her Investigative Judgement is nonsensical and contradicts Scripture in so many ways. Demons must have used her to say that all the names of the saints who first lived on the earth will come up in the Investigative Judgement, as their cases have not been decided, to decide their final outcome and fate.

Chapter Seven

God Has Forgiven and Blotted Out Our Sins

"Sins are forgiven the moment an individual repents, is converted, and comes to faith in Jesus (Acts 3:19). Our sins are not partially nor merely symbolically forgiven. They are forgiven in full, at the moment of repentance."

God does not store up our sins

Another major problem with the Investigative Judgement is that it teaches that God has not forgiven our sins. By her teaching this, Jeremiah 31:34 is negated, so as to reinforce the concept of the new or present covenant being the old covenant where sins are not forgiven and forgotten. In this teaching, God has not blotted out our sins. All the sins of believers were (and continue to be) transferred to the heavenly sanctuary and registered in the books. These sins are held against believers to determine if they can be saved when the process is over. If we are not saved, then we will be rejected and damned. In the Investigative Judgement of Adventists, God is pettily and vengefully looking for any sin to condemn believers.

If God were really doing this, no one would be able to be saved. Job 15:14-16 says, "What is man, that he can be pure? Or he who is born of a woman, that he can be righteous? [15]Behold, God puts no trust in his holy ones, and the heavens are not pure in his sight; [16]how much less one who is abominable and corrupt, a man who drinks injustice like water!" The Psalmist pointed out in Psalm 130:3, "If you, O LORD, should mark iniquities, O Lord, who could stand?" If God were truly marking our sins, storing them up in heaven to be held against us, so as to later investigate what has been "unforgiven and unrepented of," who indeed would be able to stand? Who would be acquitted or justified? Who has a supercomputer memory to ensure that they have asked for forgiveness for every single sin they have ever committed, knowingly and unknowingly? Not a single human being! We would all be hopelessly lost. This line of reasoning by Ellen White effectively blocks out the fact that we sin because we are sinners by nature, in need of a new nature. This is just another distraction to prevent people from looking at what they are instead of what they do. Biblical repentance is turning to God and not a mere regret for sins. Adventists have made repentance to be a mere regret for sin so that they can instil the need to keep their version of the Law, as a requirement for salvation. After asking that profound question, the Psalmist thankfully affirmed in verse 4: "But with you there is forgiveness, that you may be feared." Unlike the god of Adventism, the God of the Bible forgives us and does not hold our sins against us. Because of this, we revere Him.

In Psalm 103, one of the reasons the Psalmist evokes his soul to bless God is because He "forgives all your iniquities" (vs. 2). Verses 9-13 beautifully affirm:

> He will not always chide, nor will he keep his anger forever. [10]He does not deal with us according to our sins, nor repay us according to our iniquities. [11]For as high as the heavens are above the earth, so great is his steadfast love toward those who fear him; [12]as far as the east is from the west, so far does he remove our transgressions from us. [13]As a father shows compassion to his children, so the LORD shows compassion to those who fear him.

These verses disprove Ellen White's notion of the Adventist Investigative Judgement that our sins are stored in heaven; are being held against us, and will only be blotted out when our names come up in this judgement and we possibly pass its "searching scrutiny." The Adventist god is an angry, unstable, vengeful monster who needs just one unforgiven sin to reject our names in the Investigative Judgement. But the God of Scripture does not remain angry with us. He does not deal with us according to our sins nor repay us as we deserve. His love towards us is immeasurable. His forgiveness is limitless.

From our human perspective, the East from the West is infinitely far apart. The Psalmist says as far as those two points are apart from each other, it is comparably the same way that God *has removed* our sins from us! He has completely blotted them out! The Adventist Investigative Judgement argues that our sins are still registered against us and not blotted out, but this Scripture expresses clearly that we have been forgiven and that our sins have been blotted out and removed.

In penitence after committing his wicked deeds, David requested of God, "Hide your face from my sins, and blot out all my iniquities" (Psa. 51:9). Why would David ask God to blot out all of his sins if he knew that God would hold them against him in an Investigative Judgement? According to Ellen White's Investigative Judgement, David himself is not saved and must pass the Investigative Judgement and reckon with all of his sins to determine if he can be saved. But David confidently asked God here to blot out all of his sins. Why would he ask God to do this if he knew that God would not blot out sins before the Investigative Judgement would have started on October 22, 1844? David asked God to blot out his sins because He knew that God *does* blot out the sins of believers. He does not keep a record of them nor does He hold them against us to condemn us in an Investigative Judgement. David had asked God to blot out his sins; God beautifully affirmed that He does blot out the sins of his people. He does not remember them. He does not hold them against us for us to face them in an Investigative Judgement. Isaiah 43:25 says, "I, I am he who blots out your transgressions for my own sake, and I will not remember your sins."

One of the underlying premises of the Investigative Judgement is that our sins are stored in heaven, that God has not blotted them out, and that He holds them against us as He judges us, but God Himself in this text testifies that He does not do that. Adventists paint God to be a monster and a liar with respect to how He deals with believers and their sins, but God affirms that He is not that way. In Isaiah 44:22, God assured Israel, "I have blotted out your transgressions like a cloud and your sins like mist; return to me, for I have redeemed you." After God forgives us and blots out our sins, He does not count them against us. They are not reserved in the books of heaven for us to reckon with in an Investigative Judgement. David assures us, "Blessed is the one whose transgression is forgiven, whose sin is covered. Blessed is the man against whom the LORD counts no iniquity, and in whose spirit there is no deceit" (Psa. 32:1-2).

Our sins are completely forgiven in Jesus

The New Testament's theology on forgiveness of sins is no different from the Old Testament's. The New Testament makes it abundantly clear that believers' sins have been forgiven, blotted out, and are not held against us to condemn us before God. As Jesus' harbinger, John's ministry was to prepare the way for Jesus and to proclaim forgiveness of sins. Mark 1:4 says, "John appeared, baptizing in the wilderness and proclaiming a baptism of repentance for the forgiveness of sins." Sins are forgiven the moment an individual repents, is converted, and comes to faith in Jesus (Acts 3:19). Our sins are not partially nor merely symbolically forgiven. They are forgiven in full, at the moment of true repentance.

Throughout His public ministry, Jesus was forgiving people of sins, not transferring them to heaven for an Investigative Judgement to come. He blotted out sins, not reserved them to be blotted out in the future after He would have investigated the lives of believers to see if they are safe and deserving to be saved. After His passion and resurrection, He commissioned the disciples to specifically preach immediate forgiveness of sins in His name. Luke 24:46-47 records, "Thus it is written, that the Christ should suffer and on the third day rise from the dead, [47]and that repentance and forgiveness of sins should be proclaimed in his name to all nations, beginning from Jerusalem."

In their preaching and teaching, this is what the disciples proclaimed to people—immediate forgiveness of sins when they repent. They never preached that people's sins were transferred to the heavenly sanctuary for them to face when an Investigative Judgement would start in October 1844. In Acts 2:38, Peter called on the people to repent and be baptized so that they could be forgiven and filled with the Holy Spirit. In Acts 5:31 he said about Jesus and the Gospel they were preaching, "God exalted him at his right hand as Leader and Savior, to give repentance to Israel and forgiveness of sins." He preached this same message to the Gentile Cornelius and his household in Acts 10:43. Paul affirmed that he was given this same message to preach (Acts 26:18). And this is the message that Paul preached everywhere he went. For example, in Ephesians 1:7-8 he says, "In him we have redemption through his blood, the forgiveness of our trespasses, according to the riches of his grace, [8]which he lavished upon us, in all wisdom and insight."

Believers are currently redeemed in Christ. We have experienced forgiveness of our sins according to God's rich grace lavished on us with all wisdom and insight. This passage is so reassuring. Before God saved us and made so many promises towards us that He has fulfilled in Jesus Christ, He had all the insight into our post-salvation struggles, failures, sins, and dilemma. Yet He still went ahead and redeemed us, forgave us, lavished us with grace, and continues to keep us. This is mind-blowing! God factored in all the shortcomings believers will experience and still chose to forgive us and assures us that we are forgiven of all sin—past, present, and future. He did not utilize His insight to pump fear and a lack of assurance of salvation into us as Ellen White does with her Investigative Judgement. Instead, God assures us forgiveness and the total blotting out of our sins. Colossians 2:13-14 says, "And you, who were dead in your trespasses and the uncircumcision of your flesh, God made alive together with him, having forgiven us all our trespasses, [14]by canceling the record of debt that stood against us with its legal demands. This he set aside, nailing it to the cross."

Whereas the Investigative Judgement has a record of our debts (sins) stored in heaven for us to reckon with, the record of debt that did exist, as was accrued by the Mosaic Law, has been cancelled and nailed to the Cross of Christ. God does not keep a record of the sins of believers! God is not going through our sins in heaven right now to either accept or reject us, as Ellen White said. God has completely forgiven us and has made us alive with Christ. We stand complete in Jesus. Despite our repetitive failings and committing sins as believers, we, being in Christ, means that God sees us as if we have never sinned! We are completely covered by the righteousness of

Jesus. The biblical Gospel is so beautiful, humbling, liberating, and life-changing. On the other hand, the Adventist Investigative Judgement is a grotesque teaching that corrupts and contradicts the biblical Gospel. Its main aim is to pump endless fear, guilt-tripping, paranoia, and salvational uncertainty into Adventists because it depends on sinless perfectionism. Dr Steve Daily points out by saying, "This emphasis on perfectionism made the investigative judgment a very deadly and guilt-producing doctrine. Not only was it unbiblical, it was anti-biblical in its direct contradiction of the New Covenant Gospel, Christ's perfect finished work on the cross, and God's amazing grace."[80]

In Colossians 3:13 Paul said, "…if one has a complaint against another, forgiving each other; as the Lord has forgiven you, so you also must forgive." Paul grounds his exhortation instructing the Colossians to forgive each other on the grounds that the Lord "has forgiven" them. God's gracious, free, and loving forgiveness of believers should be the foundation and motivation for us to forgive each other. We can freely and lovingly forgive each other because God has done the same for us. If we knew that God's forgiveness was only partial, with our sins being stored, held against us, and for us to potentially be condemned with later on, Paul would have instructed the Colossians to follow that same pattern of forgiveness. And were this the case, tensions, unforgiveness, and bitterness would have been the norm in the Body of Christ. We would have partially forgiven each other, but written down sins and infractions to be held against each other in the future. But this is not the case. Paul exhorted the saints to completely forgive each other because God has done the same to them.

According to Hebrews 8:12, one of the promises that God made of the New Covenant is, "I will be merciful toward their iniquities, and I will remember their sins no more." And 1 John 1:9 says, "If we confess our sins, he is faithful and just to forgive us our sins and to cleanse us from all unrighteousness." This is very heart-warming and assuring for believers. The Gospel of Christ, the New Covenant,

---

[80] Steve Daily, *Ellen G. White: A Psychobiography* (Conneaut Lake, PA: Page Publishing, Inc., 2020), p. 67.

assures us of total forgiveness; complete cleansing. But the Adventist Investigative Judgement guarantees us that God is not merciful towards our sins nor does He cleanse them. Instead, He keeps them in remembrance to condemn some of us after He goes over our names in the Investigative Judgement. The Investigative Judgement is heretical, grossly anti-Gospel, and it blatantly contradicts Scripture. It makes God out to be a liar, a characteristic that befits Satan rather than God.

God already knows those who belong to Him

Another major problem with the Investigative Judgement is the fact that God is presented to be ignorant of who belongs to Him and therefore must process them through the "searching scrutiny" of the Investigative Judgement to determine who is prepared for His kingdom. By the very fact that the names of believers will be either "accepted" or "rejected" in the Investigative Judgement, it shows that in this doctrine God is ignorant of who really belongs to Him and therefore must meticulously file and sort them through the Investigative Judgement to determine who is wheat and who are tares. But Scripture presents a different picture about God's knowledge of His children. In Isaiah 43:1, God said of Israel, "But now thus says the LORD, he who created you, O Jacob, he who formed you, O Israel: "Fear not, for I have redeemed you; I have called you by name, you are mine."" This was such a beautiful reminder to Israel. God let them know that He was their creator and redeemer, He personally knew them, and they belonged to Him. God knows His faithful children. He does not need to scrutinize their lives for sins to determine who they are.

In the days of Elijah when Israel was in apostasy, he had thought that there were no other true prophets and people of God in the land. God assured him that He would judge and destroy a lot of the Israelites and confirmed to Elijah, "Yet I will leave seven thousand in Israel, all the knees that have not bowed to Baal, and every mouth that has not kissed him" (1 Kings 19:18). Amidst this widespread apostasy, God knew His faithful servants. He did not need a prolonged Investigative Judgement to know who they were.

In John 10:14 Jesus said, "I am the good shepherd; I know my sheep and my sheep know me." Jesus knows His sheep. He made this statement from the 1st century A.D. He did not need to wait to finish the Investigative Judgment beginning on October 22, 1844 so as to determine who His sheep are and for them to know Him. In verses 27-28, He confidently affirmed, "My sheep hear my voice, and I know them, and they follow me. 28I give them eternal life, and they will never perish, and no one will snatch them out of my hand." In the Investigative Judgement scheme of things, no believer currently possesses eternal life. No believer can know if they are saved. God Himself does not know true, saved believers. He needs the Investigative Judgement to determine that. But Jesus states clearly that He knows His own and they know Him. He gives to His sheep eternal life, right now, and they will never perish nor can they be snatched out of His hands. In the Investigative Judgement, believers do not have eternal life; they are not saved yet. According to Ellen White, names of believers will be accepted and names will be rejected. Their lives will undergo intense scrutiny to determine who is fit for God's kingdom. These teachings of the Investigative Judgement are antithetical to what Jesus is saying here in John 10.

God does not need such a process nor to guess who belongs to Him. He already knows. Hymenaeus and Philetus were teaching the heresy that the resurrection had already happened. This teaching of theirs was swerving some from the truth and upsetting the faith of others (2 Timothy 2:18). Amidst all of this, Paul follows up and writes to Timothy: "But God's firm foundation stands, bearing this seal: "The Lord knows those who are his," and, "Let everyone who names the name of the Lord depart from iniquity"" (2 Tim. 2:19). *God. Knows. His. Own*! Irrespective of what is going on, God knows true believers. God does not need any Investigative Judgement to know nor to determine who are true and false believers. He knows everyone (John 2:24-25). Before the foundation of the world, He knew who would be saved and who would be lost (Rev. 13:8). After all, God is omniscient (Prov. 5:21; 15:3; Psa. 139; Heb. 4:13). But in the construct of the Investigative Judgement, He is not.

Chapter Eight

Can Believers Know That They Are Saved Right Now?

"Believers are justified, saved, have peace with God, and stand uncondemned right now. We know these things because Scripture repeats them over and over."

Believers have the assurance of salvation

In the Investigative Judgement of Adventists, no one is capable of knowing that they are currently saved or that they will be saved. That assurance is not something that Adventism nor the Investigative Judgement grants. The only way SDAs will know that they had done enough and luckily made it through in the end is if they wake up in the first resurrection or if they are alive and translated when Jesus returns. Despite the fact that SDA *Fundamental Belief #10* claims that "...we...have the assurance of salvation now and in the judgement,"[81] this is nothing but another instance of forked-tongue speaking on their part. Assurance of salvation is something that is impossible to have in the SDA Investigative Judgement and environment. There are so many works that Ellen White says that they have to do that they can never be sure that they have done enough, or that they will ever be good enough to be saved. This doctrine has psychologically and spiritually wrecked the lives of millions of Adventists and Former Adventists alike. But despite the monstrosity of this doctrine, we can know that we are saved right now as Christians. We can be assured that we will never be condemned because we are in Christ. We have

---

[81] *Seventh-day Adventists Believe*, p. 133.

peace with God right now! Believers know that they are saved and are prepared for His kingdom.

In 2 Corinthians 13:5 Paul said, "Examine yourselves, to see whether you are in the faith. Test yourselves...." This is an exhortation for believers to test and confirm their faith status. Paul exhorted these believers to examine themselves to ascertain whether or not they were in the faith. This simply means that believers can know their salvific status before the Second Coming of Christ. Christians do not have to live in anxious suspense about their salvation. We do not have to be uncertain about our eternal destiny. In the construct of the Adventist gospel and the Investigative Judgement, it is impossible to be saved. This is so because their gospel is man-centred, ego-centric, and based on works. While in the biblical Gospel, it is very easy to be saved and very hard to be lost, because it is God-centred and salvation is by grace through faith in Jesus Christ (Eph. 2:8-10). John 3:16-18 puts it this way:

> For God so loved the world, that he gave his only Son, that whoever believes in him should not perish but have eternal life. [17]For God did not send his Son into the world to condemn the world, but in order that the world might be saved through him. [18]Whoever believes in him is not condemned, but whoever does not believe is condemned already, because he has not believed in the name of the only Son of God.

All we need in order to *currently have* eternal life is to believe in Jesus Christ. Jesus' first coming and vicarious death was to save us. He was not sent to condemn us. All who truly believe in Him are not condemned! In the Investigative Judgement, despite believing in Jesus, many believers will be condemned if their names are "rejected" as God scrutinizes them in the Investigative Judgement. But in the biblical Gospel, coming to faith in Christ removes us from the realm of condemnation. The only people who are and will be condemned are those who do not believe in THE true Jesus Christ. There is no possibility of condemnation for believers in Jesus Christ.

In John 5:24 Jesus said, "Truly, truly, I say to you, whoever hears my word and believes him who sent me has eternal life. He does not come into judgment, but has passed from death to life." This text is so profound. It destroys the Investigative Judgement. Jesus Himself affirmatively says that anyone who believes in God who sent Him *has* eternal life. "Has" is a present active indicative verb in the Greek. This means that eternal life is something that believers currently, actively possess! It is not something that is tentative at the summation of the Investigative Judgement.

The New Testament does present an "already-but-not-yet" construct of salvation. Some passages talk of salvation as being right now, while others present it as something that is happening, and others as still future (eg. Rom. 13:11-14). However, this does not mean that we do not currently possess salvation. Scripture presents salvation in three phases (some scholars argue four phases). Scholars have recognized these to refer to initial soul-salvation when we come to faith (Rom. 8:24; 10:10; 2 Tim. 1:9; Tit. 3:5), as continuous salvation as we are being delivered from the power of sin in our lives (1 Cor. 1:18; 15:2; 2 Cor. 2:15), and as ultimate salvation in which we will be delivered from the very presence of sin (1 Cor. 5:5).[82]

The other clause of John 5:24 destroys the Investigative Judgement even more. Jesus says the believer does not come into judgement. The judgement being referred to here is judgement that has condemnation as its end result and not the judgement that we will face to receive rewards (Rom. 14:10-12; 1 Cor. 3:10-15; 2 Cor. 5:9-10). Jesus says believers will not be condemned because we have passed from death into life. This is profound. The Greek verb for "has passed" is a perfect active indicative. It emphasizes the present or ongoing result of a completed action. It is conveying a transfer that occurred in the past and we are still enjoying the results. We have been transferred from the realm of death into the realm of life in Jesus! And we are not being bandied about between death and life either. We have been transferred to the realm of life, eternal life beginning at the moment of faith, in Jesus. This is the assurance that believers have in the Gospel. This is the assurance that Adventism

---

[82] See Arthur W. Pink, *A Fourfold Salvation* (Pensacola, FL: Chapel Library, 2006).

and the Investigative Judgement, sadly, take away from Adventists. Adventists cannot have peace with God believing in and teaching the Investigative Judgement. But Romans 5:1 assures, "Therefore, since we have been justified by faith, we have peace with God through our Lord Jesus Christ."

Justification is a status we enjoy right now in Jesus. Peace and reconciliation with God are things we experience right now in Jesus. Whereas in the Investigative Judgement, none of these things can happen right now. Believers are justified, saved, have peace with God, and stand uncondemned right now. We know these things because Scripture repeats them over and over. Paul thundered in Romans 8:1, "There is therefore now no condemnation for those who are in Christ Jesus." In the Investigative Judgement of Adventists, condemnation awaits millions of believers who are *in Jesus Christ*. The Investigative Judgement is so twisted and heretical that one cannot be secure despite being *in Jesus Christ*. Condemnation awaits many believers who do not pass this Investigative Judgement. But Paul assures us, in contradiction to Ellen White's false gospel, that *no one* who is in Jesus Christ will be condemned. The Investigative Judgement grossly contradicts the biblical Gospel.

Shortly before the end of his life, Paul stated:

> For I am already being poured out as a drink offering, and the time of my departure has come. [7]I have fought the good fight, I have finished the race, I have kept the faith. [8]Henceforth there is laid up for me the crown of righteousness, which the Lord, the righteous judge, will award to me on that Day, and not only to me but also to all who have loved his appearing (2 Tim. 4:6-8).

Paul was about to die but despite that he spoke with tremendous assurance about his salvation. He said that he had fought the good fight, finished his race, and kept the faith. He was assured that the crown of righteousness was "laid up" for him. He was equally sure that it was laid up for "all who loved" Jesus' appearing as well. Paul's tone here is so different from Ellen White's as she articulated the Investigative Judgement. In explaining what the Investigative Judgement is, Ellen White explained it with much fear, uncertainty, doom and gloom, works-orientation, and the need to be sinlessly perfect to stand a chance of passing it in order to be saved.[83] But Paul was about to die for the Gospel yet he spoke with much faith, assurance, and love. Believers can know that they are saved right now. Paul knew. We can know. 1 John 5:13 says, "I write these things to you who believe in the name of the Son of God so that you may know that you have eternal life." God's children do not have to be in a quandary about their salvation. We are saved in Jesus Christ right now. But sadly, this is not something that the Investigative Judgement can ever afford Adventists.

In Colossians 1:13-14 Paul said, "He has delivered us from the domain of darkness and transferred us to the kingdom of his beloved Son, [14]in whom we have redemption, the forgiveness of sins." This passage is expressing the same truth as John 5:24. God has delivered believers from the domain of darkness (death) and permanently transferred us into the kingdom of His Beloved Son, Jesus Christ. We are citizens of the kingdom of God (Phil. 3:20-21). We currently possess this citizenship. We are not awaiting to pass the Investigative Judgement to determine our status in God's kingdom and preparedness for it. We are already prepared for God's kingdom. We are already *in* God's kingdom because He has already forgiven us of our sins and has redeemed us. These are wonderful assurances that believers have in the biblical Gospel that Adventists can never have in their Investigative Judgement.

---

[83] See White, *The Great Controversy* (1888), chapter 26 "The Investigative Judgement."

Part III

Proof-texts

Proof-specks

Faulty Hermeneutics

Bad Assumptions

Refutations

Chapter Nine

Eleven Faulty Hermeneutical Principles And Assumptions Of Seventh-day Adventists And How To Refute Them

"Persons who use the Proof-text Method generally do not have any regard for the context they extract texts from. All relevant contextual information is ignored. Texts, or pieces of them, are indiscriminately ripped from their respective original context and smudged together to create beliefs or doctrines."

Adventists are the masters of proof-texting

Seventh-day Adventists generally do not have a basic grasp of Biblical Hermeneutics. The Proof-text Method of Bible Study was ingrained as the heart of the movement's Bible study method from the very beginning. The very text that is the foundation of the movement (Daniel 8:14), as Ellen White had said, is a proof-text. The Proof-text Method is the worst way to study the Bible. Proof-texting is essentially hunting for texts that seem to buttress what one believes and assumes, and then thinking that that is what the texts are saying. Persons who use the Proof-text Method generally do not have any regard for the context they extract texts from. All relevant contextual information is ignored. Texts, or pieces of them, are indiscriminately ripped from their respective original context and smudged together to create beliefs or doctrines.[84] Adventism's

---

[84] As a method of Bible Study, the "Proof-text Approach" is the worst and has many flaws. With this approach, various aspects of biblical interpretation are ignored, such as the immediate and historical context of the book/passage, original languages, the audience

doctrines were forged this way. The very text that they use to justify their Proof-text Method is a proof-text that means something completely different within its immediate context. This favoured text is Isaiah 28:10 and 13, which says:

> [10]For it is precept upon precept, precept upon precept, line upon line, line upon line, here a little, there a little. [13]And the word of the LORD will be to them precept upon precept, precept upon precept, line upon line, line upon line, here a little, there a little, that they may go, and fall backward, and be broken, and snared, and taken.

They believe that this text is the biblical method of how they should study the Bible. They believe that this is what this is saying. But in actuality, these texts are not saying this at all. The contextual unit is from vs. 1-13. God was rebuking Ephraim because it was full of "proud drunkards" (vs. 1). They were "overcome with wine" (vs. 1). In vs. 2-4, God presaged imminent judgement upon Ephraim by His "strong and mighty one" who will tread them underfoot. In verse 5, God promised to be a crown of beauty to the righteous remnant because He will vindicate them. The passage then laments that the prophet and priest were drunk and staggering, the tables were entirely full of vomit, and as a result they stumbled in judgement (verses 7-8). Then verses 9-10 capture the scoffing of the drunkards, "To whom will he teach knowledge, and to whom will he explain the message? Those who are weaned from the milk, those taken from the breast?"

The priest, prophet and drunkards were scoffing at the idea that Isaiah was constantly trying to teach them as if they were children just weaned from the breast. The following verse about "precept

---

addressed, the nature of the book/passage (wisdom, apocalyptic, law, narrative, etc.,) the author's style, grammar and syntax, etc., and one reads one's preconceived notions or already held beliefs into Scripture by indiscriminately connecting unrelated texts. With this approach, one can make Scripture say or teach whatever one wants it to. For a good discussion on Bible Study methods, see Dr Clinton Baldwin, *Methods of Biblical Interpretations: Perspectives on Prophecy Revised Ed.* (Spanish Town, Ja: Lithomedia Printers Limited, 2012), p. 1-44.

upon precept, line upon line, here a little and there a little" is actually how they used to take their time to teach children to write Hebrew characters of their alphabet and to read.[85] The priests and prophets and the "proud drunkards" in Ephraim were annoyed at the thought that Isaiah constantly repeated God's Word to them and was carefully going over the basics like one would do with children. Then verses 11-12 express that God will speak to them (discipline them) by a foreign nation because He desired to give them rest but they were rebellious and disobedient. Due to their obstinacy, verse 13 affirms, "And the word of the LORD will be to them precept upon precept, precept upon precept, line upon line, line upon line, here a little, there a little, that they may go, and fall backward, and be broken, and snared, and taken."

These scoffing men were annoyed that Isaiah attempted to teach and speak to them like they were little children. But now, God is saying that He will in fact use a foreign nation to discipline and punish them like children in order that they may "go, and fall backward, and be broken, and snared, and taken." This very verse that Adventists use to promote proof-texting as the legitimate way of studying the Bible is not talking about that at all! The statement was the scoffing phrase of the drunken priest, prophet, and men of Ephraim. Because of that, God was promising to discipline, judge, and punish them through a foreign nation. His discipline and judgement would be like teaching children the Hebrew alphabet. This foundation had to be laid and understood as we move on to discuss eleven faulty hermeneutical principles and assumptions of Adventists. Many more could have certainly been added to this list, but these eleven are foundational and the others can be incorporated into them.

---

[85] Matthew Henry noted, "They have been taught, as children are taught to read, by precept upon precept, and taught to write by line upon line, a little here and a little there, a little of one thing and a little of another, that the variety of instructions might be pleasing and inviting,—a little at one time and a little at another, that they might not have their memories overcharged,—a little from one prophet and a little from another...."--- *Matthew Henry's Commentary on the Whole Bible: Complete and Unabridged in One Volume* (Peabody: Hendrickson, 1994), p. 1129.

Faulty Hermeneutical Principle and Assumption #1

Ellen White is always right in whatever she says. The Bible must be interpreted in such ways that it will always agree with her statements, views, and theology.

Now, of course many Adventists will not bluntly admit this, other than those rabid Ellen White fanatics, but in reality this is the most basic hermeneutic of Adventism. Let me give a few examples that illustrate this. Ellen White says that Satan is the scapegoat and sin-bearer, therefore Adventists believe that Satan is the scapegoat and sin-bearer, irrespective of how many times the biblical data presents Jesus as being the scapegoat and sin-bearer. Ellen White says we "…must be reconciled to God through obedience to His law and faith in Jesus Christ."[86] Adventists will torture Scripture to make it say what Ellen White said despite the fact that Romans 5:8-10 teaches the opposite:

> But God shows his love for us in that while we were still sinners, Christ died for us. [9]Since, therefore, we have now been justified by his blood, much more shall we be saved by him from the wrath of God. [10]For if while we were enemies we were reconciled to God by the death of his Son, much more, now that we are reconciled, shall we be saved by his life.

Ephesians 2:8-9 is unequivocally emphatic, "For by grace you have been saved through faith. And this is not your own doing; it is the gift of God, [9]not a result of works, so that no one may boast."

Ellen White says that the Sabbath is "the seal of God"[87] without which no one can be saved. The Adventist Church doggedly believes and teaches this without reservation, despite that the Bible is replete with statements that the Holy Spirit is the Seal of God without whom we cannot be saved. Romans 5:9 says, "…Anyone who does not have the Spirit of Christ does not belong to him." 2 Corinthians 1:21-

---

[86] White, *Testimonies to the Church*, Vol. 4, p. 294, par. 2.

[87] This Adventist teaching and belief will be discussed in detail in volume II.

22 says profoundly, "And it is God who establishes us with you in Christ, and has anointed us, [22]and who has also put his seal on us and given us his Spirit in our hearts as a guarantee." Ephesians 1:13-14 affirms, "In him you also, when you heard the word of truth, the gospel of your salvation, and believed in him, were sealed with the promised Holy Spirit, who is the guarantee of our inheritance until we acquire possession of it, to the praise of his glory." And Ephesians 4:30 reiterates, "And do not grieve the Holy Spirit of God, by whom you were sealed for the day of redemption."

Lastly, Ellen White said that the Sabbath and Sunday worship will have eschatological, salvific implications. She taught that the Sabbath will determine our salvation and that Sunday is the dreaded "mark of the beast" that will cause one to be damned.[88] Adventists believe and teach this despite the consistent biblical teaching that Christians can worship God on any day; that the Sabbath is not binding on believers; that believers in the Old and New Testament periods worshipped on Sunday without displeasing God, and that days of observance are based on personal conviction (John 4:21-24; Rom. 14:5-6; Col. 2:16-17; Heb. 10:25; Rev. 1:10).

Faulty Hermeneutical Principle and Assumption #2

Adventists always ignore the contexts of texts and of Scripture (the covenantal, historical, cultural, theological, political, social, audiential, and the immediate context).

Biblical context is simply irrelevant to Adventists. The only context they seem to care about and argue to maintain is statements that Ellen White made. They are quick to bellow, "Context, context, context!" when they presume that one is misinterpreting Ellen White (which is almost never the case), but they will never bellow the same for biblical texts or passages. They themselves have no regard for biblical context, therefore they would never advocate in favor of it. Let me illustrate this. Mark 2:27 says, "The Sabbath was made for man and not man for the Sabbath," for Adventists this means that the

---

[88] Adventist beliefs, arguments, and views about the Sabbath, Sunday, the seal of God, and the mark of the beast will be thoroughly dealt with in volume II.

Sabbath is binding on all humanity.[89] But contextually, this statement is referring to the Jewish disciples to whom the Sabbath was "made for" and not for Gentiles nor all of humanity. Additionally, the statement is a defense offered by Jesus to justify His disciples' breaking the Sabbath to satisfy their need. It puts the Sabbath under Jesus' and the disciple's authority to dispense with it as they saw fit. But Adventists ignore the context and flip this statement to actually subject all "man" under the Sabbath and make it universal, mandatory, and salvational.

Romans 3:31 reads, "Do we then overthrow the law by this faith? By no means! On the contrary, we uphold the law." Adventists proof-text this verse to mean that we uphold the Ten Commandments by being under them and by keeping them. However, from the immediate context beginning with verse 21, Paul argued that God's righteousness is revealed apart from the Law. This righteousness of God is testified about in the Law and Prophets. He said that Gentiles are justified outside of the law by faith, while Jews, who were under the Law, are justified through the same faith. Everyone is justified by faith apart from the deeds of the Law and because of that, no one can boast about being saved by keeping the Law. As a result of this, the Law is upheld because it drives the Jew to faith in Christ for justification. And it confirms that Gentiles are justified by faith apart from the Law, just as the Law testifies. In other words, the job, truthfulness, and purpose of the Law is upheld. The Law is not made void through faith, it is upheld. This is what Paul is saying here, but Adventists literally make it mean that we are under the Law and can be justified by it.

1 Corinthians 3:17 is a popular proof-text of Adventists when they are preaching about, promoting, defending, or arguing for the continued obligation of the Levitical dietary distinctions and restrictions for Christians. This is proof-texted to mean that God will destroy Christians for eating pork and other unclean meats that the Law forbade. They usually couple this text with Isaiah 66:17 for their position. But contextually, the text is saying that God will destroy some people for

---

[89] Mark 2:27, along with other popular SDA Sabbath texts, will be given proper treatment in volume II.

dividing the church with strife, jealousies, carnality, fractions, and for attempting to build on false foundations instead of building on Jesus Christ.

Adventists use Exodus 20:8-11 to mandate salvational Sabbath-keeping for Christians, but they completely ignore the covenantal context of the Sabbath. The Sabbath was given to Israel as their specific covenant "sign" between God and themselves to demonstrate that He had saved them from Egyptian slavery, set them apart as His special people, and that He was their God (Exo. 31:13, 17; Deut. 5:15; Ezek. 20:12, 20). Christians are not under the Old Covenant. Therefore, they are not obligated to keep the Old Covenant sign—the Sabbath.

The Seventh-day Adventist Church proof-texts Revelation 13:11-18 to propagate the teaching that Christians will, in the future, receive the mark of the beast for worshipping God on Sundays. In this vein Ellen White wrote:

> If the light of truth has been presented to you, revealing the Sabbath of the fourth commandment, and showing that there is no foundation in the Word of God for Sunday observance, and yet you still cling to the false Sabbath, refusing to keep holy the Sabbath which God calls "My holy day," you receive the mark of the beast. When does this take place? When you obey the decree that commands you to cease from labor on Sunday and worship God, while you know that there is not a word in the Bible showing Sunday to be other than a common working day, you consent to receive the mark of the beast, and refuse the seal of God.[90]

But historically, the mark of the beast was pagans worshiping the Caesars as gods. It was a common, yearly practice mandated by the Roman Empire that sacrifices and incense burning be made to the emperor or to his image, after which compliant persons would be given a certificate that would allow them to participate in commercial

---

[90] White, *Evangelism*, p. 235, par. 2.

activities. Those who refused to worship the emperor and his image were not issued certificates and faced economic boycott.[91] The mark of the beast was never about Christians ceasing from labor on Sunday and worshipping God. And if it has any future implications and application, it will not be about that either. Worshipping God on Sundays was never forbidden in the Old Testament nor is it ever forbidden in the New. Neither is it ever presented, in Scripture or Church History as something that is satanic, the mark of the beast, and apostasy towards God that will damn Christians.

Faulty Hermeneutical Principle and Assumption #3

The Ten Commandments are exclusively God's eternal, inviolable, irrevocable, moral law that transcends all time and culture. They were written with God's own finger on stone. They are a permanent, all-encompassing, stand-alone law because they were written on stone. They are distinct and separate from the ceremonial Law of Moses that was written in the Book of the Law and placed at the side of the Ark of the Covenant. The ceremonial Law of Moses is abolished but the Ten Commandments remain to be kept by all. They are the transcript of God's character and they can never change.

A) The Ten Commandments are exclusively God's eternal, inviolable, irrevocable, moral law that transcends all time and culture.

This is simply not true. The Ten Commandments are not an eternal, inviolable, irrevocable, "moral" Law that transcends all time and culture. The Ten Commandments could not have existed before Creation, nor will they need to exist in a post-sin world. They were given to Israel at the Sinai Peninsula (Exo. 19-20; Neh. 9:13-14; Gal. 4:21-31; Heb. 12:18-21). The first set of stone tablets, which contained the Ten Commandments[92] (Heb. words), did not survive

---

[91] Dr Clinton Baldwin, *The Person of Jesus: God's Obligatory Sabbath* (Silver Spring, MD: Dikaioma Publisher, 2017), p. 285-286.

[92] The Hebrew word that is translated as "Commandments" should not be that at all. The word is *devarim* and literally means "words, sayings, things, or categories." However,

104

an entire day when Moses came down from the mountain with them. After seeing Israel's idolatry and violation of the covenant that they were entering into with God (Exo. 20:1-24:8), Moses smashed the stone tablets at the bottom of the mountain (Exo. 32:19). The Ten Commandments are not "moral" laws per se but laws that revealed Israel's immorality and sinful nature, and served to curtail it. The first 4 commandments are not naturally moralistic laws. They only take on moralistic overtones when one enters into a covenant relationship with Yahweh. Moralistic laws are inherent ought nots. They are things ingrained in us by nature. They are the consciousness of knowing what should and should not be done. The consciousness of knowing good and evil (Gen. 3:22). The first four commands of the Ten Commandments are not inherent oughts in the human psyche and nature. No one knows inherently that they ought not to have other gods other than Yahweh. No one naturally knows not to make graven images and to not worship them. On the contrary, the majority of ancient civilizations, nations, and peoples actually made graven images and false gods that they worshipped. They did not naturally know that Yahweh is the only true God and that they should not make graven images.

The Third Commandment is not a natural moralistic law either. No one naturally knows that they should not take Yahweh's name in vain. This command is not talking about using foul language and indecent speech, which differ from culture to culture, language to language. This command is forbidding hypocritical worship of Yahweh (Isa. 1:11, 13; Matt. 15:7-9). It is referring to the misuse and abuse of Yahweh's name in oaths, vows, false swearing, and legal agreements (Deut. 10:20; Eccl. 5:4-7; Matt. 5:33). Only Jews could have taken Yahweh's name in vain in those contexts because they were the ones who knew it and who actually used it under those circumstances. Gentile nations and peoples all over the world did not know Yahweh's personal name nor took oaths in it. They all spoke different languages and did not naturally know the name "Yahweh."

The Fourth Commandment is not a natural, morally-based law.

---

because of widespread use, age-old tradition, and for familiarity's sake I will use "Ten Commandments" throughout this volume. But in volume II, I will expound on this and show how the "Ten words" should be understood in the context of the Old Covenant.

The Sabbath is not a moralistic law. Morality is not a festival to be kept (Lev. 23:1-3) nor does morality hinge on a specific block of time (Exo. 20:8-11; Lev. 23:32). Michael Morrison made this potent observation:

> We find additional evidence that the Sabbath is a ritual law in that God himself does not keep the Sabbath. It is not part of his nature. He rested once, but a six-one cycle is not part of his eternal nature. Nor do we have any evidence that angels keep the Sabbath; it was not designed for them. This means that the Sabbath is not an inherent part of the way good creatures show love to God or to one another. The Sabbath is not eternal, for it did not exist before creation, and will not be relevant in the new heavens and new earth. The Sabbath is not God's nature, nor universal, nor timeless. It is a ritual law, saying that behavior that is good on Friday is not good on Saturday… Morality does not depend on the rotation of the earth, the day of the week, etc.[93]

The Sabbath cannot be kept in space because there is no sunrise and sunset (evening to evening as SDAs use to determine it). The Sabbath cannot even be kept in many parts of the world because there are places where the sun does not set for months and also where it does not rise for months. Places such as Norway, Iceland, Sweden, the Inuvik and Northwest Territories of Canada, Alaska, and Finland; the sun does not set nor rise for months. There is no consistency in sunrise and sunset. There are many tribes and peoples around the world such as the Amondawa[94] and Piraha[95] tribes of the Amazon that have no concept of time nor dates. They cannot keep the Sabbath even if they wanted to or if they were vigorously

---

[93] Michael Morrison, *Sabbath, Circumcision, and Tithing: Which Old Testament Laws Apply to Christians?* 4th ed. (Arcadia, CA: Michael Morrison, 2002, 2003), p. 80.

[94] https://www.australiangeographic.com.au/news/2011/05/amazon-tribe-has-no-language-for-time/ (Date accessed Nov. 9, 2020).

[95] Rafaela von Bredow, *Living without Numbers or Time*, 03, 05, 2006, https://www.spiegel.de/international/spiegel/brazil-s-piraha-tribe-living-without-numbers-or-time-a-414291.html (Date accessed Nov. 9, 2020).

evangelized by Adventists. But they surely have moralistic laws and codes by which they have lived for centuries. There are prison inmates who after protracted periods of solitary confinement eventually lose time calculation and the concept of time. If such inmates were Adventist Sabbatarians prior to this experience, they surely would not be able to keep the Sabbath any longer but they surely would be able to adhere to moralistic laws and maintain the concept of them.

Lastly, it has been observed that every ancient and historical nation, tribe, and people have, and continues to have, moralistic laws by which they live. These laws can be written and unwritten, enshrined in their law codes, constitutions, etc., but it has never been observed where the Sabbath was ever a part of those laws. They had many laws that were similar to Israel's moralistic and civil laws, but keeping a 7th day Sabbath holy unto Yahweh was never among those laws. This undeniably proves that the Sabbath is not a natural moralistic law that humans know by conscience that they should keep holy unto Yahweh. And even when Yahweh had revealed the Sabbath to the Israelites, it was not revealed to be a moralistic law. It was a weekly ritualistic law.

B) The Ten Commandments were written with God's own finger on stone.

Adventists make a big deal about the Ten Commandments being written with "the finger of God" (Exo. 24:12; 31:18; Deut. 4:13; 9:10). They believe that because the Ten Commandments were written with the "finger of God" they are God's special, permanent, moral Law that is different from Moses' "ceremonial" Law. But these assumptions are faulty with zero biblical support. The significance of the fingers with respect to legal documents, transactions, and laws in biblical times had more to do with authority and power, and not the literality of their fingers. The reason for this was that persons generally wore signet rings that were used to sign documents, enact laws, authenticate deals, covenants, and agreements (Gen. 38:18, 25; Isa. 3:21; Jer. 22:24; Hag. 2:23). Because of this, a person's finger was synonymous with his power and authority. The Ten Commandments being written with God's finger does not mean that God literally wrote them. God is a Spirit (John 4:24). Spirits do not have flesh, bones, and literal fingers (Luke 24:39).

The reference to His finger is an anthropomorphism, which is, representing God as having human form, features, characteristics, and performing actions. In Scripture, the phrase simply meant that the Ten Commandments had God's backing, power, and authority. In Exodus 8:18-19, when the magicians of Pharaoh could not duplicate the plague of gnats that Moses had brought upon Egypt, "Then the magicians said to Pharaoh, "This is the finger of God." They were admitting that it was by the power and authority of God that Moses was producing the plagues. They were not saying that the gnats were literally God's finger. In Psalm 8:3, the heavens and the earth are said to be the work of God's "fingers." Here again, it is not saying that God literally made the heavens and earth with His fingers. The truth is, God actually spoke the heavens and the earth into existence (Gen. 1; Psa. 33:6-9). And it is His word that continues to hold the universe together. Hebrews 1:3 says, "He upholds the universe by the word of his power." The reference to "work of His fingers" means that He created the universe by His power and authority, which was done through His spoken word.

When asked about the power and authority with which Rehoboam intended to rule Israel when he had ascended the throne, he listened to the advice of the young men and insultingly said, "My little finger is thicker than my father's thighs" (1 Kings 12:10). What he was essentially saying was that he would rule with much more force, severity, and power than his father Solomon had done (1 Kings 12:1-16).

In Luke 11:20 Jesus said, "But if it is by the finger of God that I cast out demons, then the kingdom of God has come upon you." In the context of this pericope (Luke 11:14-23), Jesus' reference to the "finger of God" is not to God's literal finger but the power of God by which He was casting out demons. I am not alone in this assessment and conclusion about the phrase the "finger of God." Merrill Frederick Unger, et al, noted that when "finger" is used figuratively it, "Denotes the special and immediate agency of anyone."[96] Charles F. Pfeiffer, et al, equally observed, "The term [finger] is also used figuratively or metaphorically to refer to the power or Spirit of God."[97]

Understanding why Scripture would refer to the Ten Commandments as being written with the "finger of God" is very significant against the backdrop that Scripture, Jewish apocryphal books, and Flavius Josephus affirm that angels were involved in the giving of the Law at Mount Sinai. They believed that it was actually an intermediary angel who gave Moses and the Israelites the Ten Commandments. When God came down on Mount Sinai, an innumerable company of angels accompanied Him. Deuteronomy 33:2 says, "The LORD came from Sinai and dawned from Seir upon us; he shone forth from Mount Paran; he came from the ten thousands of holy ones, with flaming fire at his right hand." Psalm 68:17 says, "The chariots of God are twenty thousand, even thousands of angels: the Lord is among them, as in Sinai, in the holy place" (UKJV). In his apologetic defense to the Jewish leaders in Acts 7:38 Stephen said to them, "This is the one [Moses] who was in the congregation in the wilderness with the angel who spoke to him at Mount Sinai, and with our fathers. He received living oracles [the Law] to give to us." He reaffirmed in verse 53, "You who received the law as delivered by angels and did not keep it." Paul says something similar in Galatians 3:19 when he stated, "Why then the law? It was added because of transgressions, until the offspring should come to whom the promise had been made, and it was put in place through angels by an intermediary." The author of the Book of Hebrews asserts, "...the message declared by angels proved to be reliable, and every transgression or disobedience received a just retribution" (2:2).

It was believed that Michael the Archangel was the angel and intermediary who actually gave the Ten Commandment Law to Moses on Mount Sinai.[98] And it is also Michael the Archangel who

[96] Merrill Frederick Unger, R. K. Harrison, Howard Frederic Vos et al., *The New Unger's Bible Dictionary*, Rev. and updated ed. (Chicago: Moody Press, 1988), Finger.

[97] Charles F. Pfeiffer, Howard Frederic Vos, and John Rea, *The Wycliffe Bible Encyclopedia* (Moody Press, 1975), Finger.

puts the Law, which was interpreted to be the Son of God, in the hearts of believers.[99] Flavius Josephus, the Jewish historian of the 1st century AD, said, "And for ourselves, we have learned from God the most excellent of our doctrines, and the most holy part of our law, by angels or ambassadors; for this name brings God to the knowledge of mankind, and is sufficient to reconcile enemies one to another."[100] This information is vitally important to grasp. The phrase "written with God's finger" in reference to the Ten Commandments is making a statement of authority. Angels gave the Law, but despite that fact it was God's Law. This is so because emissaries, ambassadors, chancellors, and agents acted on behalf of their kings, nobles, royalty, and superiors (Isa. 18:2; Ezek. 17:15; 2 Cor. 5:20; Eph. 6:19-20). They acted in the name or authority of their sovereign (2 Kings 18:17-37). Depending on their rank and trustworthiness, all of the authority of their sovereign was vested in them (Dan. 6:1-3). Kings did not personally write laws. They would usually dictate what they wanted to enact into law, a scribe would write it, and then they would seal it with their signet ring (finger). And whatever they said would become law.

In many cases, the royal officials of the king would write a law and all the king had to do was stamp it with his signet ring and then it was enacted as law of the land (Dan. 6:6-12). In other cases, the king did not write nor sign anything. His second-in-command would write, sign, and enact laws in the name of the king, whether or not the king agreed with such a law (Esth. 3:12; 8:1-14). This is why it was very important and highly significant for the king to give his trusted royal servant or subordinate ruler his signet ring (Gen. 41:42; Esth. 3:10; 8:2). The servant or subordinate functioned on behalf of the king, with full authority that was to be respected and obeyed. The way one treated the king's emissary reflected one's attitude towards the king. Jewish authorities recorded in their Mishnah of the 3rd century A.D. that "a man's agent is as himself."[101] The New

---

[98] Apocalypse of Moses 1 (cf. Jub. 1:25-2:1).

[99] The Third Book of Hermas (Similitudes) 8:23-26.

[100] Flavius Josephus, *Antiquities of the Jews* 15:136, translated by William Whiston.

[101] Berekoth 6:6.

Testament is replete with this principle. Consider these few texts: Mark 9:37 says, "Whoever receives one such child in my name receives me, and whoever receives me, receives not me but him who sent me." In the Parable of the Sheep and the Goats of Matthew 25, we read, "And the King will answer them, 'Truly, I say to you, as you did it to one of the least of these my brothers, you did it to me" (vs. 40). In John 5:43a, Jesus said, "I have come in my Father's name, and you do not receive me." Conclusively, the significance of the "finger of God" meant that even though it was angels who had given the Law, it was Yahweh's Law and it contained His backing, power, and authority (Exo. 32:15-16). It was to be obeyed by Israel and everyone else who entered into that covenantal agreement.

C) The Ten Commandments are a permanent, all-encompassing, and stand-alone law because they were written on stone.

This is a common misconception and faulty argument of Adventists. They create a contrast between what was written on stone versus what was written on vellum and invent the logical fallacy that just because the Ten Commandments were written on stone then that somehow indicates their permanence and durability.[102] Irrespective of their sophistry and theological gymnastics at trying to force this argument to be true, this is not true of the Ten Commandments. The stone tablets on which the Ten Commandments were written do not indicate permanence and durability. As was already observed, the first set of stone tablets did not survive their first day when they came down from the mountain. Moses smashed them at the bottom of the mountain (Exo. 32:19). The Ten Commandments being written on stone does not indicate permanence at all. It was just one of the many surfaces on which documents could have been inscribed. In the biblical world, documents were written on stone, clay tablets, wooden tablets, ostraca (broken pieces of pottery),[103] papyrus, and countless other

---

[102] *Seventh-day Adventists Believe*, p. 263, 270.

[103] Paul J. Achtemeier pointed out, "Potsherds provided a readily available medium on which to make hasty or informal notations in pen and ink during biblical times. Many prophetic oracles may have been preserved originally in the form of ostraca, written by

things.[104] The Ten Commandments being written on stone did not make them permanent.

The Ten Commandments were written in the Book of the Law in the same way that they were written on stone. Ironically, the copy of the Ten Commandments in the Book of the Law outlasted the copy on stones. The set written in the Book of the Law proved to be more durable than the set of stone tablets. The Ten Commandments are found in Exodus 20 and Deuteronomy 5. That today is on paper. That is the Book of the Law. Those portions of Scripture are not the stone tablets. No one today has the original stone tablets to read the Ten Commandments from. From the time of the Babylonian Captivity in 605 B.C., the Ark of the Covenant had been lost and was never found. Adventists and everyone else are aware of the Ten Commandments because of the fact that they were written in the Book of the Law. And it is that book, not the stone tablets, that has survived to this day. It is by means of the Book of the Law that we are cognizant of the existence of the Ten Commandments. Stone does not mean permanence nor durability. According to Deuteronomy 27:1-4 and Joshua 8:30-32, the entire Book of the Law of Moses was written on stone. This is the very law that Adventists call "ceremonial law" that was subsequently abolished at the Cross of Christ.[105] It is only logical to conclude that if stone indicates permanence, as they argue, then the very law that they claim to be ceremonial and abolished is actually permanent. And they are bound to keep all of it because it too was "written on stone."

Contrary to their argument, the biblical data informs us that what was written on "tablets of stone," "written and engraved on stones" i.e., the Ten Commandments covenant, is exactly that which was fading away, lacked glory, and was being brought to an end (2 Cor.

---

disciples of the prophets."--- Paul J. Achtemeier, Harper & Row and Society of Biblical Literature, *Harper's Bible Dictionary*, 1st ed. (San Francisco: Harper & Row, 1985), p. 736.

[104] André Lemaire observed, "Virtually any surface can be used as a medium for writing an inscription: one has only to use tools appropriate to the surface."--- André Lemaire, "Writing and Writing Materials," in Vol. 6, *The Anchor Yale Bible Dictionary*, ed. David Noel Freedman (New York: Doubleday, 1992), p. 1001.

[105] *Seventh-day Adventists Believe*, p. 274.

3:2, 7, 10-11, 13). Hebrews 8:13 says, "In speaking of a new covenant, he makes the first one obsolete. And what is becoming obsolete and growing old is ready to vanish away." This passage is extremely clear that the Old Covenant is "obsolete," "growing old," and "ready to vanish away." And without guessing what this covenant is that is vanishing away and rendered obsolete, vs. 1-5 of chapter 9 explains what that covenant is. It is the sanctuary and its services, the "Ark of the Covenant," and the "tablets of the covenant." The Ark of the Covenant contained the Ten Commandments both inside of it in the form of the tablets of stone (Deut. 10:2, 5; 2 Chron. 5:10) and at the side of the Ark in the Book of the Law (Deut. 31:26, cf. Exo. 20:1-17; Deut. 5:5-22). And of course, the "tablets of the covenant" were the Ten Commandments (Exo. 34:27-28; Deut. 4:13; 9:8-11). This is the very covenant that the author of Hebrews says is obsolete, old, and vanishing away. From these observations, there is no way that we can biblically and logically conclude that the stone tablets meant permanence and durability.

The significance and purpose of the Ark of the Covenant

Adventists believe that Revelation 11:19 is an irrefutable text that proves that the Ten Commandments covenant is still in effect and Christians are therefore bound to it. The text says, "Then God's temple in heaven was opened, and the ark of his covenant was seen within his temple. There were flashes of lightning, rumblings, peals of thunder, an earthquake, and heavy hail." They deduce from this text that the "ark of His covenant" points to the fact that the Ten Commandments are literally in heaven, as the foundation of God's throne and that they are still in effect. But this assumption not only makes total nonsense of the entire New Testament that teaches that the Ten Commandments covenant is obsolete, but it also completely misses the message that this text is conveying.

The Ark of the Covenant was never created to glorify and give permanent status to the Ten Commandments. The purpose of the Ark was not to highlight its internal contents—the stone tablets, Aaron's budded rod, and the pot of manna. The purpose of the Ark of the

Covenant was to represent the presence, glory, and power of God. In Exodus 25:10-22, God instructed Moses to make the Ark. He gave him the specifications and instructed that the "testimony" should be placed in it. The "testimony" (covenant) was the legal, binding contract between Him and Israel. Verse 22 says, "There I will meet with you, and from above the mercy seat, from between the two cherubim that are on the ark of the testimony, I will speak with you about all that I will give you in commandment for the people of Israel." The Ark symbolized God's presence. This is where the Shekinah glory-cloud was manifested as a representation of the presence of God among His people. No one could have approached the Ark of the Covenant at will, not even the high priest, lest he die. The high priest could have only approached the Ark in the Most Holy Place once a year, on the Day of Atonement. And even then, meticulous guidelines had to be followed for him to be able to do so. Leviticus 16:2-4 says:

> ...the LORD said to Moses, "Tell Aaron your brother not to come at any time into the Holy Place inside the veil, before the mercy seat that is on the ark, so that he may not die. For I will appear in the cloud over the mercy seat. ³But in this way Aaron shall come into the Holy Place: with a bull from the herd for a sin offering and a ram for a burnt offering. ⁴He shall put on the holy linen coat and shall have the linen undergarment on his body, and he shall tie the linen sash around his waist, and wear the linen turban; these are the holy garments. He shall bathe his body in water and then put them on.

The Ark was the most sacred object in the Jewish sanctuary because it represented the presence of Yahweh. When it was being transported by the priests, it had to be carried by poles (Exo. 37:5). The Ark had to be screened with a veil (Exo. 40:3) and covered with this same veil when it was being transported (Num. 4:5). Some priests had to guard it (Num. 3:31). God personally spoke to Moses from the Ark (Num. 7:89). As a symbol of God's presence, it went before Israel to indicate that God was leading and protecting them. We read in Numbers 10:33-36:

> So they set out from the mount of the LORD three days' journey. And the ark of the covenant of the LORD went before them three days' journey, to seek out a resting place for them. [34]And the cloud of the LORD was over them by day, whenever they set out from the camp. [35]And whenever the ark set out, Moses said, "Arise, O LORD, and let your enemies be scattered, and let those who hate you flee before you." [36]And when it rested, he said, "Return, O LORD, to the ten thousand thousands of Israel.

The absence of the Ark meant the absence of God's presence, glory, and power among the Israelites. During one of their notable rebellious moments Scripture notes:

> Do not go up, for the Lord is not among you, lest you be struck down before your enemies. [43]For there the Amalekites and the Canaanites are facing you, and you shall fall by the sword. Because you have turned back from following the LORD, the LORD will not be with you." [44]But they presumed to go up to the heights of the hill country, although neither the ark of the covenant of the LORD nor Moses departed out of the camp. [45]Then the Amalekites and the Canaanites who lived in that hill country came down and defeated them and pursued them, even to Hormah (Num. 14:42-45).

When Israel was about to crossover Jordan to enter Canaan, the priests bearing the Ark had to go before them. This signified God's presence, power, and leadership (Josh. 3). Because God was among them, they experienced miracles and defeated their enemies at Jericho (Josh. 6). The Ark was a means by which Israel could make enquiry from God and get direction (Judges 20:27).

Because of what the Ark represented, at various junctures the

Israelites began to idolize it like a magic charm and talisman that had existential, saving properties. We read in 1 Samuel 4:3-5:

> And when the people came to the camp, the elders of Israel said, "Why has the LORD defeated us today before the Philistines? Let us bring the ark of the covenant of the LORD here from Shiloh, that it may come among us and save us from the power of our enemies." ⁴So the people sent to Shiloh and brought from there the ark of the covenant of the LORD of hosts, who is enthroned on the cherubim. And the two sons of Eli, Hophni and Phinehas, were there with the ark of the covenant of God. ⁵As soon as the ark of the covenant of the LORD came into the camp, all Israel gave a mighty shout, so that the earth resounded.

Even the Philistines understood that the Ark represented the presence and power of the God of the Hebrews. Verses 6-9 says:

> And when the Philistines heard the noise of the shouting, they said, "What does this great shouting in the camp of the Hebrews mean?" And when they learned that the ark of the LORD had come to the camp, ⁷the Philistines were afraid, for they said, "A god has come into the camp." And they said, "Woe to us! For nothing like this has happened before. ⁸Woe to us! Who can deliver us from the power of these mighty gods? These are the gods who struck the Egyptians with every sort of plague in the wilderness. ⁹Take courage, and be men, O Philistines, lest you become slaves to the Hebrews as they have been to you; be men and fight."

God shattered the idolatry and superstition of the Israelites by allowing them to be defeated and the Ark to be taken by the Philistines (vs. 10-11). It was aptly understood by some Israelites that the absence of the Ark meant the absence of God's presence and glory. After news of the defeat of the Israelites, the death of her husband and Eli, her father-in-law, was relayed to her, Phinehas' wife was induced into immediate labour. She gave her son a name to depict this. Verses 21-22, "And she named the child Ichabod, saying, "The glory has departed from Israel!" because the ark of God had been captured and because of her father-in-law and her husband. [22]And she said, "The glory has departed from Israel, for the ark of God has been captured.""" Many more things could have been stated about the Ark of the Covenant but these sufficiently prove the point. The Ark of the Covenant was a symbol of God's presence, glory, power, and leadership. The Ark of the Covenant was never overshadowed by the Ten Commandments, Aaron's budded rod, and the pot of manna within it. Neither was it its purpose to highlight the elevated and permanent status of its internal contents.

In the context of Revelation 11:19, the Ark is representational for the power, glory, and presence of God. The context begins with verse 15, with the blast of the seventh trumpet. Voices in heaven were heard announcing the rule of God and of Christ, forever, over the kingdoms of this world. In verses 16-18, the 24 elders bow before God's throne to worship Him. As they do so, they give thanks to Him, extol His power and eternality, and His justice that rewards the righteous but judges and condemns the wicked. After this, the temple was opened, the Ark was seen, and there were ecstatic displays of God's power, induced by His presence, echoing what took place on Mount Sinai when He had descended and made the first covenant with the Israelites (Exo. 19:16-20). The sight of the Ark and the awesome display being described here by John is representational of the power, glory, and presence of God. John was in vision. He was a Jew thoroughly familiar with these symbols and themes of Judaism. He knew the Ark represented the presence, power, and glory of God. He even sees the Ark within a context that highlights the presence, power, and glory of God. His penning this vision of the Ark was never intended to convey the permanence, eternality, and current binding status of the Ten Commandments covenant for Christians. John knew that that covenant was brought to an end and that Jesus had instituted a new one. He had made this absolutely clear in the New Testament books that he wrote before Revelation (the Gospel of John, I, II, and III John).

There seems to be a good reason that the Ten Commandments were written on stone, other than the fact that it was just a convenient method of writing in biblical times. It may very well have been to depict the hardness of the hearts and stubbornness of the Israelites, the Old Covenant people. In Exodus 32:9 God said to Moses, "I have seen this people, and behold, it is a stiff-necked people." He suggested to Moses that He would destroy them and make a different nation from Moses (vs. 10). In Exodus 33:3 and 5, God said that He would not go up to the Promised Land with them because they were a rebellious people that He would destroy in a moment. Let us not forget that they had promised to do whatever God said when God had proposed the covenant to them (Exo. 19:5). But not too long after God spoke His Law and Moses had gone to the mountain to get the Law, they broke the covenant by making the Golden Calf and having orgiastic reveries (Exo. 32). This rebellion was the reason that the first set of stone tablets were broken when Moses came down from the mountain (vs. 19) and that also caused 3,000 of them to perish (vs. 25-28).

When the covenant was renewed, their rebellion and hardness of their stony hearts were still not cured. It was for that same reason that they ended up spending 40 years wandering in the wilderness until all of that adult generation died out, with the exception of Caleb and Joshua (Num. 14:33-34; 32:13). When Israel inhabited Canaan, their hearts' disposition was still the same way. From the Book of Judges to Malachi we read about endless cycles of rebellion and hardheartedness on their part. In Ezekiel 11:19 God said, "...I will give them one heart, and a new spirit I will put within them. I will remove the heart of *stone* from their flesh and give them a heart of flesh." The purpose for which God would do this is so that they would obey Him (vs. 20). Their hearts were hardened towards God. They constantly rebelled against Him. The commands on stone seemed to depict their heart's condition very well. Paul picked up on this same motif and said to the Corinthians, "And you show that you are a letter from Christ delivered by us, written not with ink but with the Spirit of the living God, not on tablets of stone but on tablets of human hearts" (2 Cor. 3:3). The stone tablets seemed to have been revealing their stony hearts. They stood as

118

a witness against their rebellion in the same way that Aaron's budded rod and the pot of manna were also witnesses against their rebellion (Num. 17:1-11; Exo. 16:1-16, 31-34).

It is interesting to note that all three of these items were eventually stored inside the Ark of the Covenant, not to highlight their permanence, supreme status above the rest of the Law, nor to depict their validity and eternal nature, but to simply be a witness against Israel's rebellion and hardheartedness (Heb. 9:3-4). It is for this very reason that God promised to give Israel faithful shepherds to feed them and that they will not even need to look to the Ark of the Covenant for guidance nor will they even remember it. We read in Jeremiah 3:15-16, "'And I will give you shepherds after my own heart, who will feed you with knowledge and understanding. [16]And when you have multiplied and been fruitful in the land, in those days, declares the LORD, they shall no more say, "The ark of the covenant of the LORD." It shall not come to mind or be remembered or missed; it shall not be made again." This will be so because God's presence will be with His people (vs. 17-18). Representation will be made redundant by reality. In New Covenant faith, God dwells in His people. His presence is with us and in us. We do not need to look to the Ark of the Covenant. Its purpose was served and now it is no longer necessary, but sadly Adventists try very hard to eternalize it and constantly want us to keep looking back to it. But God said that should not be. He also promised to make a new covenant with them which will not be like the Old Siniatic Covenant. In this New Covenant, He will write His law in their hearts and minds (Jer. 31:31-34).

Adventists have tried to twist this covenant to mean that God writes the Ten Commandments on our hearts; that they merely changed location, but the passage does not say that. This argument of theirs is very eisegetical. Firstly, God's Law for Israel is much more than the Ten Commandments. God's Law in the Old Covenant was the entire 613 commands of the Torah, not just the Ten Commandments. If this passage is to be interpreted with consistency in regards to what they argue, then the entire Torah is written on their hearts. And they must keep the entire Torah from the minutiae of laws to the weightier ones. But given that they have jettisoned over ninety eight percent of the Torah, their bad logic already defeats their own argument. Secondly, the New Testament authors interpreted this passage to refer to the Holy Spirit being placed in the hearts of believers to lead, to guide, to impart life, to have permanent abode, to give liberty, to transform us into Christ-likeness, and to assure us of complete forgiveness of sins in Jesus (Heb. 10:14-23; 2 Cor. 3). Because of this, all their desperate attempts at elevating the Ten Commandments above the rest of the Law and claiming that it is those commands which are written on the hearts of believers have failed miserably.

The belief that the Ten Commandments can be extracted and isolated from the Mosaic Law and elevated to be a stand-alone, all-encompassing, moral law is faulty and ill-thought out. The Ten Commandments are a proverbial toothless bulldog when extracted and isolated from the rest of the Mosaic Law. They are an almost pointless, legalistic code. They are mostly prohibitions against sins but most of them carry no punishment for their violation. Most of them, as they are stated, contain no rewards for obeying them. Most of them cannot be used to try, punish, nor execute anyone. They have no by-laws nor amendments for their circumstantial violation. For example, the command to not murder simple prohibits murder, but if one actually murders there is no punishment within the command itself for that violation. It contains no by-laws and does not refer to various forms of murder and their degrees of punishments (for example 1st degree murder, 2nd degree murder, and 3rd degree murder). They are not stand-alone laws nor are they all-encompassing. The Fifth Commandment obliged Israelite children to honor their parents so that they would have lived long in Canaan when God gave them the land. But the command does not obligate parents to love, nurture, provide for, respect, educate, train, nor be responsible for their children. I can prove the inefficiency of every one of the Ten Commandments as a "stand-alone" law. But you certainly get the point. If Adventists want to be dogged that the Ten Commandments are an all-encompassing, stand-alone law, then I have a small experiment that I want them to try to prove this argument. I want Adventists to abolish every law, by-laws, policies, principles, and rules in their homes, churches, medical institutions, school systems, Adventist towns, etc., and only live by and enforce the Ten Commandments as all-encompassing, stand-alone laws. Abolish all medical procedure laws, tuition fees, hygienic laws, policies, grading systems, the Church Manual, organizational laws and by-laws, etc., and keep *only* the Ten Commandments as all-encompassing.

They generally argue that all of these laws are downstream laws and concepts that have their genesis in the Ten Commandments. But that is not true. What they have really done is to recreate the balance of the Mosaic Law to suit their own needs and purposes. Dear reader, I am quite sure you can envision that if they were to do this, within minutes they would be plunged into chaos, confusion, anarchy, insubordination, and pandemonium. This experiment is the perfect thing that they should do to prove their claim. But I am sure you can see that their claim is shallow and absurd.

D) The Ten Commandments are distinct and separate from the "ceremonial" Law of Moses that was written in the Book of the Law and placed at the side of the Ark of the Covenant (Deut. 31:26).

This claim is untruthful. It is an unjustifiable assumption that has no biblical support. The Ten Commandments are a synecdoche or a pars pro toto—a part of the Law that represents the whole law. They were the very words of the Old Covenant (Exo. 34:27-28; Deut. 4:13; 9:9-11). They functioned like an executive summary. As was already proven, Moses wrote all the Law. He wrote the Ten Commandments also in the Book of the Law. The Ten Commandments are "Moses' Law" just as much as they are "God's Law." In Mark 7:9-10 Jesus said to the Pharisees, "You have a fine way of rejecting the commandment of God in order to establish your tradition! [10]For Moses said, 'Honor your father and your mother'; and, 'Whoever reviles father or mother must surely die.'" In this statement, Jesus refers to the Fifth Commandment (Exo. 20:12) and a law from Exodus 21:17 and says that both are "Moses" Law just as much as they are God's law. In John 7:19 Jesus said, "Has not Moses given you the law? Yet none of you keeps the law. Why do you seek to kill me?" Jesus is referring to the Sixth Commandment that prohibited murder (Exo. 20:13) and said it was Moses who gave it. Yet this command is one of the Ten Commandments spoken by God Himself. According to Paul in 2 Corinthians 3:14-15, when one reads the Old Covenant (tablets of stone) one is reading Moses. As was proven before, the Ten Commandments were written in the Book of the Law that was kept beside the Ark of the Covenant, and that is why they exist in our Bibles today in Exodus 20 and Deuteronomy 5. The Law of God and the Law of Moses are one and the same law. The Law simply had various nomenclatures in Scripture.

In the Old Testament, all of those various names for the Law or sections of it are used interchangeably. The Book of Nehemiah sufficiently proves this. In Nehemiah we can observe these various names for the one Law. It is called "the Law" (Neh. 8:2, 7, 9, 13; 10:36; 12:44; 13:3), "the Book of the Law" (Neh. 8:3), "the Law of God" (Neh. 8:8; 10:28), "the Book of the Law of God" (Neh. 8:18), "the Book of the Law of the Lord" (Neh. 9:3), "God's Law that was given by Moses" (Neh. 10:29), "the Book of Moses" (Neh. 13:1), and "Law that the LORD had commanded by Moses" (8:14). In the New Testament Gospel of Luke, he used God's Law and Moses' Law interchangeably also. Luke 2:22-24 reads:

> And when the time came for their purification according to the *Law of Moses*, they brought him up to Jerusalem to present him to the Lord [23](as it is written in the *Law of the Lord*, "Every male who first opens the womb shall be called holy to the Lord") [24]and to offer a sacrifice according to what is said in the *Law of the Lord*, "a pair of turtledoves, or two young pigeons [italics mine].

Additionally, one will never find in Scripture nor Jewish history where Jews considered the Ten Commandments to have been exclusively "God's Law" that was separate and different from the "Law of Moses." They have always understood it to be *one* Law.

One will also never read in Scripture that the Ten Commandments have greater weight and authority than the rest of the Law because they were "God's Law" and "written with His own finger." Never. All the Law is God's Law and all of it was equally authoritative for the Jews. What God supposedly wrote (which is not the case as was proven) is not more authoritative than what He spoke nor than what Moses wrote. The fact of the matter is God spoke the Law and Moses wrote the Law. Exodus 24:4a says, "And Moses wrote down all the words of the LORD." When God had introduced His covenant to them, He spoke from Exodus 20:1 through to chapter 24. The Israelites were afraid of His voice and the spectacular display of His glory and therefore requested that God stop speaking to them directly, that He should speak to Moses, and then Moses would let them know what He said. In recalling the events, in Deuteronomy 5:27, Moses reminded them what they had said, "Go near and hear all that the LORD our God will say, and speak to us all that the LORD our God will speak to you, and we will hear and do it." God then obliged their request (vs. 28-33), spoke everything personally to Moses on the mountain, and Moses wrote down everything in the book, after which he delivered the book to the priests and Levites (31:9, 24-26).

The Ten Commandments are no more special nor more authoritative, nor a separate law from the rest of the Law. The Law is one package. The Israelites could not have extracted pieces of the Law that they liked nor what they deemed agreeable to them, and practiced *only* those things as Adventist do today.[106] They never had

---

[106] Seventh-day Adventists have extracted the Ten Commandments from the rest of the Law and elevated them to be exclusively "God's moral Law" (*Seventh-day Adventists Believe*, p. 265), while they erroneously contend that the Book of the Law was "the ceremonial Law" and abolished (ibid, p. 274). They have also unjustifiably extracted pieces of the clean and unclean animal distinctions in Leviticus 11 and Deuteronomy 14. They only adhere to the distinctions themselves but not to the laws that govern those distinctions (being separated from the covenant community if one was rendered unclean by those animals, taking a bath at sunset and washing one's clothing before re-entering the covenant community, avoiding cross-contamination, breaking contaminated pots, stoves, utensils, etc.,). They have also extracted pieces of the tithe laws from the Law and redefine tithes to be money (*Seventh-day Adventists Believe*, p. 301-308), and have ignored basically everything else that biblical tithes was and the laws concerning it.

that privilege. They had promised to do *everything* that God spoke (Exo. 19:8; 24:3). They were bound to do *everything* that God spoke and what Moses transcribed. The one who did not abide by everything that the Law said was under a curse. Deuteronomy 27:26 says, "Cursed be anyone who does not confirm the words of this law by doing them." "And all the people shall say, 'Amen.'" In Galatians 3:10, Paul repeated this text to illustrate his point that no one can be justified by the Law. He said, "For all who rely on works of the law are under a curse; for it is written, "Cursed be everyone who does not abide by all things written in the Book of the Law, and do them." It is poignant to keep in mind too that it was the Book of the Law that was ratified as the Old Covenant, sprinkled with blood (Exo. 24:4-8). There is *nothing* in Scripture that indicates that the Ten Commandments were ratified as a separate, moral covenant, independent of the Book of the Law covenant.

E) The ceremonial Law of Moses is abolished but the Ten Commandments remain to be kept by all. They are the transcript of God's character and they can never change.

Adventists are quick to argue that the "ceremonial law" or "the Law of Moses" is abolished but not the "moral law of Ten Commandments." This is the argument they use with passages and books such as the Book of Romans, Galatians, Ephesians 2, Colossians 2, and anywhere else in Scripture that speaks of the abolition of the Old Covenant or the Law. But irrespective of the arguments, sophistries, and theological gymnastics they employ, as was proven, the Law is one package, a unified whole. It was never dissected into minute pieces and kept as one desires as Adventists attempt to do, "cherry-picking" the Law. When it was valid, all of it was valid and to be kept by Jews and Gentile converts to Judaism. Now that Scripture talks about its abolition, all of it is abolished and rendered inoperative. The entire Old Covenant is abolished, has faded away, came to an end, and is not binding on Christians as the legal document or law under which we function in our relationship with God. The New Testament is beyond clear about this.

Romans 6:14 says, "For sin will have no dominion over you,

since you are not under law but under grace." This text presupposes that sin has dominion over the ones who are "under the law." But for the ones who are not under the law but under grace, sin does not have any dominion over them. Having drawn a marriage analogy to show how we should relate to the Law in the first section of Romans 7, Paul concludes by saying:

> Likewise, my brothers, you also have died to the law through the body of Christ, so that you may belong to another, to him who has been raised from the dead, in order that we may bear fruit for God. 5For while we were living in the flesh, our sinful passions, aroused by the law, were at work in our members to bear fruit for death. 6But now we are released from the law, having died to that which held us captive, so that we serve in the new way of the Spirit and not in the old way of the written code (Rom. 7:4-6).

This passage is emphatically clear. Christians have died to the law and are married to Christ. Being dead to the Law means that we are released from it. The Law has no legal claims on believers. Sadly, Adventists want to be married to their version of the Law and to Christ at the same time. Romans 7 teaches that it is spiritual adultery and idolatry.

The entire Book of Galatians abolishes the Old Covenant Law. It is a very short book, read it in your spare time, and you will see how it does this in various ways. Ironically, the Adventist prophetess has conceded that the law in Galatians 3 is both the "moral" and "ceremonial" law. She says, "I am asked concerning the law in Galatians. What law is the schoolmaster to bring us to Christ? I answer: Both the ceremonial and the moral code of Ten Commandments."[107] She says this in a positive way to buttress the fact that the Law was a schoolmaster to lead to Christ, but this very admission refutes the Adventist position and puts them in a tight spot. Had Ellen White continued to read that same pericope, she would have

---

[107] White, *Seventh-day Adventist Bible Commentary*, Vol. 6, p. 1109, par. 9.

realized that the passage says that we are no longer under that schoolmaster! Statements like these I embrace with glee. Statements like these make me appreciate the biblical illiteracy and oblivious, unchecked contradictions of Ellen White because they refute their position and should force them to either accept biblical truth or reject Scripture and plunge into cognitive dissonance. Galatians 3:23-26 says, "²³Now before faith came, we were held captive under the law, imprisoned until the coming faith would be revealed. ²⁴So then, the law was our guardian until Christ came, in order that we might be justified by faith. ²⁵But now that faith has come, we are no longer under a guardian, ²⁶for in Christ Jesus you are all sons of God, through faith." This passage is unequivocally clear. We are not under the guardian, which is the Law. And Ellen White admits that this law is "Both the ceremonial and the moral code of Ten Commandments." Therefore, we are not under the Ten Commandments nor the "ceremonial" law. Ellen White herself inadvertently admitted this.

Ephesians 2 affirms the abolishment of the Law. In verses 1-3, Paul reminded the Ephesians that they were dead in their sins, immoral lives, and were being actuated by the devil but they now have been made alive in Christ. In verses 4-10, Paul reminded them of the ineffable grace and mercy of God in Jesus Christ that saved them. He affirmed that they had been saved by grace through faith and this salvation could have never been attained by their works, and therefore they can never boast about them attaining salvation on their own nor in partnership with God. Paul is also clear that good works were prepared by God beforehand for them to walk in. These good works are not to achieve salvation nor to maintain it, but to demonstrate it. In verses 11-13, Paul told them to remember that they are naturally Gentiles who were derisively called the "Uncircumcision" by the Jews ("the Circumcision"). Before their salvation experience they were without Christ, foreigners to the Israelite covenants of *promises*, having no hope, and devoid of God in the world. But through the vicarious atonement of Jesus Christ, they have been brought near. Then verses 14-16 says:

> For he himself is our peace, who has made us both
> one and has broken down in his flesh the dividing

wall of hostility [15]by abolishing the law of commandments expressed in ordinances, that he might create in himself one new man in place of the two, so making peace, [16]and might reconcile us both to God in one body through the cross, thereby killing the hostility.

This statement is revolutionary. Paul says that Christ is our peace. He has united Jews and Gentiles in Himself. And the way He did so was through His death, which broke down "the dividing wall of hostility," by abolishing the law of commandments expressed in ordinances.

The "dividing wall of hostility," also called the Middle Wall, was a literal wall that separated the Court of the Gentiles from the Temple precincts that was only accessible to Jews. The *Nelson's New Illustrated Bible Dictionary* says the Middle Wall was:

> ...a barrier or partition that divided the inner court of the Temple, open only to Jews, from the Court of the Gentiles. The Jewish historian Josephus described this partition as a stone wall, inscribed with warnings to Gentiles not to enter the holy place of the Temple, under threat of death.[108]

In 1871 one of the pillars of the Temple was found which contained this inscription: "No man of another race is to enter within the fence and enclosure around the Temple. Whoever is caught will have only himself to thank for the death which follows."[109] Paul used this literal wall, its literal function, and its spiritual significance to highlight the fact that Jesus has torn down the spiritual and social separation that was created by the Law, between Jews and Gentiles. Jesus reconciled Jews and Gentiles and killed the hostility that

---

[108] Ronald F. Youngblood, F. F. Bruce, R. K. Harrison and Thomas Nelson Publishers, eds., *Nelson's New Illustrated Bible Dictionary* (Nashville, TN: Thomas Nelson, Inc., 1995), Middle Wall.

[109] Peter W. L. Walker, *Jesus and the Holy City: New Testament Perspectives on Jerusalem* (Grand Rapids, MI: William B. Eerdmans Publishing Company, 1996), p. 124.

naturally existed between them by tearing down that which caused the hostility—the Law itself. Andrew T. Lincoln noticed the same thing when he said, "Christ neutralized these negative effects of the law by doing away with the law."[110]

Is the Law the transcript of God's character?

Seventh-day Adventists have always argued that the Law is a transcript of God's character.[111] Ellen White boldly asserted, "The law of God is the transcript of the character of God."[112] And of course by now you should be aware that they only mean this for the Ten Commandments. They attempt to prove this erroneous assumption by correlating what God is or is revealed to be in Scripture with what is said about the Law. For example God is love (1 John 4:8), the Law is love (Rom. 13:10). God is holy (Lev. 11:44), the Law is holy (Rom. 7:12). God is perfect (Matt. 5:48), the Law is perfect (Psa. 19:7). God is good (Psa. 34:8), the Law is good (1 Tim. 1:8). God is righteousness (Jer. 23:6), the Law is righteousness (Psa. 119:172), etc. Adventists are convinced that this is an airtight argument that undoubtedly proves that the Law is the transcript of God's character. I recall thinking that this argument was truly incontrovertible when I was an Adventist. I used it a lot as well as in my evangelistic sermons and seminars. But the fact is this argument is very weak and shallow.

The fact that some things in Scripture share some communicable attributes of God does not make them transcripts of God's character. The fact that some places, people, ordinances, and things in Scripture are described in some ways that God is described does not make them transcripts of His character. Mere created, mortal things can never, absolutely never, encapsulate who and what God is, and therefore become transcripts of His character. There are many things in Scripture that are declared to share God's communicable attributes,

---

[110] Andrew T. Lincoln, vol. 42, Ephesians, *Word Biblical Commentary* (Dallas: Word, Incorporated, 1990), p. 142.

[111] *Seventh-day Adventists Believe*, p. 265.

[112] White, *The Signs of the Times*, March 14, 1895, par. 9.

but that can never make them a transcript of His character. A quick example of this is the City of Jerusalem. The Bible describes Jerusalem as being spiritual (Gal. 4:26, Heb. 12:22-23), beloved (Rev. 20:9), faithful and righteous (Isa. 1:21, 26), holy (Dan. 9:16, 24), the perfection of beauty (Psa. 50:2, Lam. 2:15), eternal (Psa. 125:1), just (Isa. 1:21), pure (Jer. 6:2), unchangeable (Psa. 125:1), etc. Does this mean that Jerusalem is the "transcript of God's character" too? Of course not. All this means is that persons, places, and things can share in the communicable attributes of God, or that God can bequeath such honor to them, but that will never make such things transcripts of His character. That which is finite and created cannot be a transcript of the Eternal God nor can it ever fully encapsulate who He is and what He does and can do. It takes a special level of myopia and theological small-mindedness to attempt to squeeze the eternal God into a finite creation to the point of making them equal.

By claiming that the Law is a transcript of God's character, the Law is put on par with God. A common ploy that some cults constantly use is to diminish Jesus, and the Holy Spirit, in relation to the Law. This is a formula of a legalistic cult. Elevate the law; diminish Christ and the Holy Spirit. Sadly, but not surprisingly, Ellen White taught that God exalted the laws "equal to himself." She states:

> Satan grew bold in his rebellion, and expressed his contempt of the Creator's law. This Satan could not bear. He claimed that angels needed no law; but should be left free to follow their own will, which would ever guide them right; that law was a restriction of their liberty, and that to abolish law was one great object of his standing as he did. The condition of the angels he thought needed improvement. Not so the mind of God, who had *made laws and exalted them equal to himself.* The happiness of the angelic host consisted in their perfect obedience to law.[113] [Italics mine]

---

[113] White, *Signs of the Times*, January 9, 1879, par. 10.

It is idolatrous, perhaps even blasphemous, to elevate created laws so high that they become a transcript of the Eternal, Uncreated God, equal to Him. Irrespective of how convinced Adventists might be of this argument and for how long they have vainly argued this, the Law is not the transcript of God's character. While the Law shares some communicable attributes of God, as does many other things, the Law does not share many more communicable and also non-communicable attributes of God. The Law is not loving, kind, patient, merciful, others-centred, self-existent, self-sacrificing, forgiving, immutable, indestructible, able to save, life-producing and sustaining, omnipotent, omniscient, omnipresent, retaining and deserving of glory, deserving of praise, worship, and adoration, etc. For the Law to qualify to be the transcript of God's character, it must possess all of these attributes and abilities. After all, a transcript of something is an exact replica of that thing. The Law is not an exact replica of God.

Jesus Christ is the transcript of God's character

There is only one Person who is the exact replica of God, who is the transcript of God's character. It is Jesus. He is all of these things and much more. Proving that Jesus is the transcript of God's character does not necessitate matching His attributes and qualities with those of God to ascertain this fact, although we can certainly take that route as well. Proving that Jesus is the transcript of God's character is very easy. We only need a few passages of Scripture to prove this.

John begins his Gospel with a profound prologue that states the identity of Jesus in the first two verses. He says, "In the beginning was the Word, and the Word was with God, and the Word was God. [2]He was in the beginning with God" (John 1:1-2). John establishes 3 things here. Firstly, the Word always existed. Secondly, the Word existed "with God," that is, in an intimate, personal relationship with God. And thirdly, he affirms that the Word is God, just as God (the Father) is God. In verse 14, John says, "And the Word became flesh and dwelt among us, and we have seen his glory, glory as of the only Son from the Father, full of grace and truth." John profoundly notes here that the Word became flesh. God became a man. God took on human flesh and dwelt among humans in the Person of Jesus Christ. And those who lived around Him saw His glory as the unique Son of God, who overflowed with grace and truth. In the Old Covenant sanctuary system, God symbolically dwelt in a tent in the wilderness. His Shekinah glory and presence was revealed atop the mercy seat on the Ark of the Covenant (Exo. 25:21-22). That is where He had said that He would have met Moses and spoken with Him. When Israel was established in Canaan, God's presence was manifested above the mercy seat in the Most Holy Place of the sanctuary (1 Kings 8:6-10). But in the incarnation of Christ, God became flesh and personally dwelt among His people. God's presence was no longer symbolically revealed above the Ark of the Covenant; it was now enshrined in physical flesh in the Person of Jesus.

Verse 18 makes a profound statement that reveals that Jesus is indeed the transcript of God's character. It says, "No one has ever seen God; the only God, who is at the Father's side, he has made him known." In Exodus 33 Moses requested of God, "Please show me your glory" (vs. 18). And God's response to him was, "You cannot see my face, for man shall not see me and live" (vs. 20). John 1:18 is reiterating this fact. Man has lost the ability to see God's face because of sin and the physical weakness of his body. Sin debilitated our physical bodies (Rom. 8:20-23) and caused a massive separation between us and God, therefore rendering us incapable of beholding God in His glory (Isa. 59:2). But there is One who was always at the Father's side.[114] He is the only One who is qualified to reveal the Father. And He has revealed the Father. The verb "made known" is translated from the Greek word εξηγεομαι (exegeomai). It is a compound verb that means "to lead out, to unfold, to declare, to interpret." It is the word from which the English word "exegete" is

---

[114] The Greek word that is translated as "side" here is κόλπος (kolpos). When it is used in a relational sense, it is not describing proximity or juxtaposition (i.e., "standing at his side"), but it is describing intimacy and relationship. Kolpos is used to describe deep intimacy and relationship (cf. Luke 16:22-22; John 13:23; LXX Deut. 28:54, 56; Ruth 4:16; 1 Kings 1:2; 3:20). It is the English equivalent of a wife lying in her husband's arms. John 1:18 is conveying that Jesus shares a deep, intimate relationship with God and if there is anyone who can be the transcript of God's character and to reveal Him, it is certainly Jesus.

derived. When we exegete literature, we employ several literary skills, competencies, and considerations in order to correctly interpret literature. John is simply saying here that Jesus is the exegete of God. He is the One who has always had a deep, close, and intimate relationship with God, and therefore is the One who correctly interprets and reveals Him. He is the transcript of God's character. He can transcribe God because He is God. He has always existed with the Father and has always shared an intimate relationship with Him. No mortal man nor any other created thing can ever fully, correctly, and rightly be a transcription of God. Only God can be a transcript of God's character. Only God can ever be what God will always be. Jesus is God, as John had already established, and He is the only One who is the transcript of God's character, and the only One who can exegete God.

In John 14, Jesus exhorted the disciples to not be troubled but to believe in God and in Himself (vs. 1). He assured them that He was going to prepare a place for them in His Father's house so that they can be with Him. He assured them that they knew the way (vs. 2-4). Thomas questioned that they did not know where He was going, much less to know the way. Jesus then assured them that He is the Way, the Truth, and the Life and that no one can come to God except through Him (vs. 5-6). Jesus then boldly said to them that in knowing Him, they know the Father and as a result they have both known and seen the Father. Upon saying this, Philip said to Him, "Lord, show us the Father, and it is enough for us" (vs. 8). Jesus responded, "Have I been with you so long, and you still do not know me, Philip? Whoever has seen me has seen the Father. How can you say, 'Show us the Father'?" (vs. 9). Jesus' rhetorical questions are very pointed. He was clear that whoever saw Him saw the Father. He assured Phillip that the Father had been with them in His Person. This can only be true if Jesus is the transcript of God's character. And that is exactly what Jesus was saying here. As the transcript of God's character, He reveals exactly what the Father is like. He reveals exactly who God is. And having seen and experienced Him, the disciples saw and knew exactly what God was like. This observation and statement cannot be said about the Law nor the Ten Commandments. No one who beholds the Ten

Commandments or the Law beholds and knows what God is like, although it may reveal God's holiness and expectations. Beholding the Law does not reveal who God is. Instead it revives sin in us (Rom. 7:7-12), empowers sin in our lives (1 Cor. 15:56), is powerless due to our sinful flesh (Rom. 8:3), and *condemns us* (2 Cor. 3:6-9). Given that the law condemns us, if the law is a transcript of God's character, and it condemns us, then isn't that saying God condemns us? In light of Jesus' statement, it is obvious to see that He understood Himself to have been the transcript of God's character.

In 2 Corinthians 4:4, Paul said that Christ is "the image of God." He again affirmed in Colossians 1:15, "He is the image of the invisible God, the firstborn of all creation."[115] He noted further in Colossians 2:9, "For in him the whole fullness of deity dwells bodily." These passages and statements are all revealing one thing—that Jesus is the transcript of God's character. In Philippians 2:5-6, Paul expressed this same truth in a different way when he said, "Have this mind among yourselves, which is yours in Christ Jesus, who, though he was in the form of God, did not count equality with God a thing to be grasped." The part that I want to highlight is the fact that Jesus was "in the form of God." "Form" refers to the external appearance, shape, or nature. This not only reaffirms the deity of Jesus Christ, but it also repeats the fact that He was the physical manifestation of God. God was bodily revealed in Jesus. He is God in His very nature and being. He is the only One who is the transcription of God.

Hebrews 1:1-3 is another passage that indubitably proves that Jesus is the transcript of God's character and not the Law nor the Ten Commandments as Adventists assert. In verses 1-2, the author states that in times past God spoke to the fathers by the prophets, but in these last days He has spoken to us through His Son Jesus. In verse 3 he says of Jesus, "He is the radiance of the glory of God and the exact imprint of his nature...." If no other passage we have discussed proved that Jesus is the transcript of God's character, this one

---

[115] The Greek word for "image" in these texts is εικων (eikon). This is the word from which we get the English word "icon" from. The word literally means "an image, a figure or likeness, a statue." And figuratively it means a "representation or resemblance." This is exactly what a transcript is. Jesus is the transcript of God's character.

certainly does. There is no possible way that Adventists can get around this text. The Greek word for "exact imprint" is χαρακτηρ (character) and it means the "exact impression, copy, or precise reproduction" of a person or thing. This text strongly affirms that Jesus is the "character" of God. He is the exact copy or transcript of God. This text leaves no room for the Law nor the Ten Commandments to usurp the place of Jesus as the transcript of God's character. Jesus alone is the transcript of God's character. He is everything that God is. If we want to know who God is or what He is like, we should look to Jesus and not to the Law, not to the Ten Commandments. Warren Wiersbe succinctly puts it this way:

> "Express image" (Heb. 1:3) carries the idea of "the exact imprint." Our English word *character* comes from the Greek word translated "image." Literally, Jesus Christ is "the exact representation of the very substance of God" (see Col. 2:9). Only Jesus could honestly say, "He that hath seen Me hath seen the Father" (John 14:9). When you see Christ, you see the glory of God (John 1:14).[116]

Faulty Hermeneutical Principle and Assumption #4

Whenever the words "law" and "commandments" are spoken of positively in Scripture they mean the "Ten Commandments." But whenever they are spoken of negatively, they mean the "ceremonial" law.

In discussions with Adventists, Christians will often be thrown in a loop if they do not understand how the Adventist mind operates in regards to the Old Covenant Law. Because they assume that the Ten Commandments are eternal and irrevocable, they do a lot of spins and twists with biblical statements about the Law. So, whenever Scripture speaks positively about the Law, in the mind of Adventists and in their argumentation that automatically means "the moral law

---

[116] Warren W. Wiersbe, *The Bible Exposition Commentary* (Wheaton, IL: Victor Books, 1996), Heb. 1:1-3.

of Ten Commandments." But whenever Scripture speaks negatively or disparagingly about the Law, that also automatically means the "ceremonial Law of Moses" for them. But of course, I have sufficiently refuted their claims, parcelling, and differentiation of the Law so I will not be doing much of that again here other than to give a few examples where they do this and give some contextual comments.

A prime example of this phenomenon is Ecclesiastes 12:13 where Solomon says, "The end of the matter; all has been heard. Fear God and keep his commandments, for this is the whole duty of man." In the minds of Adventists, this text means that we must fear God and keep the Ten Commandments and doing so is man's entire duty. They usually couple this with the next verse and push for their doctrine of the Investigative Judgement, thinking that we will be judged by the Ten Commandments. But this conclusion of theirs is non-contextual and imposing upon the text what is not there. Contextually, King Solomon was talking about the entire Mosaic Law that was given to the Israelites for them to live by. Solomon made this appropriate conclusion after his endless pursuit of pleasure, trying to enjoy all that he could have in this life, but sadly discovered that in the end it was all "vanity." He strongly urged, "Remember also your Creator in the days of your youth, before the evil days come and the years draw near of which you will say, "I have no pleasure in them" (12:1). A life lived in pursuit of pleasure and disconnected from God is a fruitless and pointless life. Solomon says that before one reaches old age and realizes this and concludes that one's life was wasted, he says to remember God and live for Him. So to fittingly close his quest, Solomon said that one should fear God and keep His commandments because that is man's entire duty. No doubt, Solomon's call can be applicable to all humans as a call to revere God and be obedient to Him in whatever ways He has revealed Himself to them, or under specific rules or covenants that they are under. But this passage, in context, is not supporting the assumption of Adventists. This call by Solomon is not new. He is merely reiterating what the Law had said hundreds of years before him.

In Deuteronomy 5:29 God said of Israel, "Oh that they had such a heart as this always, to fear me and to keep all my commandments, that it might go well with them and with their descendants forever!" In Deuteronomy 6:1-2 Moses reminded Israel:

> Now this is the commandment—the statutes and the rules—that the LORD your God commanded me to teach you, that you may do them in the land to which you are going over, to possess it, ²that you may fear the LORD your God, you and your son and your son's son, by keeping all his statutes and his commandments, which I command you, all the days of your life, and that your days may be long."

Deuteronomy 8:5-6 says, "Know then in your heart that, as a man disciplines his son, the LORD your God disciplines you. So you shall keep the commandments of the LORD your God by walking in his ways and by fearing him." What can be noticed from these few passages so far is that the call to "fear God and keep His commandments" was consistently given to the Israelites as a condition of their covenant with Him and also a condition upon which they would have long, meaningful, and prosperous lives in Canaan, which they were about to inhabit. This call referred to the entire Law and not just the Ten Commandments that Adventists have extracted from the Law.

Deuteronomy 13:4 says, "You shall walk after the LORD your God and fear him and keep his commandments and obey his voice, and you shall serve him and hold fast to him." In Deuteronomy 17 God gave instructions concerning kings, should Israel choose a monarchy in the future. One of those things that the king should do was to make a copy of the Book of the Law in order that he may constantly read it, live by it, and thus rule justly. We read in verse 18-19, "And when he sits on the throne of his kingdom, he shall write for himself in a book a copy of this law, approved by the Levitical priests. ¹⁹And it shall be with him, and he shall read in it all the days of his life, that he may learn to fear the LORD his God by keeping all the words of this law and these statutes, and doing them."

This is what King Solomon should have done! He had neglected the Law and therefore ended up in apostasy and regrettable hedonism, as Ecclesiastes records. In his old age, he came to his senses and realized that he and everyone else should fear God and live by the Mosaic Law because that was truly their entire and best duty. That is what he was saying in Ecclesiastes 12:13. He was not propagating the Ten Commandment fetishism of Adventists.

To further highlight this faulty hermeneutical assumption of SDAs, I will engage some of their most commonly attested proof-texts. Matthew 5:17-19 is one such proof-text they are fond of using.

> Do not think that I have come to abolish the Law or the Prophets; I have not come to abolish them but to fulfil them. [18]For truly, I say to you, until heaven and earth pass away, not an iota, not a dot, will pass from the Law until all is accomplished. [19]Therefore whoever relaxes one of the least of these commandments and teaches others to do the same will be called least in the kingdom of heaven, but whoever does them and teaches them will be called great in the kingdom of heaven.

This is a pivotal Adventist proof-text that is used to bolster this faulty hermeneutic. The word "Law" for them in this passage is referring to the Ten Commandments. What they extract from this is that Jesus has not come to abolish the Ten Commandments but to establish them (that is how they interpret "fulfil"). They also argue that the Ten Commandments will forever remain because heaven and earth have not passed away, therefore neither iota nor dot will be altered from the Ten Commandments. They also believe that they are considered "great" in God's kingdom for keeping and teaching the Ten Commandments, while those who do not claim to be keeping and teaching them are considered "least" in the kingdom. Adventists go so far as to say that such believers will not even be in the kingdom. Without me even going into much detail, I am quite sure you can see the glaring problems with their interpretation of this text. They have made complete nonsense of this text and attempt to make it say the exact opposite of what it is actually saying. I will properly deal with this text in "Faulty Hermeneutical Principle and Assumption Number 6."

John 14:15 is another major Adventist proof-text. This is their go-to proof-text to demand the way to show love for God or Jesus is to keep the Ten Commandments, especially the Sabbath. This is what they almost always use it for. But just like every other proof-text of theirs, context always kills their assumptions. The text reads, "If you love me, you will keep my commandments." Jesus is not saying that love towards Him is shown by us by keeping the Sabbath nor the Ten Commandments. There is no possible way that this can be shown from the immediate context. The antecedent commands that Jesus is referring to are "love one another as I have loved you" (13:34-35), "let not your heart be troubled" (14:1-imperative in the Greek), "believe in God" (14:1- imperative in the Greek), "believe in Me" (14:1-imperative in the Greek), "believe that I am in the Father and the Father in Me" (14:11- imperative in the Greek), and "believe on account of the works themselves" (14:11- imperative in the Greek). All of these statements are imperatives in the Greek. The imperative mood in the Greek "...corresponds to the English imperative, and expresses a command to the hearer to perform a certain action by the order and authority of the one commanding."[117] These are the contextual commands that Jesus says to His disciples that if they "love Him" they would obey. There is further evidence from John's specific use of the Greek word εντολη (entole), which he always uses to refer to Jesus' commands not only in that pericope (John 13-17) but in the entire book. On the flip side, whenever John is referring to the Old Covenant Law he always uses νομος (nomos). He is the only New Testament author that makes this unique distinction between nomos and entole in his writings (the Gospel, his epistles, and the book of Revelation). Later on when John refers to the commands of Jesus that believers should obey, he specifically refers to these same commands to love one another and believe in God and Christ as Christ's commands (1 John 3:23-24; 4:7-12, 20-21; 5:1-3; 2 John 4-6).

---

[117] Larry Pierce, *Tense Voice Mood* (Bellingham, WA: Logos Bible Software), the imperative mood.

Romans 7:12 says, "So the law is holy, and the commandment is holy and righteous and good." In the mind of an Adventist this means that the Ten Commandments are holy, righteous and good. This is a true statement but it is not just true about the Ten Commandments. The entire Law is holy, righteous, and good. Sadly, they only use it to refer to the Ten Commandments. They never use it to refer to the rest of the Law that they lump as "ceremonial law." But the fact is the entire Law is holy, righteous, and good. It is because the Law is holy, righteous, and good, and our flesh is unholy, unrighteous, and sinful that the Law is incapable of helping our flesh. It condemns us. We can't ever keep it to perfection and meet its demands (vs. 7-24). It is for that very reason that through Christ's death "...we are released from the law, having died to that which held us captive, so that we serve in the new way of the Spirit and not in the old way of the written code" (vs. 6).

The Book of Galatians is a short and powerful letter that strikes at the heart of all works-based, law-centred faith systems such as Adventism. It is for this reason that every legalistic faith tradition either casts much doubt on Galatians (and most other Pauline letters) or they go to great lengths to radically redefine the Law therein, and the clear-cut statements it makes against a Law-centred salvation. Adventism does this with Galatians. Its radical redefinitions of the Law in Galatians makes the letter about the "ceremonial law," hoping to rescue the Ten Commandments from Galatians' law-negating clutches. Try as they may, the Law in Galatians is the entire Old Covenant Law. Galatians 4:21-31 draws a sharp contrast between the Old Covenant with the New by allegorizing Hagar (the Old Covenant) and Sarah (the New Covenant), and their respective sons (Ishmael and Isaac). And the conclusion of this contrast is, "Cast out the slave woman and her son, for the son of the slave woman shall not inherit with the son of the free woman." This could not be clearer. The Old Covenant, including the Ten Commandments, is to be "cast out." We are not slaves nor children of the Ten Commandments covenant. We are children of the New, freedom-giving covenant that remains. If Galatians 4:21-31 is still not clear to Adventists that the Ten Commandments are a part of the

Law that it is talking about, let me reiterate the words of their prophetess, "I am asked concerning the law in Galatians. What law is the schoolmaster to bring us to Christ? I answer: Both the ceremonial and the moral code of Ten Commandments."[118] And as I had already proven, she unsuspectingly undercuts the Adventist position and her lifelong arguments and teachings about the Law because that very passage she proof-texted states clearly that we are no longer under "the schoolmaster," which she admits is, "Both the ceremonial and the moral code of Ten Commandments."

Hebrews 7:11-12 is another text that suffers from this Adventist faulty hermeneutic. They cannot allow this text to ever be referring to the Ten Commandments, for obvious reasons. The text says:

> Now if perfection had been attainable through the Levitical priesthood (for under it the people received the law), what further need would there have been for another priest to arise after the order of Melchizedek, rather than one named after the order of Aaron? [12]For when there is a change in the priesthood, there is necessarily a change in the law as well.

Their age-old argument is that the Law cannot change, but this text says clearly that the Law had to change. Now, they cannot have their Ten Commandments changing so they pin this change only to the ceremonial law, as if the priests had no jurisdiction over the Ten Commandments. The Levitical priests had jurisdiction and authority over the Ten Commandments. God gave them authority over the entire Law to teach it, explain and interpret it, and to bind their judgements derived from it on the Israelites (Deut. 17:8-12; Matt. 23:1-3). For example, if an Israelite committed murder, committed adultery, worshipped other gods or blasphemed, broke the Sabbath, etc., the priests lawfully adjudicated on all of those matters of the Ten Commandments (Lev. 20; Num. 5: 11-22; 35:9-34; John 5:16-18; 8:58-59; 9:16; 10:33, etc.,). The author is more than clear that he is referring to the entire Law. He refers to "the law" twice in the

---

[118] White, *Selected Messages*, Book I, p. 233, par. 1.

singular, without any modifiers ("ceremonial" or "moral"). The Law was one package. The Israelites received "the Law" under the "Levitical priesthood." In Hebrews 9:1-5, when the author itemized the accoutrements of the "first covenant," he listed the "ark of the covenant" and the "the tablets of the covenant" (which was the entire law on papyrus and on stones) as part of that covenant. And this is the same covenant that he had already said was "…becoming obsolete and growing old is ready to vanish away" (8:13). Therefore, Hebrews 7:11-12 is essentially restating the same point—the priesthood has changed, therefore the Law must also change.

The last text I will use to illustrate this faulty Adventist hermeneutic is 1 John 5:2-3, which says, "By this we know that we love the children of God, when we love God and obey his commandments. ³For this is the love of God, that we keep his commandments. And his commandments are not burdensome." This speaks positively about commandments. It says His commandments are not burdensome and that we show that we love God and His children by keeping His commandments. For a moment, just think like an Adventist who essentially has no regard for context, as I demonstrated over and over. Wouldn't your mind play tricks on you too and insert "Ten Commandments" in this text as "His commandments" that John is referring to? Of course your mind would do that. In the past, my mind had played all of those tricks on me via this faulty hermeneutic and bad, unbiblical conditioning. But not anymore. Now that I know better and have regard for contextual exegesis of Scripture, I can assure you, as I reiterate, that this text is not referring to the Ten Commandments but to the commands to believe in Jesus Christ, to believe in the Father, and to love one another (3:23-24; 4:7-12, 20-21; 2 John 4-6). John is consistent in referring to these commandments in his writings.

Faulty Hermeneutical Principle and Assumption #5

1 John 3:4 (KJV) says transgressing the Law is the only definition of sin in the Bible. The Ten Commandments Law exclusively defines sin. If the Ten Commandments are abolished, then sin does not exist. But given that sin exists, then that means we are under the Ten

Commandments as the definer of sin.

In Adventism, the existence of sin is contingent upon the Ten Commandments. They cannot conceive of the existence of sin without having the Ten Commandments to identify sin. For them, if the Ten Commandments do not exist, then sin does not and cannot exist. They believe that Satan sinned in heaven by breaking the Ten Commandments or the Law.[119] This theology is based on Ellen White's teachings in the Great Controversy[120] and their erroneous interpretation of 1 John 3:4 in the KJV, which reads "Whosoever commiteth sin trangresseth also the law: for sin is the transgression of the law." This is an erroneous translation. The Greek reads "Πᾶς ὁ ποιῶν τὴν ἁμαρτίαν καὶ τὴν ἀνομίαν ποιεῖ, καὶ ἡ ἁμαρτία ἐστὶν ἡ ἀνομία." A better translation than the KJV should be, "Everyone who practices sin also practices lawlessness; and sin is lawlessness" (author's translation). The Greek word for "sin" in this verse is αμαρτια (hamartia) and it literally means "missing the mark." "Lawlessness" is ανομια (anomia) and it means "a condition of being without law, wickedness, unrighteousness, or iniquity." Missing the mark, being wicked, unrighteous, or living in a lawless state is never something that is exclusively defined by the Ten Commandments. Sin, wickedness, and unrighteousness, as used in Scripture, have to be understood within their contexts. So, what exactly does "sin" and "lawlessness" mean in this context? The answer is within the passage. We do not need to approach the passage with a

---

[119] Ellen White states, "Good angels wept to hear the words of Satan, and his exulting boasts. God declared that the rebellious should remain in heaven no longer. Their high and happy state had been held upon condition of obedience to the law which God had given to govern the high order of intelligences. But no provision had been made to save those who should venture to transgress his law. Satan grew bold in his rebellion, and expressed his contempt of the Creator's law. This Satan could not bear. He claimed that angels needed no law; but should be left free to follow their own will, which would ever guide them right; that law was a restriction of their liberty, and that to abolish law was one great object of his standing as he did. The condition of the angels he thought needed improvement. Not so the mind of God, who had made laws and exalted them equal to himself. The happiness of the angelic host consisted in their perfect obedience to law."--- White, *Signs of the Times*, January 9, 1879, par. 10.

[120] See *The Great Controversy*, chapter 29 "The Origin of Evil."

presuppositional bias towards the Ten Commandments nor do we need to arbitrarily impose Exodus 20:1-17 on it, when that is far removed from what John is talking about.

John illustrates profoundly that sin is incompatible with birth from God (vs. 1-3). He had shown that birth from God involves purification (vs. 3). He now shows that where sin is, that is, the lack of self-purification, there is no birth from God. God is pure (vs. 3). He is the standard or "law" of what we should strive to be and will ultimately be when He appears (vs. 2). But the one who continues to practice sin, that is, missing the mark of purity, is practicing lawlessness. He is simply missing God's standard, which would be God Himself, His character. John emphasizes this fact similarly in vs. 7 by using the opposite of lawlessness and unrighteousness, when he says, "...Whoever practices righteousness is righteous, just as He is righteous." Again, we see that God is the standard: He is righteous. The one who continues to sin, practice lawlessness, and unrighteousness is missing the standard of purity and righteousness, God's character. That person is not demonstrating that he was indeed born of God (vs. 8-9), and that Jesus has indeed taken away his sins (vs. 5-6).

John forcefully drove this same point home just before he closed this epistle by saying, "All unrighteousness is sin....[17]We know that everyone who has been born of God does not keep on sinning, but he who was born of God protects him, and the evil one does not touch him" (1 John 5:17-18). This is the message that 1 John 3:4 is conveying. That message has nothing to do with the Ten Commandments being the absolute definer of sin. As a matter of fact, John does not even use the Greek word that usually refers to the Law (νομος) in this entire epistle. The often repeated Johannine word "commandment/s" is not referring to the Law, as the Greek word used is εντολη (entole) and he specifically uses it to refer to the command to believe in Jesus Christ and His teachings, and to love one another (3:22-24). I had said this several times before but to make a deep impression and to disabuse the mind of the hackneyed rhetoric of Adventists, I must repeat it. The belief that the Ten Commandments exclusively defines sin and that this is what 1 John

3:4 is saying is exegetically untenable.

The New Testament has many definitions for sin

Additionally, The New Testament has at least thirteen basic words for sin, unrighteousness, lawlessness, and ungodly behaviour. They are: κακός (kakos) which means "bad" (Rom. 13:3); πονηρός (poneros) which means "evil, bad" (Matt. 5:45); ἀσέβειας (asebeias) meaning "godless" (Rom. 1:18); ἔνοχος (enochos) meaning "guilt" (Matt. 5:21); ἁμαρτία (hamartia) meaning "missing the mark, sin" (1 John 3:4); ἁμάρτημα (hamartema), which is a cognate of hamartia and also means "missing the mark, sin" (1 Cor. 6:18); ἄδικια (adikia) which means "unrighteousness or injustice" (1 Cor. 6:9); ἄνομος (anomos) which means "without law, lawlessness, unrestrained" (1 Tim. 1:9); παραβάσις (parabasis) "side step, transgression" (Rom. 5:14); ἀγνοεῖν (agnoein) "to be ignorant, to sin ignorantly" (Rom. 1:13); πλανω (plano) meaning "to go astray or to wander" (1 Cor. 6:9); παραπτώμα (paraptoma) which means "to fall away" (Gal. 6:1); and ὑποκρίσις (hupokrisis) which means "hypocrisy" (Gal. 2:13; 1 Tim. 4:2). No doubt, many of these sins and ungodly behaviours are congruent with what the Ten Commandments address but they are not confined to them nor are they exclusively defined by them.

The New Testament contains other definitions of sin and immoral behaviours that can never be bound by the meagre strictures of the Ten Commandments or any other codification of laws. After the discussion about foods and days of observances in Romans 14:23 Paul concludes, "But whoever has doubts is condemned if he eats, because the eating is not from faith. For whatever does not proceed from faith is sin." This is a very profound definition of sin. Whatever does not proceed from faith is sin. This is profound because Paul also clearly said in Galatians 3:12 that "...the law is not of faith...." In other words, the Old Covenant Law is not based on faith. The Ten Commandments are not based on faith. They are based on works—doing what the Law says. Paul made this clear in the succeeding clause, "The one who does them shall live by them." What Romans 14:23 and Galatians 3:12 reveal to us is that there are sins that exist and defined by the Law, and there are sins that exist

144

and are defined by faith. One can sin by violating the Law, as well as one can sin by violating faith. The Ten Commandments have never been the sole definer of sin and they never will be.

In James 4:17 we read another definition of sin, "So whoever knows the right thing to do and fails to do it, for him it is sin." What this text does is that it makes some sins subjective to one's personal knowledge. There are things that can be considered sin for some people while those very same things are not sin for other people. And this fact is based on individualistic, personal, and subjective knowledge. And those subjective things can be things that have absolutely nothing to do with the Law nor the Ten Commandments. But if the Holy Spirit of God convicts persons of them and if such persons know better and still do contrary to that knowledge, then it is sin. That is what this definition is saying. Life, social relations, and cultural mores are too complex and change too frequently for the Ten Commandments to ever be the eternal, all-encompassing definer of sin. The Ten Commandments are grossly inadequate when extracted and isolated from the Law and its immediate context. The Ten Commandments are inadequate to deal with real estate issues, cybercrimes, health insurance, hospital and pharmaceutical industries, road traffic, environment and natural resources, scientific and medical research, racial and social justice issues, the education sector, and countless other aspects of our lives. Despite the Ten Commandments' inability to regulate those things and its lack of speaking specifically to issues in those areas of life, many grievances, sins, moral infractions, and malpractices are committed in those areas. They exist.

We read in 1 John 5:16-17, "If anyone sees his brother committing a sin not leading to death, he shall ask, and God will give him life—to those who commit sins that do not lead to death. There is sin that leads to death; I do not say that one should pray for that. All wrongdoing is sin, but there is sin that does not lead to death." This passage says so much that challenges the Adventist assumption of 1 John 3:4. John says there is sin that does not lead to death, for which life can be given to those committing it. He also says there is a sin that leads to death, which should not be prayed about. Any form of wrongdoing is sin (another definition of sin) and there are sins that do not lead to death. If this is talking solely about the Ten Commandments as Adventists assume, this passage would not make sense and would be contradicting itself.

There are two other passages that disprove the Adventist assumption of 1 John 3:4 and show how ludicrous such a pedantic definition and conceptualization of sin it is. Let us look at them.

Romans 2:12-15 says:

> For all who have sinned without the law will also perish without the law, and all who have sinned under the law will be judged by the law. [13]For it is not the hearers of the law who are righteous before God, but the doers of the law who will be justified. [14]For when Gentiles, who do not have the law, by nature do what the law requires, they are a law to themselves, even though they do not have the law. [15]They show that the work of the law is written on their hearts, while their conscience also bears witness, and their conflicting thoughts accuse or even excuse them.

In verse 12, Paul is crystal clear that people can sin outside of the Law, as well as under the Law. If the Ten Commandments were the only thing that defined sin then we have a huge problem here. As was seen, sin can be committed outside of the Ten Commandments, as well as under the entire Mosaic Law. In verse 13, Paul said that merely being a hearer of the Law will not count one as righteous before God, but being a doer of it is what will justify one. This is a truthful statement but it does not mean that the Law has justified anyone (Gal. 3:11). The fact is no one has ever kept the Law perfectly resulting in being justified by it. And no one will ever keep it perfectly to ever be justified by it. If this could have happened, humans would not need Jesus. We would be able to justify ourselves by merely keeping the Law (Gal. 2:20).

Paul then says in vs. 14 that Gentiles do not have the Law but despite this they naturally do what the Law requires. By doing what the Law requires they are a law unto themselves, despite not having the written Law. Before this is misunderstood to mean that Gentiles had every minutiae of the Mosaic Law to live by and were naturally keeping them, it should be kept in mind (and harmonized with the entirety of Scripture) that Gentiles were not required to undergo circumcision like the Jews were. They did not eat like Jews, as the Law required of the Jews. They did not offer sacrifices in the right way to God. They did not worship at the Jerusalem temple nor keep the Sabbath and other Jewish feasts. They did not wear blue tassels on the edges of their garments to remember to do what the Law says, like the Jews did (Num. 15:37-41). They did not do countless other things in the Law. What Paul is talking about here is moralistic laws that are innate to all people (Gen. 3:22). Gentiles practiced moralistic laws by nature, as revealed in nature (Rom. 1:18-32). Some of these moralistic laws are contained in the Law and required by the Law.

Paul then states in vs. 15 that the works of the Law are written on their hearts. This is certainly about inherent morality and the evaluation of our actions that comes with having a conscience. The takeaway from this passage that disproves Adventism is that Gentiles did not have the Jewish Law. They did not have the stone tablets of the Ten Commandments yet they were conscious of sin because moral principles were written on their hearts. Their consciences served as a gauge of moral uprightness or wrongness.

In Romans 5:13, Paul says, "For sin indeed was in the world before the law was given, but sin is not counted where there is no law." Sin existed *before* the Law was given at Mount Sinai. Sin exists outside of the Law, outside of the Ten Commandments. The Ten Commandments are not and will never be the sole definer of sin. The Adventist assumption of 1 John 3:4 is contextually wrong and theologically inept.

Faulty Hermeneutical Principle and Assumption #6

Proof-speck and proof-text: whatever will support Adventism but conveniently ignore everything else in a text or passage that disproves Adventist assumptions and doctrines.

Genesis 26:4-5 is a text that Adventists run to and proof-speck[121] in order to push their faulty assumption that the Ten Commandments existed before Mt. Sinai and that the patriarchs kept them. In this text God said to Isaac, "I will multiply your offspring as the stars of heaven and will give to your offspring all these lands. And in your offspring all the nations of the earth shall be blessed, 5because Abraham obeyed my voice and kept my charge, my commandments, my statutes, and my laws." In the Adventist mind, this text means that Abraham kept the Ten Commandments, specifically the Sabbath, and it is on that basis that God promised to bless Isaac and multiply his descendants. They proof-speck "commandments" in this text to mean "Ten Commandments" and "laws" to mean Ten Commandment law, which is very redundant on their part. They completely ignore everything else that God said that Abraham did and observed. What are the "charge and statutes" this text is talking about? What is the voice of God that Abraham obeyed? Adventists do not care about any of those things. They see the words "commandments" and "laws" and their minds play the usual trick on them and insert "Ten Commandments" or "the Sabbath" there while they ignore everything else.

Scripture is clear that this statement could not be referring to the Ten Commandments as given to Israel because Abraham did not have them. When Moses was reciting the Law and the covenant to the Israelites, he said in Deuteronomy 5:2-3, "The LORD our God made a covenant with us in Horeb. 3Not with our fathers did the LORD make this covenant, but with us, who are all of us here alive today." Moses was unequivocal that Israel's patriarchs did not have the Old Covenant Law with the Ten Commandments. God did not make the Ten Commandments covenant with them. And without even guesstimating what this covenant was, Moses explicitly said what it was in verses 5-22. It was the Ten Commandments covenant.

In the same vein, Paul says in Galatians 3:17, "This is what I mean: the law, which came 430 years afterward, does not annul a covenant previously ratified by God, so as to make the promise void." This statement is made about the promise that God made to

---

121 A proof-speck is a tiny part of a text that is extracted from it, while ignoring other relevant things in it, to support a presuppositional assumption, doctrine, teaching, or view.

Abraham. The covenant and Law that he refers to here is the Ten Commandments covenant, which came into existence 430 years after God had made the promise to Abraham to bless everyone in him. So given these biblical facts, there is no possible way that Genesis 26:4-5 could be talking about the Ten Commandments covenant. Nor could it be saying that Abraham had them and was keeping them. The *Keil and Delitzsch Commentary on the Old Testament* observes that "...commandments, statutes, [and] laws denote constant obedience to all the revelations and instructions of God."[122] Gordon J. Wenham equally notes, "This verse expands 22:18b, "because you have obeyed me." The additions, "kept my instructions, commandments, statutes, and my laws," reinforce and underline the extent and thoroughness of Abraham's obedience."[123] It seems that Moses wrote this in this manner to make a point to the Hebrews that Abraham did all God commanded of him, so God expects the Hebrews to do all that is commanded of them too.

As we read Abraham's story from Genesis 12-25, we can trace his obedience to God's voice and to all of the charges, commandments, statutes, and laws that God gave him but we cannot put our finger on him keeping the Sabbath. For example, in Genesis 12:1 he was instructed to leave his country and he obeyed (vs. 4). In chapter 13:14 he was told to "Lift up your eyes and look...," which he did. In verse 17 God said to him, "Arise, walk through the length and the breadth of the land, for I will give it to you." He did just that. According to verse 18, he built an altar to God. In chapter 14:20, he gave a tithe to Melchizedek from all the spoils of war (cf. Heb. 7:4). In 15:1-6, God told him not to be afraid, that He would bless him with a son, and he believed God. In 15:9, God told him to fetch a three year old goat and ram, a pigeon and turtledove, and he did as he was instructed. In 17:1, God commanded him to "walk before Me and be blameless." He did that. In verses 9-17, God commanded him to circumcise everyone in his house as the covenant sign between

[122] Carl Friedrich Keil and Franz Delitzsch, *Keil and Delitzsch Commentary on the Old Testament* (Peabody, MA: Hendrickson Publishers, 1996), Gen. 26:5.

[123] Gordon J. Wenham, Vol. 2, Genesis 16–50, *Word Biblical Commentary* (Dallas: Word, Incorporated, 1998), p. 190.

God and himself. According to verses 23-27, he circumcised himself and all the males in his house. Chapter 18:19 says, "For I have chosen him, that he may command his children and his household after him to keep the way of the LORD by doing righteousness and justice, so that the LORD may bring to Abraham what he has promised him." Here, God affirms that Abraham will command his household in the way of God but despite this there's no evidence that Abraham's descendants were keeping the Sabbath before Mt. Sinai, as an instruction that Abraham gave to them. But we do see evidence of his descendants being circumcised, promoting the worship of Yahweh only, upholding the moral principles of Yahweh, abstaining from idolatry, building altars to Yahweh, etc. Sabbath-keeping among Abraham's descendants, before Mt. Sinai in Exodus 16, is grossly absent from all their recorded history. In Genesis 22:2, God told Abraham to go offer his son as a burnt offering on Mount Moriah, and he obeyed. In verse 12, when he was about to kill Isaac and God told him to stop, he promptly stopped. We can continue to survey the life and experiences of Abraham and his descendants, and glean countless things that they did. But glaringly absent will always be them keeping the Sabbath. This proves that they did not keep the Sabbath as Adventists argue and neither does their proof-specking of "commandments and laws" in Genesis 26:5 mean "the Ten Commandments" or the Sabbath.

Does Exodus 31:12-17 prove that the Sabbath is an eternal sign?

Exodus 31:12-17 is a major Adventist proof-text for mandatory, salvational, and perpetual Sabbath-keeping. But like many others, they proof-speck and extract from the passage a few things that will uphold their assumptions and false views, while they conveniently ignore everything else in that same passage. The passage reads:

> And the LORD said to Moses, 13"You are to speak to the people of Israel and say, 'Above all you shall keep my Sabbaths, for this is a sign between me and you throughout your generations, that you may know that I, the LORD, sanctify you. 14You shall keep the Sabbath, because it is holy for you. Everyone who

profanes it shall be put to death. Whoever does any work on it, that soul shall be cut off from among his people. [15]Six days shall work be done, but the seventh day is a Sabbath of solemn rest, holy to the LORD. Whoever does any work on the Sabbath day shall be put to death. [16]Therefore the people of Israel shall keep the Sabbath, observing the Sabbath throughout their generations, as a covenant forever. [17]It is a sign forever between me and the people of Israel that in six days the LORD made heaven and earth, and on the seventh day he rested and was refreshed.'"

The key proof-specks Adventists have extracted from this passage are: "my Sabbaths" (vs. 13), "a sign" (vs. 13, 17), "sanctify you" (vs. 13), "covenant forever," (vs. 16), and "forever" (vs. 17). And they have applied all of these things to themselves and the Christian church. But I am sure you can readily see the flaws in this. You can see their egregious proof-specking.

From the very first verse in this paragraph, we can see clearly who is in focus here and under which covenant. God told Moses to communicate this to Israel. Notice that this is not Jesus, Paul, Peter, Luke, nor any other New Testament author who is being given these rules to give to believers of their day, and by extension to us Christians today. Moses was to communicate this to "the people of Israel" under the Old Covenant. This was not for any other ancient or modern people. This was specifically for the Israelites under the Old Covenant system. Adventists completely ignore this and do all sorts of theological gymnastics and Replacement Theology with the use of Romans 2:28-29 to claim that Christians are "spiritual Jews" and therefore bound to keep the Sabbath. But this is not true at all.

The rest of vs. 13 reads, "...for this is a sign between me and you throughout your generations, that you may know that I, the LORD, sanctify you." This is exclusive to the Israelites. The Sabbath was a covenant sign between God and themselves ("me and you") throughout *their* generations. This covenant sign was exclusive. It was like a wedding ring that indicated that they were God's special, Old Covenant bride. This did not apply to Gentile nations nor does it apply to modern nations today. The specific purpose for the Sabbath was that they would know that it was God who had "sanctified" them. The word "sanctify" here means to be set apart for holy use. The Sabbath was an identity marker for the Israelites to communicate to them that they were God's holy, special people (cf. Eze. 20:10-21). Verse 14 says the Sabbath is "holy for you," that is, the Israelites. The Sabbath was not holy for the Canaanites, the Philistines, the Moabites, the Ammonites, the Hittites, nor any other Gentile nation of the day. It was holy *only* for Israel.

Verse 14 also gives the punishment for violating the Sabbath. The Israelite who violated the Sabbath should be "put to death." Whoever did *any* work on the Sabbath was to be "cut off from among his people," that is, the Israelite covenant community. Adventists completely ignore this aspect of keeping the Sabbath in this very text that they proof-speck in order to enforce it on everyone else. The Sabbath cannot be enforced in its Old Covenant construct without the death penalty for its violation! The death penalty is part and parcel of Sabbath-keeping. God was so serious about this that the death penalty is repeated twice in this command (vs. 15). And it was repeated again when other laws were given on how to correctly keep the Sabbath. Exodus 35:2-3 says, "Six days work shall be done, but on the seventh day you shall have a Sabbath of solemn rest, holy to the LORD. Whoever does any work on it shall be put to death. ³You shall kindle no fire in all your dwelling places on the Sabbath day." God was very serious about the death penalty for Sabbath violators among the Israelites. Numbers 15 even has an example of a Sabbath violator being stoned to death for gathering sticks on the Sabbath (vs. 32-36). But Adventists conveniently ignore this aspect of Sabbath-keeping while they push the specks of it that promote their faulty narrative.

Verse 16-17 repeats most of what was already stated in the previous verses, namely, that the "people of Israel" should keep the Sabbath "throughout their generations," that it is "a sign" between God and themselves that God created heaven and earth in six days and rested on the seventh day and was refreshed. The only new element that is added in these two verses is that the Sabbath is a "covenant forever" and a "sign forever" between God and the people of Israel. Adventists usually think they have found irrefutable proof to demand that Christians keep the Sabbath today as Israel did, by the reference to it being a covenant and sign "forever." We certainly cannot expect better from the masters of proof-texting and proof-specking. Their own logic always returns to hound them but they could care less. Now, if the Sabbath is to be kept forever because these verses say so, then so do the ways that it ought to be kept and the *punishments* prescribed for its violation. Adventists generally argue that the death penalty and being "cut off" from among the covenant community for Sabbath violations are no longer applicable nor binding. And of course they ignore most of the ways Scripture prescribes for the Sabbath to be kept. Essentially, only parts of the Sabbath are "forever" that Adventists deem are forever. But this is a subjective, unreliable hermeneutic. Either all of it is forever or none is.

Is this paragraph really teaching that the Sabbath is forever, as in, will it endure throughout all eternity, in its Old Covenant forms, rules, and regulations? Of course not! The word "forever" is actually defined in the pericope itself. It simply meant "throughout their generations" (vs. 13, 16), as long as their generations and that Old Covenant would last, which from the perspective of the immediate audience would seem like forever. The Hebrew word that is translated "forever" in this text is עוֹלָם (olam) and the *Enhanced Strong's Lexicon* defines it as "long duration, antiquity, futurity, forever, ever, everlasting, evermore, perpetual, old, ancient, world. 1a) ancient time, long time (of past). 1b) of future. 1b1 forever, always. 1b2 continuous existence, perpetual. 1b3 everlasting, indefinite or unending future, eternity."[124] As is the case with any biblical word, the context and the nature of the thing being discussed will determine the meaning. Surely "olam" cannot mean "world, ancient, and eternity" in reference to the Sabbath in this passage. Neither can it mean "everlasting, continuous existence, or unending future" because the Sabbath had a definite beginning at the Sinai Peninsula (Exo. 16:22-30; Neh. 9:13-15; Psalm 147:19-20). It had multiple endings under the Old Covenant (Isa. 1:13-14; Lam. 2:6;

---

[124] James Strong, *Enhanced Strong's Lexicon* (Ontario, CA: Woodside Bible Fellowship, 1995), 5769 עֹ וֹלָ ם.

Hos. 2:11; Amos 5:21-22) and it had a final ending at the Cross of Christ (2 Cor. 3; Gal. 4:21-31; Eph. 2:14-16; Col. 2:11-17; Heb. 8:13). The best definition for "olam" in reference to the Sabbath here is "long duration, perpetual" with respect to Israel's future both during and after their 40 years' wilderness wandering. The Sabbath was specifically a long- enduring or perpetual sign *to them as a nation* until the Old Covenant would cease to be in effect. The Sabbath is not "God's perpetual sign of His eternal covenant between Him and His people"[125] as Ellen White[126] and Adventists have redefined both the Sabbath and *olam* in Exodus 31:12-17.

Irrespective of their redefinitions and fanciful arguments, *olam* does not and cannot mean "everlasting, eternal" in reference to the Sabbath. There are many other Old Covenant institutions, rituals, and practices that are modified with "olam" and said to be "perpetual, everlasting, eternal, etc.," yet they have been brought to an end. Adventists themselves have accepted and argued that these "olam" institutions, practices, and rituals have ended and do not need to be adhered to in their literal Old Covenant constructs. These are: Circumcision (Gen. 17:10-14), the Passover (Exo. 12:14, 24), the Day of Atonement (Lev. 16:29-31), the Feast of Tabernacles (Lev. 23:41-43), the Feast of Unleavened Bread (Exo. 12:17), the tabernacle lamps (Lev. 24:2-4), the Bread of the Presence (Lev. 24:5-9), the Levitical priesthood (Exo. 29:7-9), animal sacrifices (Exo. 29:38-42; Lev. 7:36-38; Deut. 12:27-28), grain offerings (Lev. 6:15-18; 23:13-14), the burning of incense (Exo. 30:8), Levites to do the tabernacle work (Num. 18:22-23), priestly washings (Exo. 30:17-21), etc. There is no exegetical basis upon which Adventists can ground their position that all of these "everlasting, perpetual" institutions, practices, feasts, and regulations are not "everlasting and perpetual" but the Sabbath is "everlasting and perpetual" because Exodus 31

---

[125] *Seventh-day Adventists Believe*, p. 281.

[126] Ellen White said, "The Lord speaks to those who turn away their feet from [trampling on] the Sabbath. This is the Sabbath spoken of in the thirty-first chapter of Exodus, which God declares is *a sign between Him and His people*. By keeping this day holy, we show to the world that we recognize God as the One who created the world in six days, and rested on the seventh."--- White, *The Upward Look*, p. 76, par. 2.

says so. Absolutely none. Their argument is grounded on Ellen White's statements about the Sabbath, faulty premises, cognitive dissonance, and sheer rejection of the biblical data.

What they do with Exodus 31:12-17 is classic proof-specking that they think will uphold their views, while they ignore and discard the other things the passage does say.

Does Matt. 5:17-19 prove that the Law cannot be abolished?

Matthew 5:17-19 is another major text that Adventists proof-speck. In this passage, they think they have found arguments for the continuing obligation and validity of the Law (specifically the Ten Commandments). In this pivotal Sermon on the Mount, Jesus said:

> Do not think that I have come to abolish the Law or the Prophets; I have not come to abolish them but to fulfill them. [18]For truly, I say to you, until heaven and earth pass away, not an iota, not a dot, will pass from the Law until all is accomplished. [19]Therefore whoever relaxes one of the least of these commandments and teaches others to do the same will be called least in the kingdom of heaven, but whoever does them and teaches them will be called great in the kingdom of heaven.

When Adventists read this passage, they scratch out "the Prophets," proof-speck "the Law" and redefine it to mean "the Ten Commandments." They interpret "fulfil them" to mean to magnify and enforce them. They interpret "until heaven and earth" to mean because heaven and earth have not passed away then the Ten Commandments are still valid to be kept by everyone, using a modern cosmological view instead of how those Jews at that time understood heaven and earth in this context to mean the temple at Jerusalem where heaven and earth met. They interpret "an iota" and "a dot" to mean any one of the Ten Commandments. The word "accomplished" is generally ignored in their proof-specking frenzy. The rest of the text is interpreted to mean that Adventists are "great" in the kingdom of heaven because they "do and teach" the Law, while non-Adventist Christians will be called "least" in the kingdom of heaven because they do not keep nor teach the Ten Commandments, especially the Sabbath. This of course contradicts their Investigative Judgement and sinless perfection doctrine because such persons will not even make it into the kingdom to be privileged to be called "least."

Adventists make complete nonsense of this passage in order to make it uphold their obsession with the Ten Commandments. The reference to "these commandments" in vs. 19 is not to the Ten Commandments as they assume. The demonstrative pronoun "these" can refer to what was commanded before its use or what follows its use. From vs. 1-18, Jesus did not command the Ten Commandments nor any other command, so "these commandments" cannot be referring to any command previously stated. "These commandments" are referring to all the commands that Jesus was about to give beginning with vs. 21 and ending in chapter 7. And those commands He gave were not exclusively the Ten Commandments. He quoted many commands from the Old Covenant Law. He showed how limited they were in scope, magnified them, then assumed greater authority than Moses and gave commands that went beyond those commands. He even negated points of law, contrary to the Adventist take on verse 17.

In vs. 21-26, He gave commands about murder and anger. In vs. 27-30 he spoke about adultery and lust, while in vs. 31-32 He spoke about divorce, adultery, and sexual immorality. In vs. 33-48, He gave commands about oaths and false swearing, retaliation (vs. 38-42), and loving one's enemies (vs. 43-48). In chapter 6, He commanded concerning giving to needy persons (vs. 1-4), praying (vs. 5-14), fasting (vs. 16-18), storing up one's treasure and serving two masters (vs. 19-24), and anxiety about daily needs (vs. 25-34). In chapter 7, He commanded about judging others (vs. 1-6), requesting and seeking things from God (vs. 7-11), the golden rule (vs. 12), the narrow and the wide gate (vs. 13-14), false prophets (vs. 15-20), obeying God (vs. 21-23), and building on the rock (vs. 24-27). These are the commandments that they were not expected to relax. These contextual facts in the Sermon on the Mount do not uphold the assumptions of Adventism. It is of utmost importance to note too that in chapter 5, Jesus also gave impossible mandates, such as plucking out an eye, cutting off a hand (vs. 29-30) in order to do the impossible. It was His way of saying how impossible it is to control one's own mind and thoughts, which alone can condemn one (Rom. 14:22-23; 1 John 3:19-21).

Jesus had sat down on the mountain top to teach the multitudes (vs. 1). He taught them the Beatitudes (vs. 3-12), stated that they were the salt of the earth (vs. 13), and the light of the world (vs. 14-16). Obviously, they must have thought that His mission was to abolish the Law and the Prophets, but He quickly banished such a thought by saying that they ought not to think that. Instead, He said He had come to fulfil them, not to abolish them (vs. 17). In saying "the Law or the Prophets," Jesus does not mean "the Ten Commandments" as Adventists have proof-specked and read into the text. The Law or the Prophets was a designation for the entire Old Testament Scriptures,[127] the Law being the five books of Moses (Genesis to Deuteronomy) and the Prophets being everything else. Jesus said He came to fulfil the Old Testament Scriptures, not to abolish them. The word "fulfil" does not mean to magnify and enforce them as Adventists argue. It means to complete or to bring them to pass. Matthew 11:13 says, "For all the Prophets and the Law prophesied until John [the Baptist]...." Jesus came to fulfil the prophecies of the Law and the Prophets.

In verse 18, Jesus made a profound statement that Adventists will continue to misconstrue. Twice in this verse the Greek conjunction ἕως (heos) is used with the particle ἄν (an) to not only express the temporal covenantal era of the Law and Prophets but also to express the certainty that they will be fulfilled. This certainty is further expressed by His use of "heaven and earth" and "not an iota, not a dot" will ever pass from the Law until He accomplished all of them. The Law and the Prophets would be in full effect, in their entirety,

---

[127] "The Law or the Prophets" is the New Testament's designation for the entire Old Testament. There are variations of this nomenclature for the Old Testament in the New Testament (Matt. 5:17; 7:12; 11:13; Luke 16:16, 29, 31; 24:27, 44; John 1:45; Acts 13:15; 24:14; 26:22; 28:23; and Rom. 3:21).

until Jesus fulfilled them. Until Jesus fulfils them, the smallest point in the Law and the Prophets would still be in force. It would be easier for the universe to dissolve before the smallest aspect of the Law or the Prophets dissolves. This is what Jesus was communicating. But what did Jesus mean by saying that He came to fulfil the Law and Prophets? And, did He fulfill them? Let us explore the answers to these questions.

In John 5:39, Jesus said to the religious leaders, "You search the Scriptures because you think that in them you have eternal life; and it is they that bear witness about me." The Old Testament Scriptures testify about Jesus. Jesus said in vs. 46, "For if you believed Moses, you would believe me; for he wrote of me." Indeed, Moses wrote about Jesus in the Law (Genesis to Deuteronomy). The entirety of the Old Testament Scriptures, including the Ten Commandments, bore witness to Jesus' life, ministry, death, resurrection, and atonement for humanity. Jesus had to fulfill the Law and Prophets in their entirety in order to be the Messiah. This is a biblical fact that one would be foolish as a student of Scripture and reject. In Matthew 5:17, the Greek word for "to fulfill" is πληρῶσαι (plerosai). It is from the root verb πληρόω (pleroo) and means "to fill up, to make full or complete (to fill to the top so that nothing is lacking), and to fill full (to the brim)."[128] Pleroo connotes progressive fulfilment. This connotation reveals the ineptitude of the Adventist argument. Adventist argue that Jesus was bringing the 10 Commandments up to "full force," "filling them to the brim, magnifying them," etc., all the while claiming that the Ten Commandments are *already* "perfect," as well as eternal. Jesus came to progressively fulfil the Old Testament Scriptures until nothing was lacking or left undone. As we study Jesus' life and ministry in the Gospels, we constantly see how He progressively fulfilled the Scriptures. And the Gospel writers often signal us that in His actions, He was fulfilling parts of Old Testament Scripture. Consider these passages:

Matt. 1:22-23- "All this took place to fulfill [Gr. pleroo] what the

---

[128] W.E. Vine and F.F. Bruce, Vol. 2, *Vine's Expository Dictionary of Old and New Testament Words* (Old Tappan, NJ: Revell, 1981), p. 96.

Lord had spoken by the prophet: [23]"Behold, the virgin shall conceive and bear a son, and they shall call his name Immanuel.""

Matt. 4:14- "so that what was spoken by the prophet Isaiah might be fulfilled" [Gr. pleroo]:

Matt. 21:4-5- "This took place to fulfill [Gr. pleroo] what was spoken by the prophet, saying, 5 "Say to the daughter of Zion, 'Behold, your king is coming to you, humble, and mounted on a donkey, on a colt, the foal of a beast of burden.'""

Mark 15:28- "So the Scripture was fulfilled [Gr. pleroo] which says, "And He was numbered with the transgressors.""

Luke 4:21- "And He began to say to them, "Today this Scripture is fulfilled [Gr. pleroo] in your hearing.""

John 13:18- "I do not speak concerning all of you. I know those whom I chose; but that the Scripture may be fulfilled [Gr. pleroo], 'He who eats bread with Me has lifted up his heel against Me.'"

Many more Scriptures could have been used but these are sufficient to illustrate my point. Throughout His life and ministry, Jesus progressively fulfilled the Law and the Prophets. In the closing scenes of Jesus' ministry, we read these words in John 19:28-30:

> After this, when Jesus knew that everything was now accomplished that the Scripture might be fulfilled, He said, "I'm thirsty!" [29]A jar full of sour wine was sitting there; so they fixed a sponge full of sour wine on hyssop and held it up to His mouth. [30]When Jesus had received the sour wine, He said, "It is finished!" Then bowing His head, He gave up His spirit" (HCSB).

Jesus fulfilled the Law and the Prophets. He had stated in Matthew 5:18 that the Law would be in force until "all is accomplished." At His death, John informs us that Jesus was conscious that "everything was now accomplished," then Jesus said, "It is finished!" Jesus did exactly what He said He came to do—fulfill the Law and Prophets.

Interestingly, the Greek word used in John 19:28 and 30 is not πληρόω (pleroo) but τελέω (teleo). Whereas pleroo connotes progressive fulfilment, on the other hand, teleo connotes

159

consummatory fulfillment because it means "end, goal, to make an end or to accomplish, to complete something, not merely to end it, but to bring it to perfection or its destined goal, to carry it through."[129] Jesus executed what was written in the Law and the Prophets. To suggest that He did not would be a grave rejection of a fundamental teaching of Scripture and a denial of Jesus' messiahship. "It is finished" in John 19:30 is the Greek word τετελεσται (tetelestai). It is in the perfect tense and means completed action with unending potency and efficacy. Tetelestai literally means, "It has been and continues to be paid in full" or "It stands complete." There is nothing more that can be added to what Jesus has accomplished on the Cross. He has perfectly carried out *all* the requirements of the Law and the Prophets, just as He had said He would do.

After His resurrection, several times Jesus reminded the disciples that He had to suffer to fulfill the Law and the Prophets. We read in Luke 24:25-27, 44-48:

> And he said to them, "O foolish ones, and slow of heart to believe all that the prophets have spoken! [26]Was it not necessary that the Christ should suffer these things and enter into his glory?" [27]And beginning with Moses and all the Prophets, he interpreted to them in all the Scriptures the things concerning himself... [44]Then he said to them, "These are my words that I spoke to you while I was still with you, that everything written about me in the Law of Moses and the Prophets and the Psalms must be fulfilled." [45]Then he opened their minds to understand the Scriptures, [46]and said to them, "Thus it is written, that the Christ should suffer and on the third day rise from the dead, [47]and that repentance and forgiveness of sins should be proclaimed in his name to all nations, beginning from Jerusalem. [48]You are witnesses of these things.

Indeed, not one "iota-nor dot" had passed from the Law and the

[129]Spiros Zodhiates, *The Complete Word Study Dictionary: New Testament*, electronic ed. (Chattanooga, TN: AMG Publishers, 2000), τελέω.

Prophets until Jesus fulfilled them.

Verse 19 of Matthew 5 is not saying that Adventists are considered great in the kingdom of God for doing and teaching the Ten Commandments. Nor is it saying that Christians are least in the kingdom of God for not doing and teaching the Ten Commandments. After Jesus' death, resurrection, and the ushering in of the New Covenant the apostles and New Testament authors relaxed more than mere iotas and dots in the Law. They relaxed circumcision, Sabbath-keeping, animal sacrifices, temple offerings and services, kosher laws, Torah-induced clean and unclean designations, and scores of other things. Yet they were not considered to be the least in the kingdom of God. And the Judaizers, Pharisees, and other law-centred persons who were trying to do and teach the Law as still binding for salvation and as an identity marker for Christians were considered to be "the least" and objectionable persons in the kingdom of God. When one reads Acts 15, the Book of Galatians, Colossians 2, Titus 3, the Book of Romans, and many other parts of the New Testament one sees this clearly.

Faulty Hermeneutical Principle and Assumption #7

Anytime any of the Ten Commandments is mentioned or alluded to, that automatically upholds the validity of all the Ten Commandments and enforces them, but this is never true for ceremonial laws or laws outside of the Ten Commandments.

Does Gen. 39:9 prove that Joseph had the Ten Commandments?

Whenever Adventists are attempting to defend or prove the existence of the Ten Commandments before Mount Sinai, a quick proof-text they run to is Genesis 39:9 when Joseph said to Potiphar's wife, "...How then can I do this great wickedness and sin against God?" What they assume from this is that Joseph knew the Ten Commandments and was keeping them. "Thou shalt not commit adultery" is one of the Ten Commandments and Joseph was refusing to commit adultery because he had the Ten Commandments, he knew of them, and knew not to break them. This is the typical Adventist line of reasoning. But does Joseph's response to Potiphar's wife prove that he had the Ten Commandments and was keeping them before they were codified at Mount Sinai centuries later? Did laws against adultery exist among Gentile nations before Israel became a nation and before God gave them the Law at Mount Sinai?

When we study the laws of ancient nations, both before and during the time of Israel and its reception of the Law, we understand that they had many laws that were similar to Israel's laws, and that some of their laws even predated Israel's laws. Joseph knew adultery was wrong because of conscience (Gen. 3:22; Rom. 2:12-15), that committing adultery, although it sins against man, is ultimately sinning against God (Psa. 51:3-4), and also because Egypt had laws against adultery. This is precisely why Joseph was thrown in jail because Potiphar presumed that he was guilty of attempting to rape his wife (Gen. 39:19-20). There is nothing in the Ten Commandments that stipulates imprisonment or punishment for "Thou shall not commit adultery." But Joseph was thrown in jail because that was a punishment based on Egyptian law. Joseph's objection that to commit adultery was to sin against God was because he knew God and knew that any sin committed is ultimately against Him. His statement is not indicating his awareness of or personal possession of the stone tablets containing the Ten Commandments. Deuteronomy 5:1-3 is very clear that the Ten Commandments covenant (vs. 5-22) was not made with Israel's ancestors (which would include Joseph) but with the Israelites who were at Mount Sinai and their progeny to come after them. The existence of moralistic laws among the patriarchs and Gentile nations is not contingent upon the Ten Commandments.

In *Old Testament Parallels*, Victor H. Matthews and Don C. Benjamin documented several ancient civilizations that predated and were coeval with Israel and had laws and stories that were very similar to their law codes and stories. They specifically paralleled the *Code of Shulgi*, the *Sumerian Code*, the *Code of Hammurabi*, the *Hittite Code*, and the *Middle Assyrian Code* with the law codes we read from Genesis to Deuteronomy. Those ancient law codes contain laws about murder, perjury, rape, incest, slavery, accidental miscarriage by wounding a pregnant woman, lying and false accusations, bribery, kidnapping, treason, stealing and robbery, false measurements, sorcery, the purposeful wounding of a man's testicles, adultery, and countless other things.[130] What this proves is that Joseph was aware of the wrongness of adultery, not from possessing or having a knowledge of the Ten Commandments, but from conscience and also from the very law codes in Egypt and other nations around him. What is glaringly absent in all of these law codes are laws about the Sabbath and dietary distinctions, two key things that Adventists incessantly argue are "moral and health laws" that were always binding on *all* of humanity from creation. It is very odd to contend that the Sabbath is a "moral law" that was written on the hearts of these Gentiles yet in all of their law codes there is absolutely nothing about the Sabbath and keeping it holy. Nothing. This fact alone should prove how vacuous the Adventist claim and argument is. As a matter of fact, these law codes did not have many laws that were peculiar to Israel. They did not have laws about Yahweh and exclusively worshipping Him. They did not have laws about the sanctuary and its services, sacrifices, wearing blue tassels on their garments, the Jewish feasts, and countless other things.

In addition to this, the theme of adultery was prominent among the patriarchs. In their interactions with other nations, specifically Egypt and Gerar, we gather that those countries had severe laws against adultery and considered it to be a major and flagrant sin. Joseph would have known of these adultery narratives of his forefathers via oral tradition. He would have known how God dealt with both Pharaoh and Abimelech. Elaine Adler Goodfriend pointed out:

> The theme of adultery is found several times in the book of Genesis. Both Abraham and Isaac try to pass off their wives as their sisters, allowing them to be taken (or nearly taken) by foreigners (Genesis 12:10–20; 20; 26:1–11). Both patriarchs assume that the people of Gerar and Egypt took the "great sin" of adultery very seriously and would rather make widows out of Sarah and Rebecca than incur the guilt

---

[130] Victor H. Matthews and Don C. Benjamin, *Old Testament Parallels: Laws and Stories from the Ancient Near East Third Edition* (Mahwah, NJ: Paulist Press, 2006), p. 101-130.

of adultery (David Kimchi). YHWH's punishment for adultery in all three chapters is collective (12:17; 20:7, 17; 26:10).[131]

Conclusively, what the retort of Joseph to Potiphar's wife proves is that some moralistic laws were common among all ancient civilizations and adultery was one of them. Joseph's response is in no way proving that he had the Ten Commandments nor that He knew of them. His deterrent was that he knew it would be wickedness and a sin against God. It was a desire not to be going against God out of reverence for Him. What we witness with Adventists is the proclivity to grasp at any possible straw in support of their preconceived notion that the Law existed and was extant long before it was given to the Hebrews at Sinai.

Does Matthew 19 prove that we have to keep the Ten Commandments to be saved?

Adventists generally think that they have found incontrovertible ammunition in Matthew 19 that proves that we are saved by keeping the Ten Commandments and that we must keep them as a full package. The specific verses they have culled out from the entire pericope is vs. 17-19, which says:

> And he said to him, "Why do you ask me about what is good? There is only one who is good. If you would enter life, keep the commandments." [18]He said to him, "Which ones?" And Jesus said, "You shall not murder, You shall not commit adultery, You shall not steal, You shall not bear false witness, [19]Honor your father and mother, and, You shall love your neighbor as yourself."

Because Jesus quotes five of the Ten Commandments as examples of what this Rich Young Ruler must "keep" to "enter life," Adventists draw the conclusion that we must keep the Ten

---

[131] Elaine Adler Goodfriend, "Adultery," in Vol. 1, *The Anchor Yale Bible Dictionary*, ed. David Noel Freedman (New York: Doubleday, 1992), p. 84-85.

Commandments if we want to be saved. But as I am proving in this chapter, one can see the obvious mental tricks that Adventists perform on themselves to come to such a conclusion. If quoting some of the Ten Commandments mean that all of them are binding on believers, should not the same logic apply to Jesus' quoting the command to "love your neighbour as yourself"? The command to "love your neighbour as yourself" is from Leviticus 19:18. If quoting some of the Ten Commandments means that all are automatically binding and must be kept, should not this same logic apply to Leviticus 19, especially given that Jesus quotes it in the same statement as the five commands from the Ten Commandments? It is very difficult to keep up with the twisted logic of Adventists.

Contrary to what Adventists attempt to torture this passage to say, the story is revealing quite the opposite. It is showing that no amount of law or commandment-keeping can ever be good enough to save us or to grant us eternal life. When the Rich Young Ruler asked Jesus the question, Jesus' response was basically to reach him where he was, as a Torah-abiding Jew, and then to show him that he needed to actually have faith in Jesus, be detached from what he found meaning and existence in, and receive salvation. After Jesus responded to him, the young man's response was, "All these I have kept. What do I still lack?" (vs. 20). What this reveals is that no amount of law-keeping can ever be sufficient to save one. If law-keeping was the means to be saved, then surely this young man would have automatically been saved. He said to Jesus that he had already been keeping *all* of those commands and wondered what he was still lacking. The fact that he felt like he had lacked something to thus ask Jesus what he needed to do to be saved reveals that his keeping the entire Torah still left him devoid of the assurance of salvation. The obvious revelation from this is that one can keep the Torah perfectly and that still does not mean that one is saved. This young man had been keeping Torah as a young boy up to this point but was *still* lacking.

Jesus' response reveals exactly that. In verse 21 we read, "Jesus said to him, "If you would be perfect, go, sell what you possess and give to the poor, and you will have treasure in heaven; and come, follow me.'"" What we can glean from Jesus' diagnosis and instructions here are that no amount of law-keeping can perfect one. For the young man to have been considered "perfect" and thus saved, he would have had to part ways with his tremendous wealth (that required faith). He would have had to give everything to the poor (again, that required faith and selfless love). His actions would have stored up treasures in heaven (again, that required faith). And he would have had to come and follow Jesus, which again would require faith!

In short, what this young man needed to do to be saved was to place his faith in Jesus. And as he experienced conversion by faith, his actions would have demonstrated his faith. Faith in Jesus would bring transformation. This would be expressed in him detaching himself from his idolatrous wealth. Through the Holy Spirit's transformation, he would have acquired the ability to love his neighbour as himself to the point of sacrificing his livelihood to feed them. What he needed in order to have eternal life was faith—faith in Jesus that would produce works congruent with such faith (Eph. 2:10). But sadly, the story says, "When the young man heard this he went away sorrowful, for he had great possessions" (vs. 22). He went away from Jesus to continue to live his life practicing the Law, being attached to his wealth, but still lacking, still faithless, still devoid of eternal life and salvation. He chose the Law over faith in Jesus. And just as before this encounter, the Law still cannot save him nor fill the emptiness within. This is a sad story. This is the lesson that the story is teaching—no amount of law-keeping can ever save us. We must have faith in Jesus to be saved. Faith in Jesus will transform us to follow Him and to be like Him in the way we treat our neighbours. But Adventists have completely missed the point and invert this story to say that it is law-keeping, specifically the Ten Commandments, that will save us. Unfortunately, they are repeating the very same, grave mistake as this Rich Young Ruler. They are choosing an empty, non-saving, idolatrous life under the Law over assuring, eternal life-giving, self-sacrificing faith in Jesus.

The disciples' response to Jesus and His interaction with the Rich Young Ruler is very instructive and blows the Adventist position out of the water. Matthew 19:25-26 says, "When the disciples heard this, they were greatly astonished, saying, "Who then can be saved?" ^{26}But Jesus looked at them and said, "With man this is impossible, but with God all things are possible."" It is impossible for anyone to save themselves through their efforts of Law-keeping and wealth. No amount of Ten Commandments-keeping can save any Adventist or anybody else for that matter. Salvation is only possible through and by God and what He does. It can never be possible by what we do.

Does Ephesians 6:1-4 prove that the Ten Commandments are binding on Christians?

Ephesians 6:1-4 says:

> Children, obey your parents in the Lord, for this is right. ^{2}"Honor your father and mother" (this is the first commandment with a promise), ^{3}"that it may go well with you and that you may live long in the land." ^{4}Fathers, do not provoke your children to anger, but bring them up in the discipline and instruction of the Lord.

This is another text that Adventists believe justify the continued validity and binding nature of all Ten Commandments because Paul quoted the Fifth Commandment here. But as was already proven, Paul's use of the Fifth Commandment is not binding the Ten Commandments as a package on believers in Ephesus. Neither is it suggesting that the Ten Commandments covenant is still in force for the Ephesians, and by extension Christians today, to observe in their Old Covenant context. That is not what Paul is doing at all. The Fifth Commandment is a universal and natural law. Every tribe, culture, and civilization, ancient and modern, had laws or cultural expectations of children to respect and honor their parents. This was true for Jews under the Old Covenant and it was true for the citizens of Ephesus. Paul's usage of the command is merely to remind them of this universal principle. The way Paul adapts the Fifth Commandment even reveals that he is not intending to teach that it is binding in its Old Covenant construct. The Fifth Commandment in

Exodus 20:12 reads, "Honor your father and your mother that your days may be long in the land that the LORD your God is giving you." The way this is written shows that Israel had not yet possessed the land, hence "the land that the LORD your God *is giving* you." The longevity of their lives in the land was contingent upon them honouring their parents. But when Paul quotes the command, notice how he repackaged and adapted it, "Children, obey your parents in the Lord, for this is right." He used it to strengthen this command that children should obey their parents "in the Lord." The commandment in the law does not address immature children, but adults whose parents still live. A child was not held accountable to the law until they were around 14 years old.

The issue Paul had with them was in relation to the works or deeds of the law; things one had to "do" or avoid doing that were arbitrary, like keeping the Sabbath. Honoring one's parents was a duty in relation to one's relationship with parents. Israelites didn't have to jump through hoops to do this. There is also another aspect to this law. The law said to "honor" one's parents; a concept of respect despite how they might have treated you. Honor can be devoid of love. Whether or not children in Ephesus loved their parents, Paul said to honor them "in the Lord" because it was "right." The usage and adaptation of this command by Paul in no way suggests that the entire package of Ten Commandments is binding on believers. The utilisation of an old law to argue for the principle of that law in a new context does not place one under that old law. What Paul was relating, addressing children, is in keeping with his take on the Law being a paidagogos (Gal. 3:24); someone who had charge over children, or in this case, the spiritually immature. So it is not at all surprising he would use this commandment in relation to physical children. He does not apply this commandment to adults who are spiritually mature Christians.

There is something else to consider too. What exactly did it mean for children to "honor" their parents in the Old Covenant context? And was Paul reinforcing that command from that context? Where the Old Covenant law was concerned, parents were essentially in total control of children under their roof, whether they were adults or not. Parents could have arranged marriages for their children and children had to "honor" their parents' choice of a spouse for them (Isaac and Rebekah- Gen. 24; Jacob, Leah, and Rachel- Gen. 29, etc.). Children had to obey their parents every wish and command, almost without reservation. Children did not have much say in their own lives. If adult children disobeyed their parents or lived in a way that would bring disrepute to their parents (a stubborn drunkard), the parents could have had that child executed (Deut. 21:18-21). These are only brief examples of what it meant to "honor" one's father and mother in the Old Covenant construct. Paul was not enforcing this upon the Ephesians. Children were instructed to obey their parents "in the Lord," that is, in a Gospel-centred, Christocentric, transformative way and not "in the Law."

As I had demonstrated before, the Ten Commandments extracted from their historical and covenantal context and construct are a proverbial toothless bulldog and inadequate. While the Fifth Commandment has a promise of long life attached to it, it is still very inadequate both to the Ephesians and to us in our modern context. Hence, Paul had to do some elaboration and expansion as he used that command as a springboard. The Fifth Commandment does not oblige parents to take care of nor to be considerate towards their children. But when Paul uses and adapts the command, he places obligations on parents towards their children. Paul says, "Fathers, do not provoke your children to anger, but bring them up in the discipline and instruction of the Lord" (Eph. 6:4). Fathers were under no obligation to not aggravate and enrage their children under the law of the Fifth Commandment. None. But Paul used it as a principle and exhorts fathers to not aggravate their children. The Fifth Commandment in Exodus 20:12, extracted and isolated from the rest of the Law, as Adventists have done with it, does not obligate parents to discipline, train, nor to raise their children in the instructions of the Lord. But Paul uses that command as a principle for parents to do so for their children in Ephesus and in a New Covenant context and construct. His use of it is not intended to enforce the validity and obligation of all Ten Commandments. Instead, he used it as an established, universal principle and adapted it to Ephesus and exhorted children to obey their parents, and conversely for parents to not aggravate their children; rather, to raise them with Christian principles and ethics.

James 2:10-11, break one, break all?

James 2:10-11 is perhaps one of the most favourite and popular proof-texts of Adventists when they are attempting to show that the mention of one commandment from the Ten Commandments means that they are all valid and being enforced. They always use this to trip up unsuspecting non-Sabbatarian Christians to convince them to keep Saturday as the Sabbath. The respective verses say, "For whoever keeps the whole law but fails in one point has become accountable for all of it. [11]For he who said, "Do not commit adultery," also said, "Do not murder." If you do not commit adultery but do murder, you have become a transgressor of the law." The Adventist argumentation from these two verses is if we break one of the Ten Commandments then we break them all and are guilty of the entirety of that covenant. Additionally, they argue that since Christians keep nine of the Ten Commandments but do not keep the Saturday Sabbath then they are guilty of breaking all of the commandments, and therefore are transgressors of the Law. This argument seems hermetic. Adventists consistently use it to drag Christians under Ten Commandments legalism, and eventually the entire gamut of Adventist unorthodoxy and false doctrines.

But as with every other faulty hermeneutic and false assumption of theirs that I have been disproving, this is sloppy proof-texting and extremely weak argumentation. The Adventist argumentation actually works against them if one knows how to respond or how to reverse their logic on them. Let me illustrate. Since breaking one of the Ten Commandments means that Christians don't keep any of them and therefore are guilty of breaking all of them, this also applies to the Adventist and literally undermines their claim to be keeping the Ten Commandments. If Adventists break any of the Ten Commandments, in whatever way, they are guilty of breaking all of them. And if they are guilty of breaking all of them, then their claim and boast of keeping the Sabbath is empty. It would be a lie because they are guilty of violating it. If they told a lie, coveted, committed adultery, dishonoured their parents, or violated any other command, they are guilty of breaking the Sabbath. The very thing that they accuse and charge Christians with, they are themselves equally guilty. Therefore all of their barefaced claims and triumphalism of "keeping the Sabbath" and the Ten Commandments are as vapid as dew that will vanish when the sun shines upon it. By their logic, they do not keep the commandments and neither do Christians, therefore no one actually keeps the Ten Commandments. Consequently, no one is truly saved and obedient to God because for them salvation is hinged on obedience to the Ten Commandments. What a dismal conundrum we are all in with this bad logic of theirs! Unfortunately, this is the logical end of their argument. This is the egregious weakness.

For this to not be the case with their argument from this text, they have to literally claim to be sinlessly perfect and have never ever broken any of the Ten Commandments. If they claim to have never broken any of the Ten Commandments, then that would be claiming to be without sin—never ever committed any sin from birth to the present. And of course, we know where this would lead because 1 John 1:8 says, "If we say we have no sin, we deceive ourselves, and the truth is not in us." And verse 10 is equally clear, "If we say we have not sinned, we make him a liar, and his word is not in us." Dear Adventist, are you sure you want to continue to use this argument? You are trapped by your own logic. As the saying goes, you can't have your cake and eat it too.

Despite what Adventists argue from James 2:10-11, this text is not saying what they have wrung out of it. The context of the paragraph is not proving that Christians are under the Ten Commandments and that if they break any one of them then they break all and are guilty of all of them. The contextual unit of vs. 10-11 starts with vs. 1 and ends with vs. 13. Surprisingly, the paragraph is dealing with partiality with love and its application, not the validity of the Ten Commandments. From vs. 1 James already lets us know the subject matter that he is talking about when he said to "show no partiality" as they held the faith in Jesus Christ. In vs. 2-7 he illustrated how partiality is shown when they discriminate in the way they treat a poor man as opposed to a rich man in their assemblies. The poor man was judged based on his appearance and made to stand or sit in an undignified place, while the rich man was made to sit in a dignified place solely because of his appearance as well. James then says in vs. 8, "If you really fulfill the royal law according to the Scripture, "You shall love your neighbor as yourself," you are doing well." Ellen White erroneously claimed that the Ten Commandments is the "royal law" that James is talking about here,[132] and ever since she said that, this is what Adventists have incessantly argued it to be. But James is not saying that the Ten Commandments is the "royal law." He quoted Leviticus 19:18 which says "You shall love your neighbor as yourself," and calls that the "royal law." The command "You shall love your neighbour as yourself" is not in the Ten Commandments. Ironically, that command is from what Adventists call the ceremonial law that they claim is now abolished. It is this royal law that James says if they "really fulfill" they are doing well. They would fulfill this royal law by not showing partiality.

In vs. 9 James says, "But if you show partiality, you are committing sin and are convicted by the law as transgressors." This is not referring to the Ten Commandments. Nothing in the Ten Commandments condemns partiality. Partiality is condemned in Deuteronomy 1:17a, which says, "You shall not be partial in judgment. You shall hear the small and the great alike. You shall not be intimidated by anyone, for the judgment is God's." It is also condemned in Deuteronomy 16:19, which says, "You shall not pervert justice. You shall not show partiality, and you shall not accept a bribe, for a bribe blinds the eyes of the wise and subverts the cause of the righteous." As a Jewish Christian, teacher, and apostle writing to Jewish Christians, neither James nor his audience would have conceptualized "the Law" as just the Ten Commandments. The Law for them was the entire Torah (five books of Moses), hence his reference to Deuteronomy as "the law" that convicts them as transgressors if they showed partiality. If they showed partiality even

---

[132] In the *Great Controversy* p. 466, par. 2, Ellen White said "The apostle James, who wrote after the death of Christ, refers to the Decalogue as "the royal law" and "the perfect law of liberty" James 2:8; 1:25."

once, with just one person, just like someone is guilty for having transgressed just one point of that Old Covenant Law, they become guilty of the entirety.

James strengthens his argument in vs. 10 by saying, "For whoever keeps the whole law but fails in one point has become accountable for all of it." This further proves that he did not view the Ten Commandments as exclusively "the Law" by him referring to "the whole law." The Ten Commandments were never considered to be "the whole law" in Judaism. These Jewish believers who were still practicing the Law were failing to keep the whole law by showing partiality. James says by showing partiality (failing in that one point), they were accountable to the entire law of liberty. To properly illustrate his point he quotes two of the Ten Commandments, which are part of the "whole law," and says, "For he who said, "Do not commit adultery," also said, "Do not murder." If you do not commit adultery but do murder, you have become a transgressor of the law." His use of two commands from the Ten Commandments are no different from his use of commands from Leviticus 19:18, Deuteronomy 1:17 and 16:19.

In vs. 12 James exhorts, "So speak and so act as those who are to be judged under the law of liberty." As typical of Adventist, they claim that this text is saying that the Ten Commandments are what will judge everyone and determine salvation. This is even depicted in their artwork where they have an illustration of a heavenly courtroom scene where a man is standing in front of two massive stones with the Ten Commandments inscribed on them, an angel standing beside the man, and another angel sitting at a desk transcribing sins or deeds. But this is not what James is saying at all in this pericope. James is saying that these Jewish Christians should not only talk a good talk about "the faith in our Lord Jesus Christ, the Lord of glory" (vs. 1) but they should also act according to that faith as those who will be "judged under the law of liberty." The law of liberty is not the Ten Commandments as Adventists generally argue. The Ten Commandments are never called the law of liberty in the New Testament. As part of the Old Covenant and the Mosaic Law, they are always called or alluded to as a law of bondage, the opposite of liberty

(Acts 15:1, 5, 7-11; Rom. 7:1-6; Gal. 3:23; 4:21-31; 5:1-4). The law of liberty is "the faith" in Jesus (vs. 1). It is the Gospel.

In chapter 1, James had already established what is this "law of liberty" just before he got into the sin of partiality. In vs. 19-25, he said:

> Know this, my beloved brothers: let every person be quick to hear, slow to speak, slow to anger; [20]for the anger of man does not produce the righteousness of God. [21]Therefore put away all filthiness and rampant wickedness and receive with meekness the implanted word, which is able to save your souls. [22]But be doers of the word, and not hearers only, deceiving yourselves. [23]For if anyone is a hearer of the word and not a doer, he is like a man who looks intently at his natural face in a mirror. [24]For he looks at himself and goes away and at once forgets what he was like. [25]But the one who looks into the perfect law, the law of liberty, and perseveres, being no hearer who forgets but a doer who acts, he will be blessed in his doing.

James refers to the Gospel by several terms here. He calls it the "implanted word" that is able to save our souls (vs. 21). The Ten Commandments are not the implanted word that is able to save our souls. He calls it "the word" that we should be doers of and not merely hearers (vs. 22). In vs. 25, he calls it the "perfect law" and "the law of liberty," which we should persevere in. James adequately defined his terms. We do not need to assume nor inject anything into his statement to make it say something else. It is the Gospel of Christ that will judge us. We will be judged based on how we respond to the Gospel (John 12:47-48) and how we lived out its demands. Living out the demands of the Gospel will be demonstrated in how we treat people. We will be judged by that (Matt. 25:31-46). This is the subject matter that James is dealing with (partiality). Liberty in New Covenant faith is being delivered from the power of sin through the Gospel, and being transformed to not only be like Jesus but to love and treat each other the same way He loves and treats us. This is expressed in a variety of ways in the New Testament.

Jesus said in John 13:34-35, "A new commandment I give to you, that you love one another: just as I have loved you, you also are to love one another. [35]By this all people will know that you are my disciples, if you have love for one another." He stated again in 15:12-13, "This is my commandment, that you love one another as I have loved you. [13]Greater love has no one than this, that someone lay down his life for his friends." In Romans 15:1-7, Paul exhorted the saints to welcome, build up, please, and bear each other's burdens in accordance with the example that Christ had set and commanded. In 1 Corinthians 9:21, he referred to this considerate, others-centred, self-sacrificial living as "the law of Christ." In Galatians 6:2 Paul states, "Bear one another's burdens, and so fulfill the law of Christ." This is the law of liberty that James is talking about that we will be judged by. This sin of partiality, contextually, does not result in condemnation, given the context of the New Covenant law of liberty. In the context of the New Covenant law of liberty, one learns to become more Christlike over time.

James then closed this paragraph with an axiom, "For judgment is without mercy to one who has shown no mercy. Mercy triumphs over judgment" (vs. 13). Contextual analysis always disproves Adventist faulty assumptions and arguments. And that was clearly demonstrated with James 2:1-13.

Faulty Hermeneutical Principle and Assumption #8

Radically redefine biblical terms, concepts, or theological words in ways that Adventist doctrines will always be upheld.

Under grace

The redefinition of biblical terms and concepts is another faulty hermeneutic and assumption of Adventists where Christians need to be aware. Like any other cult, they use the same words and terms as Christians use but they mean different things for them. Those that have close meanings to Christian orthodoxy are conceptualized differently, subconsciously by Adventists. For Adventists the term "under grace" means when we break the Ten Commandments we receive grace. Grace averts immediate punishment and empowers us to keep the Ten Commandments. Grace is what helps us get back up when we fall so that we can continue to try our best to keep the Ten Commandments. Conversely, when Scripture says we are not under the Law (Ten Commandments), this means that we are not under it unless we transgress it. There is another logical twist to this argument of theirs. We are not under grace unless we break the Law. So, what this means is that we are in a normal state of being neither under law nor grace. The only way that we can be under either of them is when a violation of the Law has taken place.

In the Adventist worldview, grace cannot exist where there is no law, no Ten Commandments. The existence of grace is contingent upon the Ten Commandments. As a matter of fact, in their sermons and evangelistic outreach they usually use illustrations that have the Law as being the heart and foundation of the reason why grace exists and is needed. They usually line up seven persons who would represent sin, the Law, grace, a saviour (Jesus), the Gospel, a preacher, and the church. The argument usually goes like this, "Sin is breaking the Law. When we break the Law we receive grace, which is pardon for sin. The saviour (Jesus) died so that we might have grace and put an end to sin. A preacher preaches the Gospel. Preaching the Gospel is committed to the church." After illustrating this with the persons (I used to do this), the preacher would then remove the person that represents the Law from the line and then proceed to show how everything else cannot exist or is totally unnecessary once the Law is removed. So, when the Law is removed there is no sin. If there is no sin, then we do not need nor can we receive grace. If there is no need for grace then there is no need for Jesus. If there is no need for Jesus then there is no Gospel. And if there is no Gospel, there is nothing for the preacher to preach. And if there is no need for the preacher, then there is no need for the church. This is how it is usually illustrated.[133] Sin, grace, Jesus, the Gospel, the preacher, and the church owe their existence to the Law. That is

---

[133] The legendary Adventist preacher the late C. D. Brooks used to use this illustration a lot. See "Law and Grace Explained" by C. D. Brooks, https://www.youtube.com/watch?v=KyfBAXG8q78 (Date accessed Dec. 30, 2020).

the underlying argument and thrust of the illustration. This is what Adventists typically mean when they refer to being "under grace."

This popular illustration and argument of Adventists is not only a sad case of exalting the Law beyond its place, but it also shows how limited their understanding of biblical concepts is. The existence of grace and the other things in their illustration is not contingent upon the Law. Grace exists as a part of God's nature and flows from His being. When Moses asked God to show him His glory (Exo. 33:18), after shielding him in the cleft rock, God passed by and proclaimed His character to Moses. An essential part of His character is that He is gracious (Exo. 34:8). John says of Jesus, "For from his fullness we have all received, grace upon grace" (John 1:16). Grace resides in and flows from the nature of God. It is not a by-product of the Law. It is for this reason that Peter referred to God as "the God of all grace" (1 Pet. 5:10). Grace simply defined is God's unmerited favor. A. W. Tozer expanded the definition of grace and noted, "Grace is the good pleasure of God that inclines him to bestow benefits on the undeserving."[134] Before the existence of the Law, God bestowed His grace on persons. Genesis 6:8 says of Noah, "Noah found favor in the eyes of the LORD." This grace was not bestowed upon Him after he had broken the Law or the Ten Commandments. The Law did not exist yet (Rom. 5:13). Out of the goodness and graciousness of His character, God spared Noah and his family and preserved them through the Flood. They did not deserve grace. But God bestowed it nonetheless, because of who He is. Grace is not a by-product of the Law. This fact disproves the entire faulty illustration of Adventists.

In addition to grace being God's unmerited favor, there are various shades of meaning and contextual connotations of grace in Scripture, specifically in the New Testament. It is not my intention to discuss all of those. I will only focus on the concept of being "under grace." The Greek phrase ὑπὸ χαριν (hupo charin) meaning "under grace" does not mean the Adventist redefinition and assumption at all. The preposition "hupo" as used with the accusative χαριν means to be under the authority, supervision, discipline, execution,

---

[134] A. W. Tozer, *The Knowledge of the Holy* (New York: Harper and Row, 1961), p. 100.

administration, and power of.[135] So, to be "under grace" means to be under grace's authority, administration, power, discipline, execution, supervision, etc. In the New Testament, grace is often interchangeable with terms such as "New Covenant," "faith," "new dispensation," etc. With respect to us being "under" it, it is an entirely different system of operation from the Law. John 1:16-17 says, "For from his fullness we have all received, grace upon grace. For the law was given through Moses; grace and truth came through Jesus Christ." In this text, John presents grace as something that stands in contrast to the Law. Grace is something that was ushered in through Jesus Christ, from whom we receive it in copious measure. It also demonstrates that grace did not exist, was not extant, under the administration of the Law. Hence, it did not come from the Law as Adventists claim, as cited above. Grace came through Jesus, and not the Law. Truth also came through Jesus, and not the Law. Romans 5:21 presents grace as currently reigning through righteousness.

Roman 6:13-14 says, "Do not present your members to sin as instruments for unrighteousness, but present yourselves to God as those who have been brought from death to life, and your members to God as instruments for righteousness. [14]For sin will have no dominion over you, since you are not under law but under grace." Grace is again presented as being the dominant power under which we operate. This is not merely a little help to get up to keep the Ten Commandments after we have fallen. Grace is the sovereign power under which we currently function as Christians. Commenting on this verse, *The Reformation Study Bible* drew a similar conclusion on grace and said, "The controlling principle in the life of the believer is the reign of grace that sets free from the reign of sin (5:21) and transforms into the likeness of Christ."[136]

Galatians 3:23-25 is another conclusive passage that reveals what it means to be under grace, although it does not use the word "grace."

---

[135] Zodhiates, *The Complete Word Study Dictionary: New Testament*, electronic ed., ʹυπο, hupo.

[136] Luder G. Whitlock, R. C. Sproul, Bruce K. Waltke and Moisés Silva, *The Reformation Study Bible: Bringing the Light of the Reformation to Scripture: New King James Version* (Nashville, TN: Thomas Nelson, 1995), Rom. 6:14.

It uses "faith" instead of grace, but the concept is still the same. It contrasts being under faith ushered in by Jesus with being under the Law. It says, "Now before faith came, we were held captive under the law, imprisoned until the coming faith would be revealed. [24]So then, the law was our guardian until Christ came, in order that we might be justified by faith. [25]But now that faith has come, we are no longer under a guardian." This text presents the Law in antithesis to faith. Under the Law meant that one was bound and imprisoned by it. It functioned like a guardian that disciplined, guided, taught, and managed a child. But when Christ came and enacted New Covenant faith, the job of the guardian was rendered counterproductive and obsolete. Paul concludes that we are no longer under the Law but under faith. Faith is now our guardian, not the Law.

Under the law

Similar to Adventists' twisted concept of what it means to be "under grace," they also have a warped redefinition of what it means to not be "under the law." Their concept of what it means to not be under the law is when we sin, we come "under the law," and therefore will face the penalty of the law. But when we do not sin we are not under the law. Adventists usually use traffic lights, stop signs, and speed limits to illustrate this concept. For example, when one breaks the stop sign and is caught one is "under the law" and will face its penalty. But when one obeys the stop sign then one is not under the law. This is nothing but arguing semantics on their part.

Not only is this very bad logic and argumentation but it does not represent the actual facts at all. The fact is one is able to break the law because one is actually under it, irrespective of one's actions at different junctions. Americans can break American traffic laws because they live in America and therefore are subject to those laws. But someone like me who lives in Jamaica cannot break American traffic laws because I am not under them. Being under the law does not mean one's actions or disposition towards the law at a particular time. It means being within the jurisdiction of the law and therefore subject to it and all of its demands. It is because one is subject to it that one can commit offenses against it. The Adventist redefinition is ridiculous and self-defeating. Let me illustrate this. We are not under the law of murder unless we murder someone. We can still hate their guts, the spirit of murder, but we are in the clear as long as we don't act on our evil thoughts. Same with the Sabbath as well. We are not under the Sabbath law unless we break it, even though we can do "lawful" work on the Sabbath. The amazing and flabbergasting thing here is that members accept these inane definitions.

The Greek phrase ὑπὸ νόμον (hupo nomon) does not mean that one is under the Law only when one sins or breaks the Law. The preposition "hupo" as used with the accusative noun "nomon" means to be under the authority, supervision, discipline, execution, administration, and power of. So, to be "under the law" means to be under its authority, administration, power, discipline, execution, supervision, etc. It is because one is under the Law that one can actually break the Law, and subsequently be charged for breaking it. But if one is not under a specific law or law codes, one can break them with impunity. American traffic laws require that motorists drive on the right side of the road. I, here in Jamaica, break that law with impunity every time I drive my vehicle. I drive on the left side of the road, in contradistinction to America's law that stipulates that motorists must drive on the right side. Despite my breaking America's traffic law, I cannot be prosecuted because that law has no authority over me. I am in a completely different jurisdiction with its own laws. Of course some of these laws may be similar to America's laws but it is still a different jurisdiction.

The Adventist redefinition of what it means to be "under the law" would automatically make Jesus a sinner because Galatians 4:4 says that Jesus was "born under the law." Now, while Jesus did break many points of the Law (e.g. John 5:16-18), He never sinned because not all transgression of the Law resulted in a charge of sin (David and the Bread of the Presence- Matt. 12:3-5). But He was nonetheless "under the law" as a Jew and therefore under its authority, discipline, demands, obligations, supervision, etc. Their redefinition also makes nonsense of Paul's statement here, "To the Jews I became as a Jew, in order to win Jews. To those under the law I became as one under the law (though not being myself under the law) that I might win those under the law" (1 Cor. 9:20).

The law of liberty

As was already discussed in James 2, Adventists have radically redefined the "law of liberty" to mean the Ten Commandments and keeping them. But as I had demonstrated, this is not true. The Ten Commandments and the entire Old Covenant are spoken of as "a yoke" that the Jews could not bear in Acts 15:10 (cf. 15:1, 5). Paul saw the Law as an opportunist that enslaves us in sin in Romans 7:7-25. In Galatians 5:1 he calls it "a yoke of slavery." As was proven already, the "law of liberty" is the Gospel that liberates us and enables us to love our neighbours as ourselves. This is encapsulated in the "law of Christ" that commands us to love one another as He loved us (John 13:34-35), to carry one another's burdens (Gal. 6:2; Phil. 2:1-5), to treat others as we want them to treat us (Matt. 7:12), to be sensitive towards people's cultural and customary contexts (1 Cor. 9:19-23), and acting in consideration towards others without unrighteous judgmentalism and condemnation (Rom. 14).

Unclean

Another biblical word that Adventists have radically redefined is "unclean." When used in a dietary context, Adventists redefine it to mean "unhealthy or unfit for human consumption."[137] But this is not true. Unclean just meant "ceremonially impure." Persons who became unclean would be separated from the "clean" covenant community. In the Old Testament, hordes of things were considered unclean. This includes Gentiles (Acts 10:28), their countries, homes, and practices (Ezra 9:11), or anything they touched. Bodily discharges of any kind made one unclean—semen via wet dreams or copulation (Lev. 15:16-18; Deut. 23:10-11). Persons were rendered unclean by leprosy and other skin diseases (Lev. 13:1-3) and childbirth (Lev. 12). Certain animals were unclean for Jews but they still ate them under certain conditions (Lev. 11; Deut. 14:3-21; 2 Kings 6:24-25; Isa. 65:4; 66:17). Clean animals prepared incorrectly

---

[137] See *Seventh-day Adventists Believe*, p. 318-319; Samuele Bacchiocchi, *The Sabbath in the New Testament: Answers to Questions* (Berrien Springs, MI: Biblical Perspectives, 2000), p. 83.

or that had died naturally could have made a Jew unclean (Lev. 11:39-40; Deut. 14:21). If they did eat them, they merely had to be separated from the covenant community, then return at sunset, wash their clothing, take a bath, and they were clean again (Lev. 11:24-28, 39-40).

Unclean animals such as pigs, rabbits, rodents, scaleless and finless sea creatures, shellfish, etc., were not forbidden for Jews because they were "unfit for human consumption." They were fit for human consumption. They were forbidden for Jews as a means of ceremonially separating them from their Gentile neighbours who ate those things (Lev. 11:44-47). The dietary laws were a part of the holiness code that was meant to separate Jews from Gentiles. The New Testament makes it very clear that dietary clean and unclean distinctions have been made obsolete for believers. Mark 7:18-19 says, "And he said to them, "Then are you also without understanding? Do you not see that whatever goes into a person from outside cannot defile him, [19] since it enters not his heart but his stomach, and is expelled?" (Thus he declared all foods clean.)" Romans 14:14 is very emphatic, "I know and am persuaded in the Lord Jesus that nothing is unclean in itself, but it is unclean for anyone who thinks it unclean."

The Gospel

Christians are easily fooled by Adventists when they hear them use the term "gospel." They usually think that they both are using the same word to mean the same thing, but the reality is that they are not. When Adventists use the term "gospel," they are referring to "The 3 Angels' Messages of Revelation 14."[138] This gospel or "Three Angels Messages" of Adventists is interpreted to be themselves calling people to keep the Ten Commandments and the Sabbath, announcing the start of the Investigative Judgement in 1844, announcing the fall of Babylon, which for them is Roman

---

[138] Ellen White said, "Christ is coming the second time, with power unto salvation. To prepare human beings for this event, He has sent the first, second, and third angels' messages. These angels represent those who receive the truth, and with power open the gospel to the world."--- *SDA Bible Commentary*, Vol. 7, p. 978, par. 11.

Catholicism and apostate Protestantism, and warning the world against worshipping God on Sunday, which for them is the mark of the beast. And they have added to this other idiosyncrasies of their faith. This is the Adventist gospel. This is what they mean when they refer to the gospel. But Scripture does not define the Gospel as Adventists do at all. The Gospel is aptly defined in John 3:16. It is God giving His beloved Son to die vicariously for us. And through His death and resurrection and placing our faith in Him, we receive the remission of our sins and eternal life. We become a new creation, God's children, instead of His enemies as before. When we read the New Testament, everywhere the Gospel is defined by the authors it is always about Jesus' vicarious atonement for our salvation and justification, and eternal life. It is never defined as how Adventists have re-defined it.

Keep the Sabbath

Keeping the Sabbath biblically, socially, and culturally for Jews involved following the rules contained in the Law and Prophets, the Talmud, and the interpretations of those laws by their respective rabbis. And while attending Temple worship services was certainly a part of Sabbath-keeping for the Jews (Lev. 23:1-3; Num. 28:9-10; Eze. 46:1-8, Psalm 92), it was not what Sabbath-keeping was mainly about. Sabbath-keeping was mainly about resting, staying in one's home or precincts, abstaining from labor and commercial activities, not bearing burdens, etc., (Exo. 16:23-30; 20:8-10; Num. 15:32-36; Neh. 10:31; 13:15-22; Jer. 17:19-27). But when an Adventist talks about keeping the Sabbath, it primarily means attending an Adventist Church on Saturday.

In addition to this, it includes refraining from doing certain secular works and activities, and subjectively keeping a small portion of the Sabbath rules of the Bible and those of Ellen White[139] that they want, while discarding a large percentage of those rules. Sabbath-keeping is centred on church attendance for them. Adventists would never agree for one to keep the Sabbath by staying

---

[139] This will be discussed and proven in volume II.

at home and resting, and then going to church on Sunday if one is already a member of a Sunday-gathering congregation. That sort of Sabbath-keeping is unacceptable and discounted. One must attend an Adventist Church to keep the Sabbath. Attending other Sabbatarian churches still does not equate to keeping the Sabbath for them because while they may commend those other churches for at least keeping the Sabbath, they still frown on them and consider them to not have "the truth" nor to be "God's remnant church." But Adventists do an amazing flip flop with this because wherever they see Jesus, Paul, or anyone else in Scripture going to a synagogue on the Sabbath, they say they were keeping the Sabbath.

Saved

When Adventists talk about being saved, they do not mean what Scripture means by that term nor what Christians generally mean by it. When Christians talk about being saved, we mean experiencing salvation in Jesus Christ right now (Rom. 10:9-13), being freed from condemnation (John 5:24; Rom. 8:1), freedom from the power of sin over our lives (Rom. 6:12-14, 18, 22), being forgiven of sin (Col. 1:14), being transformed, filled, led, and sealed by the Spirit of God (Rom. 8:9, 12-17; 1 Cor. 6:9-11; 2 Cor. 3:17-18; Gal. 5:18, 22-23; Eph. 1:13-14; 4:30), being delivered from the domain of darkness and transferred to God's kingdom (Col. 1:13-14), and currently possessing eternal life and having full assurance of salvation (John 3:16; 11:26; 1 John 5:11-13). But when Adventists talk about being saved, they do not mean these things. Salvation for the Adventist is joining an Adventist Church by having their names officially on the church roll, learning and adapting to the Adventist distinctive church life, culture, doctrines, and mores. It is also beginning the process of *potentially* being saved *if* they eventually pass the Investigative Judgement through rigorous diet reform, dress reform, entertainment reform, evangelistic efforts, character reform, faithful tithing, Sabbath-keeping, church attendance, and strict adherence to all that Ellen White has laid down for them do. Ellen White is more than clear that Adventists should never say or think that they are saved until they make it to heaven. She said:

We are never to rest in a satisfied condition, and cease to make advancement, saying, "I am saved." When this idea is entertained, the motives for watchfulness, for prayer, for earnest endeavor to press onward to higher attainments, cease to exist. No sanctified tongue will be found uttering these words till Christ shall come, and we enter in through the gates into the city of God. Then, with the utmost propriety, we may give glory to God and to the Lamb for eternal deliverance. As long as man is full of weakness–for of himself he cannot save his soul–he should never dare to say, "I am saved."[140]

When Adventists are resurrected, and discover that they are not saved, but condemned, all this will still reinforce what they believe now. They would not conclude they stand condemned for the real reasons, having rejected Christ and the true gospel. Even beyond death, Ellen White will be messing with their minds.

For these reasons, Adventists generally do not have any assurance of salvation. When asked if they are saved, they usually respond that they "hope" to be saved. It is very common in discussions, debates, or any biblical talks with Adventist pastors, apologists, and laypeople to get a lot of pushback against the notion of having assurance of salvation right now. This is so because for them salvation is something that must be earned and possibly achieved through their efforts by following what Ellen White said and hoping to be lucky enough to pass the Investigative Judgement. This causes a lot of stress, consternation, and depression among Adventists. I was a popular Adventist preacher. I knew the Advent Message well and brought people into it, kept people in it, but I had no assurance of salvation. I was constantly daunted by my failings, imperfections, and inability to live up to the rules of Ellen White and the church that were necessary to attain sinless perfection, and ultimately salvation.

At one point I felt like I could not have been saved but despite this

---

[140] White, *A New Life*, p. 43, par. 1.

I pledged to God to just use me to potentially save others. This anxiety and anguish upon myself was not because I had committed grave offenses or experienced moral falls. I was morally upright and in good standing with the church. I wasn't living in secret sins, addictions, cognitive dissonance, and neither did I backslide. I felt this way because I kept relapsing on menial things such as eating cheese and dairy products, ironing on the Sabbath, occasionally falling behind on witnessing, for often lapsing in tithing, for getting in petty arguments with my wife for eating meat, wearing beauty products, lip gloss, and other trivial matters, all of which Ellen White counsels against and makes necessary for salvation. I know of many persons who gave up on God, the Adventist Church, and spirituality altogether because of Adventist soteriology and the lack of the assurance of salvation, and also because of the insurmountable mountain of rules and demands necessary to potentially achieve salvation. Ironically, those who read Ellen White's writings the most in Adventism are those who are most likely to suffer much mental anguish, anxiety, be internally conflicted, be more judgemental, legalistic, and be the furthest away from having any form of an assurance of salvation because of the unattainable demands that she binds on them in order to be saved, potentially sealed with the Sabbath in the "Time of Trouble," and to be prepared for "translation."

Whereas salvation for Adventists is something that is hanging in the balance, which conjures up insecurity, trepidation, causes depression, and an overall unpleasant Christian living experience, for Christians assurance of salvation is a wonderful gift that brings much peace, joy, and resilience when we fall. Scripture speaks of what we have in Jesus as a "now" experience and reality. We *now* have eternal life (John 6:47). We *now know* we have eternal life (1 John 5:13). We *now* have peace with God (Rom. 5:1). We *now* have been reconciled to God (Rom. 5:10). We are *now* to consider ourselves to be dead to sin (Rom. 6:11). We are *now* free from sin (Romans 6:18, 22; 1 John 3:8-9). We are *now* dead to the Law (Rom. 7:4). We *now* have been released from the Law (Rom. 7:6). We *now* serve in the newness of the Spirit and not in the oldness of the letter (Rom. 7:6). There is *now* no condemnation for those who are in Christ Jesus

(Rom. 8:1). We have *now* received the spirit of adoption (Rom. 8:15). We *now* overwhelmingly conquer through Him who loved us (Rom. 8:37). We are *now* sealed with the Holy Spirit (Eph. 1:13). We are *now* saved through faith (Eph. 2:8). We are *now* the dwelling place of the Holy Spirit (Eph. 2:22). We are *now* chosen in Christ (Eph. 1:4). We *now* have redemption through His blood (Eph. 1:7). God is *now* at work in us to will and to do His good pleasure (Phil 2:13). We are *now* qualified to share in the inheritance of the saints in light (Col. 1:12). We have *now* been transferred to the kingdom of His beloved Son (Col. 1:13). All believers have *now* received spiritual gifts from God (Rom. 12; 1 Cor. 12; Eph. 4). We have *now* been predestined to be like Christ (Rom. 8:29). We are *now* seated in heavenly places in Christ, with Christ (Eph. 2:6; Col. 3:1).[141]

Bible only

When Adventists claim to be "Bible alone" or "Bible only," they never mean it the way that Protestant Christians mean it. In the Adventist mind, Ellen White and the Bible are so closely intertwined that they cannot differentiate where the Bible stops and where Ellen White begins and vice versa. As was already shown, Adventists are not Bible alone. They do not believe in the Bible alone nor can their peculiar doctrines, interpretations, and assumptions be substantiated from the Bible alone, contextually exegeted. The Bible and Ellen White's writings are one and the same for them. The two are imperceptibly merged. However, Ellen White's writings have the authoritative and interpretive edge over Scripture. This was made extremely clear in the chapter about Ellen White and her role in Adventism. You read the claims that she made for herself and her writings. You read the doctrinal positions of the Seventh-day Adventist Church on Ellen White and her writings. There is nothing else that I need to prove here about that.

Faulty Hermeneutical Principle and Assumption #9

---

[141] Adapted from Dale Ratzlaff, *Gospel Transformation: What The Good News Does In Your Life* (Camp Verde, AZ: LAM Publications, LLC, 2015), p. 147-161.

The Ten Commandments are the summation of love. If we have love, we will keep the Ten Commandments. If we don't love God we will not keep the Ten Commandments. The first 4 commandments show love for God and the last 6 show love for our neighbours.

This is a standard, faulty hermeneutic and assumption of Adventists. The Ten Commandments is the summation of love—love for God and love for fellow man. They never include the other 603 laws nor the rest of the Old Testament, just the Big Ten. This is not something that the Bible teaches. This is an Ellen White assumption and teaching. She said, "To love God supremely and our neighbor as ourselves is to keep the first four and the last six commandments."[142] A common punch line of Adventists when discussing the Law with them is to state that the Ten Commandments summarize love because the first four show love for God and the last six show love for our neighbours. This is not something that they read anywhere in the Bible. This is an Ellen White assumption and teaching. She says:

> In love, with a desire to elevate and ennoble us, God provided for us a standard of obedience. In awful majesty, amid thundering and lightning, he proclaimed from Mount Sinai his ten holy precepts. This law reveals the whole duty of the human family; the first four precepts define our duty to God, and the last six our duty to man.[143]

After quoting Matthew 22:36-40, Ellen White commented:

> The first four of the Ten Commandments are summed up in the one great precept, "Thou shalt love the Lord thy God with all thy heart." The last six are included in the other, "Thou shalt love thy neighbor as thyself." Both these commandments are an expression of the principle of love. The first cannot be kept and the

---

[142] White, *The Signs of the Times*, Sept. 22, 1890, "Love is the Fulfilling of the Law."

[143] White, *The Signs of the Times*, March 4, 1897, "Christ and the Law."

second broken, nor can the second be kept while the first is broken. When God has His rightful place on the throne of the heart, the right place will be given to our neighbor. We shall love him as ourselves. And only as we love God supremely is it possible to love our neighbor impartially. And since all the commandments are summed up in love to God and man, it follows that not one precept can be broken without violating this principle. Thus Christ taught His hearers that the law of God is not so many separate precepts, some of which are of great importance, while others are of small importance and may with impunity be ignored. Our Lord presents the first four and the last six commandments as a divine whole, and teaches that love to God will be shown by obedience to all His commandments.[144]

Despite correctly quoting the Bible passage, Ellen White butchered it to teach her false concept and idolatry of the Ten Commandments. So when Scripture says love fulfils the Law, Ellen White insist this is done by keeping this Law. You will see she did this shortly, as Adventists continue to do the same to this very day. The SDA Church paraphrased and regurgitated what Ellen White said above in their exposition on their Fundamental Belief entitled "The Law of God":

Jesus says something similar in Matthew 22 when the Pharisees asked which is the greatest commandment of the Law: "You shall love the Lord your God with all your heart and with all your soul and with all your mind. This is the great and first commandment. And a second is like it: You shall love your neighbor as yourself. On these two commandments depend all the Law and the Prophets" (Matthew 22:37-40, ESV). These two great commandments are the ten laws summed up. The first

---

[144] White, *The Desire of Ages*, p. 607, par. 2-3.

four are a reflection of our love for God. The following six have to do with loving God's people, our neighbors.[145]

Ellen White and her church correctly quoted Matthew 22:36-40, but they completely butchered it in order to uphold their false assumption about the Ten Commandments exclusively being the summation of love. Thus, instead of everything hanging on the two great love laws, everything hangs instead on the Ten Commandments.

Another biblical text they butcher in their attempt to prove this false assumption also is Romans 13:8-10, which says:

> Owe no one anything, except to love each other, for the one who loves another has fulfilled the law. [9]For the commandments, "You shall not commit adultery, You shall not murder, You shall not steal, You shall not covet," and any other commandment, are summed up in this word: "You shall love your neighbor as yourself." [10]Love does no wrong to a neighbor; therefore love is the fulfilling of the law.

Ellen White and the Adventist Church butchered Matthew 22:36-40 in this glaring detail. The passage says "all the Law and the Prophets" are what depends on the love commands. That term is a designation for the entire Old Testament Scriptures. Ellen White and her Adventist Church ignore, reject, and discard the entire Old Testament Scriptures as what this is talking about and have redefined Jesus' statement to refer exclusively to the Ten Commandments from those Scriptures! The gross distortion, redefining, and rejection of what Scripture explicitly says by Ellen White and SDA is uncanny and brazen. This is so natural to them that they do it subconsciously, all the time.

Another way they have butchered Jesus' statement is the fact that Jesus quoted the love commands from Deuteronomy 6 and Leviticus 19, which Adventists call the "ceremonial law" that is abolished, and have made Him to be talking about the Ten Commandments,

---

[145] https://www.adventist.org/the-law-of-god/ (Date accessed August 1, 2021).

exclusively. Jesus never said that the first four commands from the Ten are what shows love for God and the last six are what shows love for our neighbours, and conclude that those Ten Commandments summarize into the two love commands. Jesus explicitly said that it is the entirety of the Law (Genesis-Deuteronomy) and the Prophets (the rest of the Old Testament) that are summarized into those two love commands. He never said that it was only the Ten Commandments that are summarized by them. Ellen White and Adventists do what they do with Matthew 22:36-40 because it logically kills their arguments and assumptions and exposes their hypocrisy and unwillingness to keep the whole Law, while paying lip service to keeping the Law. They argue and conclude that if we love God we'll keep the first four commands, and if we love our neighbours we'll keep the last six. And as Ellen White said above, they are "a divine whole" of which one set cannot be kept while the other set is broken. All must be kept in its entirety. If they accepted exactly what Jesus said, that the entire Old Testament Scriptures depend on the love commands, by their logic they would be bound to keep the entirety of the Old Testament Scriptures. They would have to keep every law of the Old Covenant, but they are not willing to do that so they butchered Jesus' statement and make it refer only to the Ten Commandments and then vehemently argue for keeping all of the Ten Commandments as the way of showing love for God and love for our fellow man. Adventist assumptions, arguments, and logic are very convoluted, dissonant, and incoherent. It is a wearying task trying to make sense of their arguments, assumptions, proof-texts, and conclusions most of the time.

The second passage they proof-text (Romans 13:8-10) sums up the entire Law with the statement "and any other commandment." Paul quoted four of the Ten Commandments in that pericope, then grouped every other command of the Old Covenant Law under the heading "any other commandment" and concluded that "love is the fulfilling of the law." The entire Old Covenant Law is fulfilled when we love, not just ten commands from it. The very proof-texts Adventists use to push their bad theology and conclusions disprove their views.

Love is not predicated on negative, external prohibitions

Not only do these passages not support the Adventist assumption, but it is also ludicrous to think that love is predicated on mostly negative, external prohibitions: you shall not steal, you shall not commit adultery, you shall not murder, you shall not bow down to idols, you shall not take God's name in vain, you shall not covet, and you shall not have other gods before Me. One can keep all these negative prohibitions and still not have an ounce of love for God nor for others. Merely abstaining from doing something does not equate to automatically being loving. One may avoid criminal behaviour just to avoid the penalty or consequences that may result from such behaviour. An individual can go through their entire life adhering to these "you shall not" commands and still lack the love of God in their hearts. One can refrain from murder, yet still hate someone; the spirit of murder. But, people do not murder those they love. The Ten Commandments commands one not to murder, but does not address the heart and spirit of murder. So, one can keep the letter of the Law, despite the heart of hatred, and apparently, to Adventists, this makes you right with God anyway. Fulfilling the Law transcends the letter of the Law, where one's motive is love, and not motivated by a fear of reprisal.

In the story of the Good Samaritan in Luke 10, we can deduce that the priest and the Levite kept every one of the Ten Commandments. They did not break any of them, yet they still lacked love. They did not show any love towards the wounded man. Instead, it was a man who was considered to be a dog, a half-breed mongrel with whom Jews had "no dealings" (John 4:9), who actually showed love to the wounded man, who most likely was a Jew. A number of things can motivate one to conform to behavioural expectations. A number of things can restrain one from being a sociopath. The Ten Commandments do not summarize love nor do they express love. Having love in one's heart can motivate one to keep them, but it does not logically follow that external adherence to them automatically means that one is full of love, nor does it mean that not adhering to them means that one is devoid of love either.

In Matthew 19, the Rich Young Ruler had kept the Ten Commandments and *all* of the other laws of the Torah from childhood and yet he still did not have love. 1 John 4:8 says that "God is love." God is ontologically love. In his nature and being He loves. This love was pivotally displayed by sending His Son Jesus Christ to die in our place. When we love Jesus and act like Him, we will demonstrate love. He cared for people, fed them, restored their worth and value, forgave them, and did not condemn them even when they were deserving of it. He spoke truth to the corrupt powers of His day. He was very gracious and others-centred, always considerate. He tore down social, religious, and ethnic barriers, and worked for the overall good of humanity. That is love. That is how we show love. Jesus was love personified. In John 13:34-35 He says, "A new commandment I give to you, that you love one another: just as I have loved you, you also are to love one another. By this all people will know that you are my disciples, if you have love for one another." Love is expressed in loving others the way that Jesus loved. He loves unconditionally. He asks us to love unconditionally too. He is the quintessential example of love, not the Ten Commandments. Love is not expressed by paying lip service to the Adventist's truncated version of the Old Covenant Law. Our primary way of showing that we love God and have been transformed by Him is to love one another as He loved us. Doing this is the fulfilment of the Law. Doing this is a fruit of the Spirit, which no law can be brought up against one to condemn one (Gal. 5:22-23).

Paul says in Galatians 5:13-14, "For you were called to freedom, brothers. Only do not use your freedom as an opportunity for the flesh, but through love serve one another. For the whole law is fulfilled in one word: "You shall love your neighbor as yourself."" Love is demonstrated in sacrificial service (Gal. 6:2). Love fulfils "the whole law." Love goes way beyond the written rules and demands of the Law. Love flows from the very nature of God to us, then from us back to Him, and also to one another. This is exactly what He commands: "And this commandment we have from him: whoever loves God must also love his brother" (1 John 4:21).

The Adventist conceptualization of love is very shallow. Imagine if a wife asked her husband if he loves her and his response is "Yes I love you," and then he proceeds to rhetorically ask her, "Did I murder you, steal from you, covet your belongings, bear false witness against you in court, dishonour my parents, or commit adultery against you?" If she affirms that he did not do those things, by the Adventist logic he can just retort, "That proves I love you." If love for neighbour is encapsulated in ostentatious adherence to these six commandments, then he surely can claim to love her, despite the fact that he may verbally abuse her, degrade her, beat her, neglect her, does not satisfy her needs, and makes her feel worthless. None of these things are forbidden in the Ten Commandments. Doing them would not be breaking the Ten Commandments. He can be doing these things and much worse, but as long as he does not break the letter of any of the Ten Commandments he can claim to love her. But the fact is, he would not truly love her. Adherence to the wording of the Ten Commandments does not encapsulate love. Love is too deep, too wide, too high, too transcendent, and too mysterious to be encapsulated by and confined to the Ten Commandments.

Faulty Hermeneutical Principle and Assumption #10

The Ten Commandments are eternal and can never come to an end. They are the permanent laws written on our hearts.

Just like the others, this is a very misguided and faulty assumption of Adventists. The Ten Commandments are not eternal. Scripture teaches that the Ten Commandments came to be at the Sinai Peninsula (Deut. 5:1-22). Scripture does not teach that they are eternal. They were not in existence before the creation of the world and they will not be in the new creation either. Adventists assume and believe that this is the case, but this assumption is not grounded in exegetical study of Scripture but rests on the false assumption of Ellen White. She said, "The law of the Ten Commandments lives and will live through the eternal ages. . . . [sic]"[146] She again asserted, "The Ten Commandments are a transcript of the divine character, and are as unchangeable as the eternal throne."[147] This assumption of Adventists

---

[146] White, *The Faith I Live By*, p. 106, par. 5.
[147] White, *The Southern Work*, p. 42, par. 1.

about the Ten Commandments creates more problems for them than it solves. And it flies in the face of all the biblical data about the Ten Commandments. They believe that the Ten Commandments are eternal because they believe that sin is contingent upon the Ten Commandments. So they reason that Satan, and Adam and Eve sinned by breaking the Ten Commandments. But based on what Scripture reveals, these assumptions are wild and ridiculous.

The Bible never says that Satan sinned by breaking the Ten Commandments. The few passages that can point to Satan's sin and rebellion say nothing about him breaking the Ten Commandments. Isaiah 14:12-14 that seems to be speaking about him reveals that his downfall was precipitated by pride and an attempted coup against God. We may conclude that he took his faith away from God and applied a self-faith in himself. He wanted to be like God. Ezekiel 28 gives us another insight into his downfall. It, again, had nothing to do with breaking the Ten Commandments. This passage, too, presents his situation as eventuating due to pride because of his beauty (vs. 2, 6, 12-14, 17). His sin is presented as something that fomented in him (vs. 15) until it grew into open rebellion against God, violence, corruption, and other ungodly practices (vs. 16, 18). Nothing else in Scripture that speaks of Satan and his angels before creation presents the Ten Commandments as being the Law that they broke and sinned. This is only done in Ellen White's fertile imagination in *The Great Controversy*.

The thought of the Ten Commandments being eternal and predating creation and being kept by angels is absurd and would not even make sense in a perfect, pre-creation heaven. All of the angels, before Satan's rebellion, were sinless. They would not have had any urge to sin and therefore needed the Ten Commandments to regulate their activities and sinful desires. If we briefly analyse the Ten Commandments we will see how impossible it is that they were eternally existent in heaven before creation and were being kept by angels.

The First Commandment begins with the prologue of God delivering the Israelites of out Egyptian slavery as the reason that He is giving them these commandments to keep (Exo. 20:2). Which of the angels did God deliver out of Egyptian slavery and therefore commanded them to have no other gods beside Him (vs. 3)? The Second Commandment forbids carving an image in the likeness of objects in the sky, the earth, and the waters under the earth (vs. 4-6). How can angels have been tempted to do this when nothing in the universe and our solar system was created yet? This command also includes God visiting the sins of the parents to the fourth generation and conversely blessing thousands of their posterity that love and obey Him. Do you see the glaring problem here? Pre-creation angels did not have children and grandchildren to the fourth generation to be cursed or to be blessed.

The Third Commandment states, "You shall not take the name of the LORD your God in vain, for the LORD will not hold him guiltless who takes his name in vain" (vs. 7). The majority of Christians interpret this commandment to be forbidding profanity and vulgar speech, misusing God's name in sentences, using it as a coarse slang or curse word, or just using it too flippantly, frequently. Although those things are bad and condemned in Scripture (Eph. 4:29; 5:3-4; Col. 3:8; Jam. 3:7-12), this command is not talking about those things at all. Taking God's name in vain meant becoming a worshipper of Yahweh and a part of the covenant community but failing to live according to the covenant stipulations, rules, and laws of Yahweh (Prov. 30:7-9; Isa. 56:6; Eze. 20:9-14; 36:22). Doing so emptied God's name of its power and reverence, and caused Gentile nations to profane and disdain Yahweh, His laws, and the covenant people (Rom. 2:17-24). Angels could not have done this in heaven before the creation of this universe.

The Fourth Commandment commands rest on the 7th day Sabbath and prohibits labour for the man of the house, his children, slaves, cattle, and sojourners in his house. How can this possibly be applicable to angels before creation? Angels do not need to rest, as they do not get tired. Angels are not bound to earth's weekly cycle nor time. Work for angels is not laborious, nor do they work for six days and need to rest on the Sabbath. Angels do not have houses, children, slaves, cattle, nor do they have strangers lodging with them who they need to ensure that they rest on the Sabbath day. Again, none of these things were yet created when these angels were supposedly keeping this law in heaven!

The Fifth Commandment rests the responsibility on children to honour their parents so that they may live long upon the land that God was about to give them (Exo. 20:12). You should already figure it out by now that angels do not have fathers and mothers who they should honor, nor were they about to possess the Promised Land. They could not have been keeping this commandment in heaven. The Sixth Commandment says, "You shall not murder." Who exactly would angels be tempted to murder in heaven? Immortal angels do not seem to possess the ability to murder other immortal angels. Despite all the recorded spiritual wars, battles, and feuds between angels we observe in Scripture, we never read of an angel killing another angel. This command would not make sense to them, nor does it seem to be a crime that they can commit. The Seventh Commandment says, "You shall not commit adultery." According to Jesus' statement in Matthew 22:30, angels do not marry nor are given in marriage in heaven, so committing adultery does not seem to be something that they would have been capable of and therefore needed to be restrained from.

The Eighth Commandment says, "You shall not steal." I don't know what angels would be tempted to steal from other angels in a sinless, pre-creation heaven, but I guess we will have to leave that for Adventists to explain to us. The Ninth Commandments says, "You shall not bear false witness against your neighbor." Bearing false witness is not simply telling lies and untruths. It is telling lies and untruths in the context of a court setting when one is summoned to testify. When one testifies, this command forbids bearing false testimony *against* one's neighbour that can cause them to be condemned or unjustly found guilty. Again, what would be the need for angels to do this? 2 Peter 2:11 says that angels "...do not pronounce a blasphemous judgment against..." guilty angels that had sinned, much less for them to bear false testimony against each other. This law would not apply to them in heaven, before creation.

Lastly, the Tenth Commandment says, "You shall not covet your neighbor's house; you shall not covet your neighbor's wife, or his male servant, or his female servant, or his ox, or his donkey, or anything that is your neighbor's." Angels do not have houses they live in, so it would be farfetched to think that they would covet their neighbour's house. They do not have wives, servants, oxen and donkeys, and therefore would not covet those nor anything else that belongs to their angelic neighbours. It is worth repeating that those things did not exist yet, therefore they could not have been tempted to covet them. This brief analysis of the Ten Commandments proves how unthinkable the Adventist assumption of an eternal Ten Commandments that angels were keeping is.

The Ten Commandments essentially address those deemed to be "bad trees" (Matt. 7:15-20) so as to curb their desire to do bad things or produce bad fruits. Even with the Sabbath, the fruits of the Israelites were bad/evil according to God. Jesus said it was lawful to do good works on the Sabbath (Matt. 12:12); something that they were not capable of doing, being bad "trees" who could only produce bad fruits due to their nature. In order to actually do good; produce good fruits, one has to undergo the new birth.

Did Adam and Eve sin by breaking the Ten Commandments?

The assumption that Adam and Eve had the Ten Commandments in the Garden of Eden and it is those that they broke and fell into sin is just as inane as the assumption that angels were keeping the Ten Commandments in heaven, before the creation of the universe. As inane as this assumption is though, that is what Ellen White said and that is what Adventists believe. Ellen White stated, "I saw that Jesus did not come to abolish his Father's law. The ten commandments were to stand fast forever. Adam and Eve broke God's law and fell, and the family of Adam must perish."[148] Subsequent to their fall, Ellen White claimed that Adam taught his descendants the Ten Commandments, and that that tradition continued through successive generations until God declared them on Mount Sinai: "Adam taught his descendants the law of God, and it was handed down from father to son through successive generations.... The law was preserved by Noah and his family, and Noah taught his descendants the Ten

---

[148] White, *Spiritual Gifts*, Vol. 2, p. 274.

Commandments."[149]

Without having to repeat the same analytical process of the commandments that I did with the angels, one can simply apply those same principles and questions that were raised to Adam and Eve in a pre-sin world and one will see that the outcome is the same. Adam and Eve did not have the Ten Commandments to live by. They did not sin by breaking the Ten Commandments. Ellen White's claims are ridiculous and contradicts Scripture. Scripture is clear regarding what they did that incurred sin. Genesis 2:16-17 says, "And the LORD God commanded the man, saying, "You may surely eat of every tree of the garden, but of the tree of the knowledge of good and evil you shall not eat, for in the day that you eat of it you shall surely die." This is the command that God gave Adam, and then Adam rehearsed it to Eve (Gen. 3:2-3). It is this command that Adam and Eve broke and were plunged into sin and disobedience. Genesis 3:11-13 says:

> He said, "Who told you that you were naked? Have you eaten of the tree of which I commanded you not to eat?" [12]The man said, "The woman whom you gave to be with me, she gave me fruit of the tree, and I ate." [13]Then the LORD God said to the woman, "What is this that you have done?" The woman said, "The serpent deceived me, and I ate."

This passage speaks with profound clarity. Adam and Eve sinned by violating the command to not eat from the Tree of the Knowledge of Good and Evil. They did not sin by breaking the Ten Commandments that they did not even have in the Garden of Eden. Adventist assumptions and arguments make total nonsense of Scripture. They constantly reject the clearest statements of Scripture over and over in order to believe the lies and unorthodox theology of Ellen White.

The Ten Commandments are not eternal

---

[149] White, *Patriarchs and Prophets*, p. 363.

Scriptural evidence is forthright that the Ten Commandments cannot be eternal. Romans 5:13 says, "...for sin indeed was in the world before the law was given, but sin is not counted where there is no law." Sin predates the law. Adam and Eve sinned before the Ten Commandments Law was given. As was shown, they sinned by breaking the specific command God gave them regarding the Tree of the Knowledge of Good and Evil. That violation caused man's nature to be changed to a sinful and death nature, as Romans 5 reveals. Adam and Eve's sin was counted because there was a law (that command that God had given them). Romans 4:15 justifies this point by saying, "For the law brings wrath, but where there is no law there is no transgression." But they were not held accountable to anything in the Ten Commandments because they did not have those laws. Galatians 3:17 further proves that the Ten Commandments are not eternal. It says that the Law was given 430 years *after* the patriarch Abraham. It was added "because of transgressions, until the offspring should come to whom the promise had been made" (vs. 19). Romans 5:20 makes a similar point by saying, "Now the law came in to increase the trespass...." The law was set up at a specific junction and for specific purposes. It was given way after Abraham existed. It was given because of sin and to increase it so that man's sin could have been reckoned and they could have felt their hopelessness, and accept their great need of a Saviour. The Law is what strengthens sin in our sinful nature (1 Cor. 15:56). The Law brings a consciousness and revivification of sin (Rom. 7:7-9).

All of these facts prove that the Law could not have existed before creation and before sin. The Law will not exist post-sin either. It is not eternal. To eternalize the Ten Commandments is to eternalize the sins that they empower, revive, make conscious, deceive us to commit, and to demand a reckoning of those sins in the post-sin new heavens and earth. There is no way we can read these facts about the Ten Commandments and conclude that they pre-existed creation and will eternally exist in the new heavens and earth, way after sin would have been dealt with once and for all. Neither can we conclude that it is the Ten Commandments that God has written on our hearts. 2 Corinthians 3 is a great passage that teaches that the Ten Commandments are not eternal nor are they the laws that are written on our hearts.

The Ten Commandments are not the laws that God writes on our hearts

Paul considered the Corinthian believers to be a "letter of recommendation" written on the apostles' hearts (vs. 2). He considered them to be a letter from Christ written with the Spirit of God on tablets of the heart and not "on tablets of stone" (vs. 3). This reference to the tablets of stone is to the Old Covenant Ten Commandments. In verse 6 Paul says that God "has made us sufficient to be ministers of a new covenant, not of the letter but of the Spirit. For the letter kills, but the Spirit gives life." Paul is still talking about the Ten Commandments covenant. He contrasts the Old Covenant as one that is "of the letter" that kills with the New Covenant as the one that is of the Spirit that gives life. In verse 7, Paul identified the Old Covenant as the "ministry of death" that was "carved in letters on stone" as a ministry that was instituted with glory that the Israelites could not look at. Paul specifically says that that glory "was being brought to an end." Adventists want to immortalize the glory of the Ten Commandments but Scripture says it was being brought to an end. It was never intended to last forever. In verse 8, Paul continued with the contrast by asking a rhetorical question, "Will not the ministry of the Spirit have even more glory?" His point here is that the glory of the Ten Commandments was fading but the glory of the New Covenant ministry of the Holy Spirit will have much more glory than the Ten Commandments could have ever had. This is exactly what he concludes in verse 9, "For if there was glory in the ministry of condemnation, the ministry of righteousness must far exceed it in glory."

Verse 10 says, "Indeed, in this case, what once had glory has come to have no glory at all, because of the glory that surpasses it." These words are pregnant with meaning. The Ten Commandments covenant did have some glory while it was still in effect. But once the ministry of the Holy Spirit in New Covenant faith was activated, it completely outshined the glory of the Ten Commandments and left it without glory. Ellen White claimed to have had a vision in which she was taken to heaven into the Most Holy Place of the temple and that Jesus showed her inside the Ark of the Covenant, in which she saw the Ten Commandments shining with glory, and that the Sabbath had a halo around it and it shined more glorious than the other commandments.[150] But this is a fantastical hallucination by Ellen White. This passage is very clear that the Ten Commandments do not possess any more glory. The glory of the Holy Spirit has made the glory of the Ten Commandments obsolete. The glory of the Ten is over. It was brought to an end.

In verse 11 Paul says, "For if what was being brought to an end came with glory, much more will what is permanent have glory." Up to this point Paul was talking about the glory of the Ten Commandments covenant as that which was ending by the glory of the Holy Spirit in New Covenant faith, but now he specifically says that the Ten Commandments themselves "was being brought to an end" despite that they were attended with glory. He continued with the contrast by saying that the ministry of the Holy Spirit is permanent and has much more glory than the one that has been brought to an end. This is a beautiful contrast so far between the transient nature and glory of the Ten Commandments with the permanent, eternal glory of the New Covenant of the Holy Spirit. Adventists have been working desperately to restore the faded glory of the ended Ten Commandments covenant, but this passage affirms that it is impossible. That glory has passed and no mortal person, irrespective of how deceived and fanatical they may be, can restore its administration and glory. God has ended it and instituted the New Covenant ministry of the Holy Spirit with permanent, resplendent glory.

In verses 12-13, Paul contrasts the boldness and hope that we have because of this glorious ministry of the Holy Spirit against

---

[150] She says in *Early Writings*, p. 32, par. 3, "In the ark was the golden pot of manna, Aaron's rod that budded, and the tables of stone which folded together like a book. Jesus opened them, and I saw the Ten Commandments written on them with the finger of God. On one table were four, and on the other six. The four on the first table shone brighter than the other six. But the fourth, the Sabbath commandment, shone above them all; for the Sabbath was set apart to be kept in honor of God's holy name. The holy Sabbath looked glorious--a halo of glory was all around it."

Moses veiling his face to prevent the Israelites from gazing into the Ten Commandments ministry that "was being brought to an end." Paul has repeated this phrase many times in this chapter already. He really wanted the Corinthians (and us today) to understand that the Ten Commandments were abolished and there is something much better and more glorious that has taken their place, and that is the Holy Spirit. He is in our hearts. He is the law that has been written on our hearts.

In verses 14-16, Paul made some disheartening comments about the condition of the Israelites and anyone who is still trying to reinstate the Ten Commandments covenant. He says, "But their minds were hardened. For to this day, when they read the old covenant, that same veil remains unlifted, because only through Christ is it taken away. ¹⁵Yes, to this day whenever Moses is read a veil lies over their hearts. ¹⁶But when one turns to the Lord, the veil is removed." The minds of the Israelites were hardened then and the minds of Adventists are hardened today as they seek to reinstate and practice[151] the Old Covenant, although just in meagre portions. Paul says the veil remains on their hearts, it is unlifted because they are transfixed on an expired covenant that no longer has any glory. The only hope of them having the veil removed is for them to submit to Christ and New Covenant faith and sever ties with the Old Covenant.

This passage perfectly explains why Adventists are so hardened

---

[151] The Greek word αναγνωσις (anagnosis) translated as "read" in verse 14 does not mean that any form of studying or reading the Old Covenant hardens the hearts of Christians and blinds us. The word has the connotation of reading in order to internalize and practice. This is how this word is used in the New Testament and the Old Testament. In Acts 13:15, the Law and Prophets (Old Covenant) were read in the synagogues to be internalized and practiced by the Jews (cf. Acts 15:21). In 1 Timothy 4:13, Paul used this word in encouraging Timothy to read so that he can live out the principles of the Gospel so that he can not only save himself but also his listeners, as they hear him preach and observe him live (vs. 14-16). In Nehemiah 8:8 of the LXX, this word is used to express that the Levites read the Law to the people and explained it so that the people can practice the Law. The text says, "They read from the book, from the Law of God, clearly, and they gave the sense, so that the people understood the reading." This was necessary because the Exiles had been in dereliction and violation of the Law in countless ways, so the Levites had to read and explain it to them for them to align themselves with it, which they began to do thereafter.

and antagonistic towards the New Covenant and Christians. They are blinded and hard-hearted by the Ten Commandments that they are so monomaniacal about. Their only hope of freedom and transformation is in turning to the Lord and by beholding Him, un-blinded by the Ten Commandments (vs. 17-18). The glory that they so desperately want to achieve through the Ten Commandments, He will give them as He transforms believers "into the same image from one degree of glory to another" by His Holy Spirit.

God does not take the "ministry of condemnation and death" from the tablets of stone and transcribe them on our hearts. Instead, He does something much better. He has transcribed the Holy Spirit on our hearts, and through the Holy Spirit we are led into a life of obedience and transformation. No doubt, some laws and principles we naturally obey as Christians in New Covenant faith are from the Ten Commandments, and from many other laws of the Old Covenant, as they are reinterpreted, magnified, and administered in the New Covenant law of faith. But those laws are not the Ten Commandments themselves as they were administered under the Old Covenant.

Faulty Hermeneutical Principle and Assumption #11

The Roman Catholic Church and the Pope are wrong on just about every biblical thing they say and believe, but they are absolutely right about any claims they make about the Sabbath and Sunday.

In Adventist theology, the Roman Catholic Church is the dreaded little horn of Daniel 7 and Daniel 8 that persecuted God's people during the Dark Ages and sought to "change times and laws" (Dan. 7:25). The Roman Catholic Church is also the first beast of Revelation 13 and the harlot woman of Revelation 17 and 18. They believe that the antichrist Roman Catholic Church and the Pope are the biggest enemies of God, of Scripture, and of men's spirituality and souls.[152] In Adventist theology, Roman Catholicism and the Pope should not be trusted about anything relating to biblical and theological matters. They are utterly corrupt and antichristian. The Pope and the Roman Catholic Church should always be observed and

---

[152] *Seventh-day Adventists Believe*, p. 182-190.

constantly watched with great suspicion. Adventists are constantly on their "Pope watch." They watch the Pope like a prey animal watches a predator. They follow his every move and are always expecting him to cajole the United States of America and other countries to pass the Sunday Law and begin the slew of persecutions on Adventists for going to church on Saturday. Because Roman Catholicism and the Pope are evil fiends where they are concerned, they conspiratorially argue that we should never expect them to be truthful on theological and biblical issues.

Despite their credulity about the Pope and the Roman Catholic Church, Adventists believe that Catholicism, the Pope, and any Catholic priest are unreservedly truthful and factual about anything they have said concerning the Sabbath and Sunday. They believe that whatever claims they make about the Sabbath and Sunday should be believed without reservation. Adventists reject Catholicism's claim to apostolic succession and Peter being the first Pope. They reject their views on transubstantiation, the Eucharist, the perpetual virginity and sinlessness of Mary, the supremacy, authority and infallibility of the Pope. They reject Catholicism's claim to be the only true "mother church." They reject penance, the Mass, confession to priests, Catholic statues, relics, and apparitions. Through and through, Adventism is an anti-Roman Catholic organization. Adventists are always paranoid that the Catholic Church and her Sunday-worshipping "apostate daughters"[153] are out to get them.

Despite these views of theirs about Roman Catholicism, the Pope, and Protestant churches, they accept, without question, anything that either of them say about the Sabbath and Sunday worship that matches up with their theology and assumptions. They would quote, ad nauseam, ministers of various Protestant churches as proof to substantiate their Ten Commandments, Sabbath, and Sunday views and theology.[154] This is very inconsistent, ludicrous, and unbelievable but this is actually a hermeneutical principle and assumption of Adventists.

---

[153] Adventists believe and teach that churches that worship on Sunday are apostate daughters of Roman Catholicism, who they consider to be the "whore of Babylon." Thus they call Sunday churches "apostate Protestantism" (*Seventh-day Adventists Believe*, 194-195; Ellen G. White, *The Faith I Live By*, 286, par. 4).

[154] See https://www.biblesabbath.org/confessions.html (Date accessed Nov. 25, 2020).

Adventists literally cannot show a single text of Scripture, contextually exegeted, that justify their views about Sunday. Their entire "Sunday is the mark of the beast" rhetoric and eschatology cannot be found in Scripture. Roman Catholics make certain claims about Sunday, Adventists accept them without investigation and question, and then read them back into Scripture because of their view that Catholicism is the antichristian beast power. These are some common Catholic statements about the Sabbath and Sunday that Adventists believe to be true and use as ammunition to prop up their faulty views about both days[155]:

> Prove to me from the Bible alone that I am bound to keep Sunday holy. There is no such law in the Bible. It is a law of the Catholic Church alone. The Catholic Church says, by my divine power I abolish the Sabbath day and command you to keep holy the first day of the week. And lo! The entire civilized world bows down in reverent obedience to the command of the Holy Catholic Church.[156]

James Cardinal Gibbons is quoted as saying, "The Catholic Church by virtue of her divine mission, changed the day from Saturday to Sunday."[157] Another Catholic publication states, "Protestants do not realize that by observing Sunday, they accept the authority of the spokesperson of the Church, the Pope."[158] These two following statements drive Adventists wild. They get hyped up in their erroneous belief about the Sabbath and Sunday by these two: "Of course the Catholic Church claims that the change [from Saturday to Sunday] was her act.... And the act is a mark of her ecclesiastical authority in religious things."[159] "Sunday is our mark of authority...the church is above the Bible, and this transference of

---

[155] These statements can easily be sourced on the internet.

[156] Thomas Enright, CSSR, President, Redemptorist College [Roman Catholic], Kansas City, MO, Feb. 18, 1884.

[157] *The Catholic Mirror*, official publication of James Cardinal Gibbons, Sept. 23, 1893

[158] *Our Sunday Visitor*, February 5, 1950.

[159] C.F. Thomas, Chancellor of Cardinal Gibbons, in answer to a letter regarding the change of the Sabbath, November 11, 1895.

Sabbath observance is proof of that fact."[160] The reason that Adventists get frenzied over these two statements and think them to be irrefutable facts is because it is claimed that Sunday is the "mark" of the authority of the Catholic Church.[161]

With these apparently truthful statements, it is easy to see how Adventists are so adamant that Sunday worship is the "mark of the beast," given that they already assume and believe that the Roman Catholic Church is the beast of Revelation 13. In their evangelistic campaigns and Daniel and Revelation Seminars, this quote is usually used as the final hook to urge unsuspecting listeners to become Adventists: "People who think that the Scriptures should be the sole authority, should logically become 7th Day Adventists, and keep Saturday holy."[162]

These claims seem to be very airtight and irrefutable. Any novice in Scripture and Church history would swallow them up completely, upon hearing them being presented by Adventist enthusiasts. I know I did when I first heard them in 2005. For the next 10 years, I would ardently defend and propagate them, and convert others to Adventism, especially persons from Sunday churches.

But despite how airtight and irrefutable these claims seem, they are only claims—baseless, ignorant, and untruthful. They are a house of cards waiting to topple over when one foundational card is struck. The fact of the matter is the Roman Catholic Church *did not change* the Sabbath from Saturday to Sunday and then bequeath it to the Protestant world. The Roman Catholic Church did not even become a distinct church from the rest of the Church until the Great Schism of 1054 A.D., when it broke away from the Church. The Eastern section of the Church became Eastern Orthodoxy and the Western became Roman Catholicism. George T. Dennis notes:

---

[160] *Catholic Record of London*, Ontario Sept 1, 1923.

[161] These statements can be perused on this Adventist website: https://amredeemed.com/vatican-admits-the-change-of-sabbath-was-their-act-not-the-bible/ (Date accessed Nov. 25, 2020).

[162] Sentinel, Pastor's page, *Saint Catherine Catholic Church*, Algonac, Michigan, May 21, 1995 (quoted on https://www.sabbathtruth.com/sabbath-history/denominational-statements-on-the-sabbath/id/catholic).

On Saturday, July 16, 1054, as afternoon prayers were about to begin, Cardinal Humbert, legate of Pope Leo IX, strode into the Cathedral of Hagia Sophia, right up to the main altar, and placed on it a parchment that declared the Patriarch of Constantinople, Michael Cerularius, to be excommunicated. He then marched out of the church, shook its dust from his feet, and left the city. A week later the patriarch solemnly condemned the cardinal. Centuries later, this dramatic incident was thought to mark the beginning of the schism between the Latin and the Greek churches, a division that still separates Roman Catholics and Eastern Orthodox (Greek, Russian, and other).[163]

This simple fact already knocks down the Adventist house of cards. There is no evidence that Christians were unanimously worshipping God on Saturday prior to the Great Schism, then when Roman Catholicism came to prominence in the 11th century A.D. it changed the Sabbath from Saturday to Sunday and enforced it on the rest of the Christian church. There is absolutely no evidence for that, therefore all the claims that those Roman Catholic priests and others make are baseless. Nothing more.

It is ironic though that Adventists believe such claims unreservedly despite rejecting every other claim of Catholicism, while simultaneously viewing Catholicism as a dangerous, mendacious system that should not be trusted. It is obvious to see that they readily believe these claims without historically investigating them because they are fodder for their false doctrines, theological views; good hooks to yank unsuspecting Christians into Adventist Sabbatarianism. Without these false Roman Catholic claims, the false Sabbath and Sunday views of Adventists would not have a leg to stand on. Therefore, they must latch onto them for dear life, no matter how historically false and inaccurate those claims are.

---

[163] George T. Dennis, "The East-West Schism (1054)," *Christian History Magazine-Issue 28: The 100 Most Important Events in Church History* (1990).

What the Apostolic Fathers tell us
about the Sabbath and Sunday

Another reason that these wild 19th and 20th century claims of Roman Catholicism and Adventism cannot be true is because the Apostolic Fathers and historical Christian authors, who wrote way before the existence of Catholicism in 1054 A.D., had a lot to say about the Sabbath and Sunday. What they said disproves the false claims and narratives of Roman Catholics and Adventists.

Days of worship in the early and apostolic church varied from church to church. Some churches kept Saturday while some kept Sunday. Some kept both days. Some worshipped every day, but emphasized specific days such as Friday, the Lord's Day (Sunday), Passover, Easter, etc. Their writings are extant. They state exactly why they worshipped on Sunday. Worshipping on Sunday for them had absolutely nothing to do with a change of the Sabbath from Saturday to Sunday by Roman Catholicism, which did not exist, nor apostasy on their part, nor hatred for God, nor because they had adopted "Sun-worship" from the pagans around them. These statements that you are about to read from the Apostolic Fathers and early Christians[164] are all dated before the 4th century A.D. This is more than 700 years before the existence of Roman Catholicism. Some of these statements go as far back as within the lifetime of the disciples of Jesus and their immediate disciples.

In chapter 14 of the *Didache* we read, "But every Lord's Day gather yourselves together and break bread, and give thanksgiving after having confessed your transgressions, that your sacrifice may be pure."[165] Ignatius of Antioch, circa 107 A.D., in his *Epistle to the Magnesians* said, "Let every friend of Christ keep the Lord's Day as a festival, the resurrection-day, the queen and chief of all the days of

---

[164] The majority of these statements are sourced from *The Ante-Nicene Fathers*, Vol. 4, translated by Frederick Crombie, edited by Alexander Roberts, James Donaldson, and A. Cleveland Coxe (Buffalo, NY: Christian Literature Publishing Co., 1885), Revised and edited for New Advent by Kevin Knight, http://www.newadvent.org/fathers/04168.htm.

[165] The earliest dating for the Didache is 70-80 A.D. and the latest dating is 120 A.D. This puts the *Didache* right in the lifetime of the disciples of Jesus (especially John the Revelator) and their immediate disciples.

the week." Ignatius further wrote, "Those who were brought up in the ancient order of things [i.e. Jews] have come to the possession of a new hope, no longer observing the Sabbath, but living in the observance of the Lord's day [Sunday], on which also our life has sprung up again by him and by his death." In the *Letter of Barnabas* we read, "We keep the eighth day [Sunday] with joyfulness, the day also on which Jesus rose again from the dead."[166] What is interesting about this last statement is that it is believed that this is the same Barnabas who was a fellow worker and companion of the apostle Paul in the Book of Acts.

Justin Martyr is considered to be the first Christian apologist. In his *First Apology*, chapter 67, he says:

> And on the day called Sunday, all who live in cities or in the country gather together to one place, and the memoirs of the apostles [New Testament] or the writings of the prophets [Old Testament] are read, as long as time permits; then, when the reader has ceased, the president verbally instructs, and exhorts to the imitation of these good things.

He continues, "But Sunday is the day on which we all hold our common assembly, because it is the first day on which God, having wrought a change in the darkness and matter, made the world; and Jesus Christ our Saviour on the same day rose from the dead." Justin wrote this around 150 A.D. in his defense of the beliefs and practices of Christians. He states clearly when Christians held their "common assembly" and why. Notice too that this practice of Christians to worship on Sunday had nothing to do with apostasy nor with Roman Catholic Church's influence and dictation. Recall that Roman Catholicism did not exist at that time.

In 200 A.D., Tertullian gave an expert defence and rebuttal against Judaizers on why Christians do not need to observe the Sabbath. He states:

> In fine, let him who contends that the Sabbath is still to

---

[166] Letter of Barnabas 15:6-8 [c. 74 A.D.].

be observed as a balm of salvation, and circumcision on the eighth day because of the threat of death, teach us that, for the time past, righteous men kept the Sabbath, or practised circumcision, and were thus rendered friends of God. For if circumcision purges a man since God made Adam uncircumcised, why did He not circumcise him, even after his sinning, if circumcision purges? At all events, in settling him in paradise, He appointed one uncircumcised as colonist of paradise. Therefore, since God originated Adam uncircumcised, and inobservant of the Sabbath, consequently his offspring also, Abel, offering Him sacrifices, uncircumcised and inobservant of the Sabbath, was by Him commended; while He accepted what he was offering in simplicity of heart, and reprobated the sacrifice of his brother Cain, who was not rightly dividing what he was offering. Noah also, uncircumcised—yes, and inobservant of the Sabbath— God freed from the deluge. For Enoch, too, most righteous man, uncircumcised and inobservant of the Sabbath, He translated from this world; who did not first taste death, in order that, being a candidate for eternal life, he might by this time show us that we also may, without the burden of the law of Moses, please God. Melchizedek also, "the priest of the Most High God," uncircumcised and inobservant of the Sabbath, was chosen to the priesthood of God. Lot, withal, the brother of Abraham, proves that it was for the merits of righteousness, without observance of the law, that he was freed from the conflagration of the Sodomites.[167]

In the *Didascalia* chapter 2, circa 225 A.D, we read:

The apostles further appointed: On the first day of the week let there be service, and the reading of the Holy

---

[167] Tertullian, *An Answer to the Jews*, chap. 2, https://www.newadvent.org/fathers/0308.htm (Date accessed Nov. 25, 2020).

Scriptures, and the oblation, because on the first day of the week our Lord rose from the place of the dead, and on the first day of the week he arose upon the world, and on the first day of the week he ascended up to heaven, and on the first day of the week he will appear at last with the angels of heaven.

While we may not agree with everything stated here, we can certainly appreciate that these early Christians explained their views, understanding, and theology about Sunday. Note carefully that they said that it was the apostles who appointed that they have worship services on Sunday. Of course there is no direct command in the New Testament for worship services to be held on Sundays, but what we do see is a precedent being set in Acts 20:7 and 1 Corinthians 16:1-3. Furthermore, the *Didascalia* could be referring to a tradition that was passed on by the apostles but was never penned in their epistles. The apostles taught early Christians many traditions that were not penned in Scripture. Some were taught orally while some were via penned correspondence. Paul stated this practice when he said to the Thessalonians, "So then, brothers, stand firm and hold to the traditions that you were taught by us, either by our spoken word or by our letter" (2 Thess. 2:15).

Origen is another Apostolic Father who wrote concerning Sunday as well. In his apology *Against Celsus* he wrote:

If it be objected to us on this subject that we ourselves are accustomed to observe certain days, as for example the Lord's day [Sunday], the Preparation [Friday], the Passover, or Pentecost, I have to answer, that to the perfect Christian, who is ever in his thoughts, words, and deeds serving his natural Lord, God the Word, all his days are the Lord's, and he is always keeping the Lord's Day.[168]

What Origen reveals here is that not only were Christians

---

[168] Origen (A.D. 184-253), *Against Celsus*, Book 8, Chapter 22, https://www.newadvent.org/fathers/04168.htm (Date accessed Nov. 25, 2020).

observing specific holy days, but he also conceptualized that the Lord's Day and the significance of that day was a lifestyle for mature Christians.

In his commentary on Genesis 1 and 2, St. Victorinus of Pettau said:

> The sixth day [Friday] is called Parasceve, that is to say, the preparation of the kingdom.... On this day also, on account of the passion of the Lord Jesus Christ, we make either a station to God or a fast. On the seventh day he rested from all his works, and blessed it, and sanctified it. On the former day we are accustomed to fast rigorously, that on the Lord's Day [Sunday] we may go forth to our bread with giving of thanks. And let the Parasceve become a rigorous fast, lest we should appear to observe any Sabbath with the Jews, which Sabbath he [Christ] in his body abolished.[169]

Although Victorinus is interpreting some of these things allegorically, nevertheless, we can appreciate some of his points and theological understanding, as well as the historical facts we can glean from his statement. He informs us that Christians fasted rigorously on Friday. This fast was so rigorous, it seemed to have rolled over into Saturday as well, so that they could have purposefully avoided countenancing the Sabbath with the Jews. His statement affirmed that they understood Christ to have abolished the Sabbath, just as Christians today understand Colossians 2:16-17 has done. He further affirmed that they anticipated Sunday, the Lord's Day, as the day they went forth to their bread with thanksgiving. This is another early and potent statement that disproves the Roman Catholic statements and Adventist arguments about the Sabbath and Sunday that we had looked at.

In *Ecclesiastical History*, Eusebius of Caesarea drew a great comparison between the Old Testament saints and Christians of his

---

[169] Victorinus, *On the Creation of the World* [circa 270 A.D.], https://www.newadvent.org/fathers/0711.htm (Date accessed Nov. 25, 2020).

day. He argued that the Old Testament saints did not observe circumcision and the Sabbath, therefore Christians are no different in not observing those things. He said:

> They [the early saints of the Old Testament] did not care about circumcision of the body, neither do we [Christians]. They did not care about observing Sabbaths, nor do we. They did not avoid certain kinds of food, neither did they regard the other distinctions which Moses first delivered to their posterity to be observed as symbols; nor do Christians of the present day do such things.[170]

In *The Proof of the Gospel*, Eusebius makes another profound point concerning the Sabbath and Sunday and how Christians understood those days in light of Christ and the Gospel. He says:

> The day of his [Christ's] light was the day of his resurrection from the dead, which they say, as being the one and only truly holy day and the Lord's day [Sunday], is better than any number of days as we ordinarily understand them, and better than the days set apart by the Mosaic Law for feasts, new moons, and Sabbaths, which the Apostle [Paul] teaches are the shadow of days and not days in reality.[171]

They conceptualized Sunday to have been better than the Old Covenant feasts and Sabbaths that were merely shadows. They were enjoying the reality and much better Lord's Day on which Jesus Christ our Lord rose from the dead.

All of these are early Christian witnesses about the Sabbath and Sunday. Many more statements like these could have been given but these sufficiently prove the point—the claims of those Catholic priests and publications are flatly wrong. They are unjustified, ahistorical, and meaningless opinions. They are shoddy attempts of

---

[170] Eusebius, *Ecclesiastical History*, 1:4:8 [c. 312 A.D.].

[171] Eusebius, *The Proof of the Gospel*, 4:16:186 [c. 319 A.D.].

historical revisionism. The Catholics make the claims they do in regards to Sabbath and Sunday as an attempt to wreck the Protestant claim regarding Sola Scriptura. It is sad to see Adventist scholars, educated pastors, apologists, and laymen alike embrace them as truthful, historically accurate, and factual, in this age of information and easy access to data. This shows extreme desperation on the part of the Seventh-day Adventist Church to use those false claims to buttress their Sabbatarian theology and paranoid eschatology about Sunday. They are wrong and we should recognize and reject their scam.

Part IV

Michael the Archangel

Jesus' Deity

The Scapegoat

Ultimate Sin-Bearer

Chapter Ten

Michael The Archangel: Is He Jesus Christ Or Just An Archangel?

"The Apostolic Fathers were essentially unanimous that Michael the Archangel was not Jesus Christ. They were clear that angels and archangels are created beings, that Jesus was not a created being, nor was He an angel or an archangel such as Michael and Gabriel."

Michael the Archangel: Identity and Theology In The Judeo-Christian Faith

Michael's first mention in Scripture and Judaism was during the Hellenistic period where he is called "a prince" (Dan. 10:13, 21) and an archangel (1 Enoch 20:1-7; 71:3; 2 Enoch 22:6; 4 Bar. 9:5; cf. Jude 9).[172] His name in Hebrew means "who is like God."[173] This can be either a question or a declarative statement. Michael is mentioned a lot in Jewish and Christian literature (which will be shown), but he is only mentioned 5 times in the Bible (Dan. 10:13, 21; 12:1; Jude 9; and Rev 12:7). Michael, Raphael, Gabriel, and Phanuel (or Uriel), are the four archangels that stand before the throne of God (1 Enoch 9:1; 40; 54:6;

---

[172] This section is adapted from Duane F. Watson, "Michael (Angel)" in Vol. 4, *The Anchor Yale Bible Dictionary*, ed. David Noel Freedman (New York: Doubleday, 1992), p. 811.

[173] Adventists often argue that Michael's very name "Who is like God" indicates that he is God, but this is a very flawed argument because there are 11 other persons in Scripture who name Michael (Num. 13:13; 1 Chron. 5:11, 13-14; 6:39-40; 7:3; 8:16; 12:20; 27:18; 2 Chron. 21:2-4; and Ezra 8:8). If the very definition of his name means that he is God then all these other individuals are God too because of the definitional meaning of their names. But we can see that this is not true and this argument is flawed. There are other persons in Scripture whose names mean "who is like God" or similar to it and that does not in any way make them divine. Elijah means "Yahweh is God," and so does Joel. Daniel's friend Mishael's name also means "who is like God," and so does Micah the prophet. But none of this proves that these persons are God by virtue of the definitional meaning of their names.

71:8-9, 13; cf. 1 Enoch 87:2; 88:1; 1QM 9:14-15).[174] There is a larger group of archangels, seven in all, and Michael is one of them (1 Enoch 20:1-7; Tobith 12:15; cf. 1 Enoch 81:5; 90:21-22).

In the apocryphal Christian work *Ascension of Isaiah* 3:16, Michael is called "the chief of the holy angels," who will open the sepulchre (of Jesus) on the third day. Michael the Archangel is presented as having several roles in Scripture and the apocryphal books. He is the guardian angel of the nation of Israel (Dan 10:21; 12:1; 1 Enoch 20:5; 1QM 17:6-8; cf. Test. of Moses 10:2). Daniel presents Michael as fighting for Israel against the rival princes of the Persians (Dan. 10:13-14, 20-21) and the one who will "arise" to deliver Israel from the great "time of trouble" (Dan. 12:1; cf. Rev 12:7-9; Test. of Levi 5:5-6). He is the champion of Israel against the forces of Edom (Rome; Exod. Rab. 18:5).[175] His name is written on one of the four towers used in the holy war against Kittim (the Romans; 1QM 9:14-15). Michael is called "the LORD's archistratig" or "chief captain" in 2 Enoch 22:6 and 33:10.

Michael is one of the archangels who present the prayers of the saints to God and intercedes for Israel (Tob. 12:15; cf. Test. of Dan 6:2; Test. of Levi 5:5-6). He also intercedes for the entire world (1 Enoch 9; Ascension of Isaiah 9:23 [Latin]). Serving in this role, he is said to be merciful (1 Enoch 20:5; 40:9; 68; cf. 71:3), righteous (4 Baruch 9:5; cf. 1 Enoch 71:3), and as the one who opens the gates of heaven for the righteous (4 Bar. 9:5). He is the guardian of the soul of Abraham (Test. of Abraham 19:4) and the one who contended with Satan about Moses' body (Jude 9). This incident is recorded in Jude but it is believed to be from the lost ending of the *Testament of Moses* and the *Assumption of Moses*. The incident presents a confrontation between Michael the Archangel with Satan, who had claimed that Moses did not deserve an honourable burial because he had murdered the Egyptian (cf. Exod. 2:12). Richard J. Bauckham in his commentary on Jude reconstructed the story from a variety of ancient sources and apocryphal writings, and pointed out that the

---

[174] 1QM Milḥāmāh (War Scroll)

[175] A Rabbah is an exposition or interpretation of specific texts of the Law, individual books of the Law, or the entire Law.

story concludes that Michael did bury Moses after that confrontation and that no one saw his burial, and therefore "...no one knows the place of his burial to this day" (Deut. 34:6). He observed:

> The devil brought against Moses a charge of murder, because he smote the Egyptian and hid his body in the sand. But this accusation was no better than slander (βλασφημία) against Moses, and Michael, not tolerating the slander, said to the devil, "May the Lord rebuke you, devil!" At that the devil took flight, and Michael removed the body to the place commanded by God, where he buried it with his own hands. Thus no one saw the burial of Moses.[176]

Michael is the archangel who is believed to be keeping the heavenly record books. The reference in Daniel 12:1 to Michael defending those of Israel whose names are found "written in a book" led to the notion that Michael himself was the recording angel (cf. Ascension of Isaiah 9:19-23 [Latin]). Michael was the intermediary between God and Moses when the Law was delivered to Moses on Mount Sinai (Gk. Apocalypse of Moses 1; cf. Jubilees 1:27-2:1; cf. Acts 7:38, 53; Gal. 3:19-20). Michael is the one who puts the Law, which is explained to be Jesus Christ and the Gospel, in the hearts of believers and visits them to see if they have kept it (Shepherd of Hermas 8:25). Michael is the guardian of the secrets by which heaven and earth are established (1 Enoch 60:11-25).

According to the biblical record, Michael is the leader of the angels that warred against Satan and his angels and cast them out of heaven (Rev. 12:7-9). The fact that Michael leads the heavenly angels in Revelation 12 does not mean that he is Jesus Christ nor God. In Jewish angelology that developed during the Second Temple Period, it was believed that God or an archangel can lead the good angels into battle against evil angels. Gerald F, Hawthorne, et al, notes in the *Dictionary of Paul and His Letters*, "One notable new development is the notion of two opposing forces of angelic powers: a force of good angels led by God or *an archangel*, and a force of evil angels led by an

---

[176] Richard J. Bauckham, Vol. 50, *2 Peter, Jude, Word Biblical Commentary* (Dallas, TX: Word, Incorporated, 1998), p. 73.

evil angelic power known as Satan, Mastema or Belial" [emphasis mine].[177] Michael is believed to be one of the four archangels who will bind the armies of Satan and throw them into the furnace (1 Enoch 54:4-8).1 Thessalonians 4:16 states that Jesus' Second Coming will be accompanied "with the voice of an archangel," this archangel may very well be Michael or a different archangel.

Michael the Archangel in the writings of the Apostolic Fathers

Michael the Archangel does not get extensive mention and attention in the Apostolic Fathers but they said enough about angels, archangels, and specifically Michael sometimes, for us to reconstruct how they conceptualized him. In their deliberations about him, we will not see where they understood Michael to have been Jesus, another name for Jesus, or that he was God. They conceptualized and understood Michael to have been just an archangel who is assigned roles just like any other created angel. They saw Michael as a created archangel among other angels and archangels. It is very important to keep in mind that the Apostolic Fathers were persons who were disciples of the disciples of Jesus. They were there at the formation of the Christian church. They were the ones who identified the authentic autographs of Scripture. They copied them, passed them down, defended them, taught them, and many were martyred for them. These Apostolic Fathers would have read the very same texts that Adventists proof-text to prove that Jesus is Michael the Archangel, and yet they never concluded that Jesus was Michael the Archangel. This is very telling.

Clement of Alexandria (c. 150-215 A.D.) said:

> ...these primitive and first created virtues are unchangeable in substance, and along with subordinate angels and archangels whose names they share, effect divine operations. Thus Moses names the virtue of the angel Michael, by an angel near to himself and of the lowest grade.... Moses heard him and spoke to him face

---

[177] Gerald F. Hawthorne, Ralph P. Martin, and Daniel G. Reid, eds., *Dictionary of Paul and His Letters*, (Downers Grove, IL: InterVarsity Press, 1993), p. 21.

to face. On the other prophets through the agency of angels an impression was made as of beings hearing and seeing.[178]

In the 2nd century work *The Shepherd of Hermas* chapter 3, a vision of a tree with many branches cut off from it yet it continued to "sound" and seemed like nothing had happened to it is explained to the shepherd. The great tree is said to be "the Law of God that is given to the whole world; and this Law is the Son of God." It is said that the people under the shadow of the tree are those who heard the proclamation (of the Gospel) and believed it. It continues, "And the great and glorious angel Michael is he who has authority over this people, and governs them; for this is he who gave them the law into the hearts of believers: he accordingly superintends them to whom he gave it to see if they have kept the same." So, here we are seeing where Michael the Archangel was believed to have been just an angel who impressed the Gospel into the hearts of believers and superintends their progress in it.

Tertullian (c. 160-220 A.D.) was a 2nd century North African theologian and apologist. He was a prolific writer. In one of his apologetics against the heretics Marcion, Apelles, and Valentinus, who had denied the physical body of Christ and the resurrection, he wrote:

> He [Jesus] has been, it is true, called the Angel of great counsel, that is, a messenger, by a term expressive of official function, not of nature. For He had to announce to the world the mighty purpose of the Father, even that which ordained the restoration of man. But He is not on this account to be regarded as an angel, as a Gabriel or a Michael.[179]

Tertullian was clear in his assessment that Jesus Christ was not a created angel as the Archangel Michael or Gabriel were, but that He was only called an angel in "official function." Had Tertullian

---

[178] *Fragments of Clement Alexandria*, in Ant-Nicene Fathers, Vol. 1, p. 575.

[179] Tertullian, *On the Flesh of Christ*, chap. 14.

thought that Jesus was an angel or Michael, there is no way he could have drawn this contrast between Jesus and the archangels Michael and Gabriel.

Origen (c. 185-254 A.D.) referred to Michael and two other archangels as angels of God assigned to specific tasks and duties in the world and their very names engender their assignments. He said, "And when one is able to philosophize about the mystery of names, he will find much to say respecting the titles of the angels of God, of whom one is called Michael, and another Gabriel, and another Raphael, appropriately to the duties which they discharge in the world, according to the will of the God of all things."[180] He elaborated on this concept much further in another work when he said:

> ...or are we to suppose that it is the result of accident that a particular office is assigned to a particular angel: as to Raphael, e.g., the work of curing and healing; to Gabriel, the conduct of wars; to Michael, the duty of attending to the prayers and supplications of mortals. For we are not to imagine that they obtained these offices otherwise than by their own merits, and by the zeal and excellent qualities which they severally displayed before this world was formed; so that afterwards in the order of archangels, this or that office was assigned to each one, while others deserved to be enrolled in the order of angels, and to act under this or that archangel, or that leader or head of an order.[181]

In *Against Celsus*, Book VII, chapter 40, Origen rejected the notion that Christians made idols of fanciful creatures to worship. He said they rejected idols in accordance with the teachings of Jesus and would not make an image of Michael the Archangel, whom he had mentioned earlier. He said, "...but it is in accordance with the teaching of Jesus that we oppose all such notions, and will not allow to

---

[180] Origen, *Against Celsus*, Book I, chap. 25.

[181] Origen, *On the First Principles*, Chapter VIII, "On the Angels."

Michael, or to any others that have been referred to, a form and figure of that sort." In *Against Celsus*, Book VIII, chapter 13, Origen named "Gabriel and Michael, and the other angels and archangels" as beings that Christians do not worship. He explained further by saying neither do they worship the demons of the heathen, but they worship "the one God, and His only Son, the Word and the Image of God."

The late 2nd to early 3rd century theologian Hippolytus (c. 170-235 A.D.) in his commentary on Daniel 10:13 said, ""And lo, Michael." Who is Michael but the angel assigned to the people? As (God) says to Moses, I will not go with you in the way, because the people are stiff-necked; but my angel shall go with you."[182] In this commentary, Hippolytus clearly understood Michael to have been just an angel assigned to assist the Jewish people.

In the 4th century, St. Athanasius (c. 296-373 A.D.) said, "But as regards ministrations there are, not one only, but many out of their whole number, whomever the Lord will send. For there are many Archangels, many Thrones, and Authorities, and Dominions, thousands of thousands, and myriads of myriads, standing before Him, ministering and ready to be sent."[183] In attempts to make their theology of Michael the Archangel to be Jesus Christ, Adventists argue that there is only one archangel, but St. Athanasius stated here that there are many archangels who minister to God and are always prepared to be sent to minister (cf. Heb. 113-14; 13:2).

Basil the Great (c. 330-379 A.D.), another 4ht century Church Father, wrote:

> It appears, indeed, that even before this world an order of things existed of which our mind can form an idea.... The birth of the world was preceded by a condition of things suitable for the exercise of supernatural powers, outstripping the limits of time, eternal and infinite. The Creator and Demiurge of the universe perfected His works in it, spiritual light for

---

[182] Hippolytus, *Fragments from the Scriptural Commentaries of Hippolytus*, Third fragment (Scholia on Daniel) (https://www.newadvent.org/fathers/0502.htm).

[183] Athanasius, *Discourse II Against the Arians*, chap. 17, section 27.

the happiness of all who love the Lord, intellectual and invisible natures, all the orderly arrangement of pure intelligences who are beyond the reach of our mind and of whom we cannot even discover the names. They fill the essence of this invisible world, as Paul teaches us. "For by him were all things created that are in heaven, and that are in earth, visible and invisible whether they be thrones or dominions or principalities or powers" or virtues or hosts of angels or the dignities of archangels.[184]

Basil is expressing the "orderly arrangement" of the visible and invisible creation and he considered archangels to be a part of the invisible order of creation. Despite not naming Michael the Archangel, Basil said there are many archangels and stated clearly that they are created beings.

Cyril of Jerusalem (c. 313-386 A.D.) draws a stark contrast between the created angels, archangels, powers, and other heavenly intelligences with the Holy Spirit and said that they have "no equality with the Holy Ghost." He even names Michael and Gabriel as two created angels who need God and are not "equal in honor to Him." He said:

Thou hast seen His power, which is in all the world; tarry now no longer upon earth, but ascend on high. Ascend, I say, in imagination even unto the first heaven, and behold there so many countless myriads of Angels. Mount up in thy thoughts, if thou canst, yet higher; consider, I pray thee, the Archangels, consider also the Spirits; consider the Virtues, consider the Principalities, consider the Powers, consider the Thrones, consider the Dominions— of all these the Comforter is the Ruler from God, and the Teacher, and the Sanctifier. Of Him Elias has need, and Elisseus, and Esaias, among men; of Him Michael and

---

[184] Basil the Great, *The Hexameron*, Homily 1, 5.

Gabriel have need among Angels. Naught of things created is equal in honor to Him: for the families of the Angels, and all their hosts assembled together, have no equality with the Holy Ghost. All these the all-excellent power of the Comforter overshadows. And they indeed are sent forth to minister, but He searches even the deep things of God....[185]

In another lecture, Cyril was unequivocally clear that archangels are created beings. They were created by God. He said:

There is then One Only God, the Maker both of souls and bodies: One the Creator of heaven and earth, the Maker of Angels and Archangels: of many the Creator, but of One only the Father before all ages,—of One only, His Only-begotten Son, our Lord Jesus Christ, by Whom He made all things visible and invisible.[186]

Speaking on prayer, the eminent 4th century father John Chrysostom said:

From beneath, out of the heart, draw forth a voice, make thy prayer a mystery.... Yea, for thou art joined to the choirs of angels, and art in communion with archangels, and art singing with the seraphim. And all these tribes show forth much goodly order, singing with great awe that mystical strain, and their sacred hymns to God, the King of all. With these then mingle thyself, when thou art praying, and emulate their mystical order.[187]

He saw the angels and archangels as examples of "goodly order" to imitate. In prayer and orderly worship of God, we are joined to the choirs of angels and are in communion with archangels, who are singing sacred hymns to God, the King of all. He advised that we

---

[185] Cyril of Jerusalem, *Lecture XVI*, 23.

[186] Cyril of Jerusalem, *Lecture IV*, p. 12.

[187] John Chrysostom, *Homily 19 on St. Matthew*: On the Lord's Prayer.

emulate their mystical order in our prayers and worship of God.

All of these Church Fathers are unanimous in their expositions and statements that archangels, Michael the Archangel, Gabriel, and all other angels are created beings who they did not worship, who were not Jesus, nor equal to God and the Holy Spirit, but were created beings given specific tasks, ministries, responsibilities, etc., by God. They worship God in an orderly way and we should emulate them in doing the same.

Let me briefly reiterate. All of these Church Fathers read the very texts that Adventists proof-text to build a theology that Michael the Archangel is our Lord Jesus Christ and yet they could not, with sound exposition, come to such conclusions. Like the Jews during the Second Temple Period of the 3rd century B.C., they had an elaborate theology of angels, yet they never conceived of Michael the Archangel being Jesus Christ nor Yahweh our God. This stubborn Church history fact should cause Adventists to shudder at the thought of deifying Michael and making him and Jesus Christ to be one and the same person.

Michael the Archangel in the writings of the Reformers

In the 16th century (the 1500s), some began to toy with the idea that Michael the Archangel was Jesus Christ. John Calvin in his *Commentaries on the Book of the Prophet Daniel,* commenting on Daniel 10:21, said, "Some think the word Michael represents Christ, and I do not object to this opinion.... But as this is not generally admitted, I leave it in doubt for the present and shall say more on the subject in the twelfth chapter."[188] In a polemic against Michael Servetus, who was "boasting himself to be Michael, the guardian of the Church, and the mighty prince of the people,"[189] Calvin retorted that "Michael may mean an angel; but I embrace the opinion of those who refer this to the person of Christ, because it suits the subject best to represent him as standing forward for the defence of his elect

---

[188] John Calvin, *Commentaries on the Book of the Prophet Daniel*, translated by T. Myers (Grand Rapids, MI: Baker Book House, 1979), p. 243.

[189] Ibid, p. 369.

people."[190] When read in context, Calvin did embrace that Jesus was Michael the Archangel, not as a created angel, but that Jesus is the guardian of His Church and that He can delegate this role to angels as well, who can certainly be Michael. He says:

> By Michael many agree in understanding Christ as the head of the Church. But if it seems better to understand Michael as the archangel, this sense will prove suitable, for under Christ as the head, angels are the guardians of the Church. Whichever be the true meaning, God was the preserver of his Church by the hand of his only-begotten Son, and because the angels are under the government of Christ, he might entrust this duty to Michael.[191]

It is difficult to conclude who at that time began to propagate the idea that Michael the Archangel was Jesus, but we are aware that from that time period some Reformers and Bible commentators began to entertain it. These include Phillip Melanchthon, Amandus Polanus, Andrew Willet, Thomas Scott, Isaac Watts, John Butterworth, John Brown, Matthew Henry, etc.[192] This ranged from the 1500s to the mid-1800s. After that, the belief that Michael was Jesus basically died out. It did not gain any traction among major Bible commentators and theologians. There is no historical, reformed, nor orthodox Christian church that believes, as part of its theology or views, that Michael the Archangel is our Lord Jesus Christ. The hermeneutic and comparisons that these authors used to assume that Michael the Archangel was Jesus Christ is very similar to what Adventists use today.[193] They proof-texted titles and functions of Christ and arbitrarily compared those with what seems to be revealed or said about Michael the Archangel and came to the

---

190 Ibid, p. 369.

191 Ibid, p. 369.

192https://christianity.stackexchange.com/questions/18465/what-is-the-origin-of-the-idea-that-michael-is-jesus (Dec. 12, 2020).

193 Edwin M. Cotto, *Who Is Michael the Archangel?*, https://adventistdefenseleague.com/2020/04/who-is-michael-the-archangel.html

conclusion that they were one and the same person. This was certainly not a good approach. In this regard, they greatly erred.

Another issue with the Reformers and Bible commentators on this matter seemed to have been that they did not have nor were aware of the writings of the Apostolic Fathers on this issue. The Apostolic Fathers were essentially unanimous that Michael the Archangel was not Jesus Christ. They were clear that angels and archangels are created beings, that Jesus was not a created being, nor was He an angel or an archangel such as Michael and Gabriel. No Jewish apocryphal book ever equated Michael the Archangel with Yahweh either. They never matched the titles and attributes of God with those of Michael and concluded that Michael was one and the same as God. Early Christians never applied the same hermeneutic to Jesus and concluded that either. The lack of access to these early witnesses seems to have been a major weakness for these Reformers and commentators, and thus caused them to immaturely entertain such an idea. But Adventists believing that Michael the Archangel is our Lord Jesus Christ is not because of a lack of information. A plethora of information exists today, with ease of access to them. Contrary to the available data, it is because Ellen White said over and over that Jesus and Michael are one and the same person that they believe and teach this. They cannot admit that she is wrong. They cannot disavow the teaching, so they resort to immense biblical contortions to try to make Jesus be Michael the Archangel. Let us turn to that chapter and analyse the implications of this for Jesus' deity.

Chapter Eleven

Michael The Archangel Is
Jesus Christ In Adventism:
The Implications For Jesus' Deity

"The belief that Michael the Archangel is Jesus Christ in Adventism is rooted in the Arianism of Ellen White and the Adventist pioneers."

Ellen White and the SDA pioneers were Arians and Semi-Arians

The belief that Michael the Archangel is Jesus Christ in Adventism is rooted in the Arianism of Ellen White and the Adventist pioneers. They were all Arians and spoke against the Trinity, the personhood of the Holy Spirit, and the deity of Jesus Christ and His eternal existence. The Adventist pioneer Joseph Bates (1792-1872) said, "Respecting the trinity, I concluded that it was an impossibility for me to believe that the Lord Jesus Christ, the Son of the Father, was also the Almighty God, the Father, one and the same being."[194] James White, the husband of Ellen G. White, said, "To assert that the sayings of the Son and his apostles are the commandments of the Father is as wide from the truth as the old Trinitarian absurdity that Jesus Christ is the very and Eternal God."[195] In a negative comparison of Protestants with Roman Catholics, the Adventist pioneer Merritt E. Cornell listed a number of orthodox

---

[194] Joseph Bates, *The Autobiography of Joseph Bates (1868)* (Washington, DC: The Ellen G. White Estate, 2008), p. 204, par. 2.

[195] James White, *The Advent Review and Sabbath Herald*, Vol. 3 (1852-1853), August 5, 1852 (Washington, DC: The Ellen G. White Estate, 2008), p. 52, par. 42.

Christian doctrines that he considered to be "contrary to the spirit and letter of the New Testament." He said:

> Protestants and Catholics are so nearly united in sentiment, that it is not difficult to conceive how Protestants may make an image to the Beast. The mass of Protestants believe with Catholics in the Trinity, immortality of the soul, consciousness of the dead, rewards and punishments at death, the endless torture of the wicked, inheritance of the saints beyond the skies, sprinkling for baptism, and the PAGAN SUNDAY [sic] for the Sabbath; all of which is contrary to the spirit and letter of the New Testament.[196]

Another revered Adventist pioneer John N. Andrews said, "The son of God...had God for his Father, and did, at some point in the eternity of the past, have beginning of days."[197] Uriah Smith, editor of the *Review and Herald*, believed that Jesus was a created being. He said Jesus was "the first created being, dating his existence far back before any other created being or thing, next to the self-existent and eternal God."[198] Scores of other statements could have been provided from various Adventist pioneers stating their Arian views, their rejection of the Trinity, the deity and eternal existence of Jesus Christ, and other historically orthodox Christian beliefs and teachings, and them giving their opinions that those doctrines are apostate beliefs and teachings not grounded in Scripture. But certainly these are sufficient.

The prolific Adventist historian Dr George R. Knight noted in one of his stellar trilogy works on Adventist heritage and history:

> Most of the founders of Seventh-day Adventism would not be able to join the church today if they had to agree to the denomination's "27 Fundamental Beliefs."[199]

---

[196] Merritt E. Cornell, *Facts for the Times* (Washington, DC: The Ellen G. White Estate, 2008), p. 76, par. 1.

[197] John N. Andrews, *Review and Herald*, Sept. 7, 1869 (Washington, DC: The Ellen G. White Estate, 2008), p. 84.

[198] Uriah Smith, *Thoughts, Critical and Practical, on the Book of Revelation* (Battle Creek, MI: Seventh-day Adventist Publishing, 1865), p. 59.

More specifically, they would not be able to accept belief number 2, dealing with the doctrine of the Trinity…. In like manner, most of the founders of Seventh-day Adventism would have trouble with fundamental belief number 4, which holds that Jesus is both eternal and truly God.[200]

This Arian root of Adventism must be understood in order to grasp its historical and present Christology. These Adventist pioneers were staunch Arians or semi-Arians. Ellen White was an Arian. Even when she morphed her Arianism with a veneer of Trinitarianism, she never renounced her Arianism, nor did she ever seek to correct the Arian views and statements of her husband and fellow Adventist colleagues with a prophetic "Thus says the Lord." To the contrary, she memorialized and cemented their Arian views by saying:

> I have been instructed that we should make prominent the testimony of some of the old workers who are now dead. Let them *continue to speak through their articles* as found in the *early numbers of our papers*. These articles should now be *reprinted*, that there may be a living voice from the Lord's witnesses. The history of the *early experiences in the message* will be a power to withstand the masterly ingenuity of Satan's deceptions. This instruction has been repeated recently [italics mine].[201]

In this statement, Ellen White makes it clear that the words and early views expressed by the Adventist pioneers must continue to be reprinted so that their voices will continue to be a witness, testifying of their early doctrines and experiences, which she believed must be continuously held by Adventists. Ellen White was unequivocal about this conviction. She reiterated:

> We are to *repeat the words of the pioneers* in our

---

[199] When Dr Knight wrote his book, the Adventist Church had 27 Fundamental Beliefs, but currently they have 28.

[200] George R. Knight, *A Search for Identity: The Development of Seventh-day Adventist Beliefs* (Hagerstown, MD: Review and Herald Publishing Association, 2000), p. 17.

[201] White, *The Publishing Ministry*, p. 31, par. 2.

work, who knew what it cost to search for the truth as for hidden treasure, and who labored to *lay the foundation of our work*. They moved forward step by step under the influence of the Spirit of God. One by one these pioneers are passing away. The word given me is, "Let that which these men *have written in the past be reproduced*."[202] [Italics mine]

If Adventists ought to "repeat the words of the pioneers" and "reproduce" them in print, what exactly should we expect to be reprinted and propagated from them regarding the Trinity and the deity and eternal existence of Jesus Christ? Surely it will not be biblical and historical orthodoxy but Arianism or Semi-Arianism. That's because that is what the majority of them believed and taught.

Adventists who are avid readers of Ellen White's writings, and who endeavour to be staunch followers of them, almost always return to their Arian roots. As a matter of fact, because of these statements of Ellen White about the reproduction of the works of the pioneers and returning to their foundational theology, there is a growing movement in Adventism called "The Forgotten Pillar Project" whose main mission is to get Adventists to remember the "forgotten pillar" of Arianism in historic Adventism and return to it.[203] They consider Adventism's recent acceptance of the Trinity to be a grave apostasy. Some of the most rabid defenders of Ellen White and Adventism from the official *Adventist Defense League* are Arians or Semi-Arians.[204]

Ellen White's Arian Christology: Jesus was promoted to Godhood

I demonstrated all of this to show that Ellen White and the Adventist pioneers were not orthodox, Trinitarian believers. They were Arian heretics. Specifically for Ellen White, her Christology was pointedly Arian. She conceptualized Jesus as a created being who was not equal with God, truly God, nor of one essence with the

---

[202] White, *Counsels to Writers and Editors*, p. 28, par. 1.

[203] https://forgottenpillar.com/ (Date accessed Dec. 11, 2020).

[204] https://adventistdefenseleague.com/

Father, as Scripture and Church history consistently affirm. In Ellen White's Christology, Jesus, who she says was heaven's commander, was merely one step above Satan. But in actuality, it will be proven from her statements and her archangel theology that Jesus was equal with Satan.

In her worldview and the pronouncements she made, Jesus was *promoted* to equality with God and to Godhood. Jesus was privileged to be *invited* into consultations with God and to assist Him in the creation of the world, while Satan was excluded from the Divine Council. This promotion that Jesus received evoked the jealousy and ire of Satan, and thus began this "Great Controversy between Christ and Satan," as Satan thought that he was the one who should have been promoted to equality with God and not Jesus.[205] Ellen White said, "Our great Exemplar was exalted[206] to be equal with God. He was high commander in heaven."[207]

Ellen White explained this promotion of Jesus to Godhood and equality with God in greater detail:

> The great Creator assembled the heavenly host, that he might in the presence of all the angels confer special honor upon his Son. The Son was seated on

---

[205] Ellen White says, "Before the fall of Satan, the Father consulted his Son in regard to the formation of man. They purposed to make this world, and create beasts and living things upon it, and to make man in the image of God, to reign as a ruling monarch over every living thing which God should create. When Satan learned the purpose of God, he was envious at Christ, and jealous because the Father had not consulted him in regard to the creation of man. Satan was of the highest order of angels; but Christ was above all. He was the commander of all Heaven. He imparted to the angelic family the high commands of his Father. The envy and jealousy of Satan increased."--- *Spiritual Gifts*, Vol. 3, p. 36, par. 1, "The Temptation and Fall."

[206] Ellen White's use of the word "exalted" in these two statements means "promotion from a lower office to a higher one, to be raised in rank." This is how the *Noah Webster's 1828 Dictionary* defines the word "exalt,": "1. To raise high; to elevate. 2. To elevate in power, wealth, rank or dignity; as, to exalt one to a throne, to the chief magistracy, to a bishopric." And this is how it defines "exalted," "Raised to a lofty height; elevated; honored with office or rank." Her very use of the word "exalted" and the clear concept of what she said in those statements mean that she believed that Jesus Christ was not always God. Godhood was something that Jesus was promoted to and this promotion angered Satan, who had thought that he was deserving of that promotion to be above Jesus.

[207] White, *Testimonies for the Church*, Vol. 2, p. 426, par. 2.

the throne with the Father, and the heavenly throng of holy angels was gathered around them. The Father then made known that it was ordained by himself that Christ, his Son, should be equal with himself; so that wherever was the presence of his Son, it was as his own presence. The word of the Son was to be obeyed as readily as the word of the Father. His Son he had invested with authority to command the heavenly host. Especially was his Son to work in union with himself in the anticipated creation of the earth and every living thing that should exist upon the earth. His Son would carry out his will and his purposes, but would do nothing of himself alone. The Father's will would be fulfilled in him.[208]

When Jesus was in the wilderness being tempted by Satan (Matt. 4:1-10), Ellen White posits that Satan was still jealous over Jesus' promotion to equality with God, and since he could not get godhood in heaven and be promoted above Jesus Christ, he tried to get homage from Jesus here on earth. She says:

Satan's dissatisfaction first commenced in Heaven because he could not be first and highest in command—equal with God, exalted above Christ. He rebelled and lost his estate, and he, and those who sympathized with him were turned out of Heaven. In the wilderness he hoped to gain advantage through the weak and suffering condition of Christ, and obtain from him that homage he could not obtain in Heaven.[209]

Is Jesus Christ the Lord God Almighty or is He not?

Ellen White expressed her Arianism more when she explicitly said that "the Man Christ Jesus was not the Lord God Almighty" and that "the Deity did not sink under the agonizing torture of Calvary." She says:

---

[208] White, *The Spirit of Prophecy*, Vol. 1, p. 17, par. 2.

[209] White, *Spiritual Gifts*, Vol. 4b, p. 84, par. 1.

There is no one who can explain the mystery of the incarnation of Christ. Yet we know that He came to this earth and lived as a man among men. The man Christ Jesus was not the Lord God Almighty, yet Christ and the Father are one. The Deity did not sink under the agonizing torture of Calvary, yet it is nonetheless true that "God so loved the world, that he gave his only begotten Son, that whosoever believeth in him should not perish, but have everlasting life."[210]

This statement of Ellen White has long been a sore thumb in Adventist Christology. Many Adventist apologists have laboured hard and long defending it and attempting to make it seem like it is not saying what it is actually saying. But twist and squirm as they may, Ellen White truly believed that Jesus was not "the Lord God Almighty" despite that He and the Father were one. Without engaging their age-old, hackneyed arguments that defend the rightness of this statement, let me briefly point out that the Man Christ Jesus was indeed the Lord God Almighty. Therefore, irrespective of the way they torture this statement and Scripture to make them agree, it just does not work because Scripture affirms that Jesus was the Lord God Almighty, yet Ellen White denies this.

In Revelation 1:8 Jesus said to John, "I am the Alpha and the Omega," says the Lord God, "who is and who was and who is to come, the Almighty." The Book of Revelation uses the phrase "Lord God Almighty" in six other places (4:8; 11:17; 15:3; 16:7; 19:6; and 21:22). In those instances, the phrase equally refers to "the Man Christ Jesus" just as they refer to God the Father. The nature and deity of "the Man Christ Jesus" cannot be separated from the nature and deity of God the Father. Hebrews 1:3 affirms that, "He is the radiance of the glory of God and the exact imprint of his nature...." In John 5:16 when He said, "My Father is working until now, and I am working," the Jews clearly understood Him to be "making Himself equal with God" and therefore wanted to kill Him for it on the grounds that He was committing blasphemy (vs. 18). In John 8:48 when He said, "Truly, truly, I say to you, before Abraham was, I am," they saw the clear implications of His claim to divinity and

---

[210] White, *Lift Him Up*, p. 235, par. 3.

equality with God, and again wanted to stone Him. In John 10:30 when Jesus said, "I and the Father are one," the immediate response was, "The Jews picked up stones again to stone him" (vs. 31). The consistent reason for their reaction in all of these instances is because "the Man Christ Jesus" was claiming to be the "Lord God Almighty." That is the underlying crux of Jesus' statements. What is true of the Father is true of the Man Christ Jesus, even the title "Lord God Almighty." This can be observed in various statements about God the Father and Jesus in Revelation.

For example, in chapter 1:8 Jesus said, "I am the Alpha and the Omega." In chap. 21:6, God the Father says, "I am the Alpha and the Omega, the beginning and the end." In chap. 22:12-13 "the Man Christ Jesus" affirmed the very same about Himself. He said, "Behold, I am coming soon, bringing my recompense with me, to repay each one for what he has done. I am the Alpha and the Omega, the first and the last, the beginning and the end." Whichever way Adventists try to spin these passages and attempt to dissect the nature of "the Man Christ Jesus," that will never change the thrust of these passages—the Man Christ Jesus *is* the Lord God Almighty. Ellen White's Arianistic denial of that will not change that fact. It is sad to see that Adventists are willing to commit some historical Christological heresies in order to uphold this egregious statement of Ellen White rather than to admit that she was flatly wrong and Arian in her Christology, especially in the statement under discussion.

Ironically, in contradiction to herself, Ellen White, years later, made statements that affirm exactly what I just proved about the equality of Jesus with the Father in nature, titles, and attributes! But the challenge for Adventists is that they affirm and defend both views of Ellen White despite their mutually exclusive nature and contradiction. Adventists have mastered doublethink. Ellen White said, "Jesus said, 'I and my Father are one.' The words of Christ were full of deep meaning as He put forth the claim that He and the Father were of one substance, possessing the same attributes."[211] Now that I have shown the foundational Arian Christology of the Adventist pioneers and that of Ellen White herself, let us unravel this

[211] White, "The True Sheep Respond to the Voice of the Shepherd," *Signs of the Times*, November 27, 1893, p. 54.

theology of theirs some more and why they believe Michael the Archangel to be Jesus Christ.

Jesus is Michael the Archangel: a pivotal SDA Christology

Jesus being Michael the Archangel in Adventism seems to have been a merger of Mormon theology with the views of the Protestant Reformers and Bible commentators aforementioned. Joseph Smith had a theology of Michael the Archangel. For Smith, Michael is the name by which Adam was known in the premortal life. Michael is Adam in *Doctrines & Covenants* 27:11.[212] Mormons believe that Michael, the Lord's archangel, shall sound his trump that will awaken the dead.[213] Adventists make the same assertion from 1 Thessalonians 4:16.

Whereas for Mormons Michael the Archangel is Adam, for Adventists it is Jesus Christ. That is the change that Ellen White seemed to have made. She said:

> Again: Christ is called the Word of God. John 1:1-3. He is so called because God gave His revelations to man in all ages through Christ. It was His Spirit that inspired the prophets. 1 Peter 1:10, 11. He was revealed to them as the Angel of Jehovah, the Captain of the Lord's host, Michael the Archangel.[214]

Whereas Scripture is silent about Moses being resurrected, Ellen White boldly asserted that Jesus resurrected Moses and correlates Him with Michael the Archangel in Jude 9. She said:

> Christ resurrected Moses, and took him to Heaven. This enraged Satan, and he accused the Son of God of invading his dominion by robbing the grave of his lawful prey. Jude says of the resurrection of Moses, "Yet Michael the archangel, when contending with the devil, he disputed about the body of Moses, durst not bring against him a railing accusation, but said, The

---

[212] Joseph Smith, *Doctrines and Covenants* (Salt Lake City, Utah: The Church of Jesus Christ of Latter-day Saints, 2013), 27:11.

[213] Ibid, 29:26.

[214] White, *Patriarchs and Prophets*, p. 761.

Lord rebuke thee."[215]

What is interesting to note about Jesus being Michael the Archangel theology, is that the Jehovah's Witnesses seem to have gotten this theology from Adventists in the 1870s. The theology of Jehovah's Witnesses on this is that Michael is a created, spirit being and that he was Jesus before His incarnation, and after His ascension he resumed His Michael persona.[216] This theology of Michael is still the current theology of Jehovah's Witnesses. The Adventist view and argumentation is still very similar to theirs. The only difference is that Adventists have added divinity to Jesus while Jehovah's Witnesses continue to deny it. But by virtue of Jehovah's Witnesses getting this theology from Adventists, it is obviously clear that this is what Adventists believed at that time until they upgraded it later on but still retained the Arian roots of it.

The current Adventist belief about Michael being Jesus started to get reworked in 1897 when Ellen White started to plagiarize some orthodox Christian authors. The shift from Arianism to a veneer of Trinitarianism came with the publication of Ellen White's article "Christ the Life-giver" in *Signs of the Times* in 1897, and the book *The Desire of Ages*[217] in 1898 where she said, "In Christ was life original, unborrowed, underived."[218] As beautiful and biblically orthodox this statement is, it is not original to Ellen White. It was plagiarized from Rev. John Cumming who had written in 1856, "In him [Christ] was life,"—that is, original, unborrowed, underived."[219] The evidence is overwhelming that Ellen White and her literary assistants indiscriminately plagiarized from others. But despite these orthodox, plagiarized Trinitarian statements, Ellen White still continued to make many Arian and Semi-Arian statements. She

---

215 White, *Redemption*, p. 24, par. 2.

216https://www.jw.org/en/library/books/bible-teach/who-is-michael-the-archangel-jesus/ (Date accessed Dec. 12, 2020).

217 The evidence strongly reveals that Ellen White heavily plagiarized this book from authors such as Daniel March, William Hanna, Geike Cunningham, John Harris, Frederic W. Farrar, John Cumming, and John Fleetwood (https://www.nonegw.org/rea/rea6.htm).

218 White, *The Desire of Ages*, p. 530, par. 3.

219 Rev. John Cumming, *Sabbath Evening Readings in the New Testament: St. John* (Boston, MA: John P. Jewett and Company, 1856), p. 5.

never rescinded her prior Arian writings, statements, and views. She seemed to have just sought to perhaps balance her Arian views with some Trinitarian language and statements as she plagiarized from orthodox Christians and Trinitarians. Ellen White never rescinded Arianism and neither did many of the Adventist pioneers. Adventists who read her writings see this glaring fact. What they began to do thereafter was to proof-text various texts and smudge them together to make Michael and Jesus to be one and the same. In that way, their Arianism[220] would be covered with a veneer of Trinitarianism. But there are problems with this attempt. Everywhere they turn, Ellen White's theology and statements tie them up in a knot.

Adventists continue to believe in, argue, and vociferously defend that Jesus Christ is Michael the Archangel, not because Scripture clearly says this; not because early Jewish and Christian sources said this, but because Ellen White said so and they subconsciously believe that she cannot be wrong on any issue. Francis D. Nichol in *The Seventh-day Adventist Bible Commentary*, commenting on 1 Thessalonians 4:16, says:

> Gr. *archaggelos*, "chief angel," "first angel," compounded from *archi*, a prefix denoting "chief," or "high," and *aggelos*, "angel," hence, "chief of the angels." The word *archaggelos* appears in the NT only here [1 Thess. 4:16] and in Jude 9, where Michael is said to be the archangel. This commentary holds the view that Michael is none other than our Lord, Jesus Christ.[221]

Francis affirms their belief that Michael the Archangel is Jesus Christ. He sought to justify this by defining the Greek word αρχαγγελος (archangelos) to mean "chief of the angels." But the fact

---

[220] Keep in mind that I stated that there is a growing movement in Adventism to return to their Arian roots and that many rabid Ellen White and Adventist apologists are Arians and Semi-Arians. They hold to and defend their Arianism from Ellen White's earlier Arian writings and hold in suspicion her latter Trinitarian statements plagiarized from Trinitarian Christian authors, or they interpret them in light of her early Arianism and harmonize the later statements with the earlier ones.

[221] Francis D. Nichol, *The Seventh-day Adventist Bible Commentary: The Holy Bible With Exegetical and Expository Comment.*, Commentary Reference Series (Washington, D.C.: Review and Herald Publishing Association, 1978), p. 249.

is there is nothing that warrants pluralizing the word "angel." The word is singular in Greek. The two times it is used in the NT, which he rightly noted, it is used in the singular form and simply means "chief angel" or "high angel" and not "chief of the angels." By doing this, he assumes that there is only one archangel, Jesus Christ, who is "chief of the angels."

The author of the *Seventh-day Adventist Encyclopedia*, Don F. Neufeld, attempted to make this same point when he said, "Most Seventh-day Adventists have held that Michael is Christ.... Seventh-day Adventists conclude that Michael is none other than Christ— "archangel" not in the sense of being the highest angel (chief among equals), but of being ruler over the angelic hosts (as infinitely superior to them)."[222] Siegfried H. Horn in the *SDA Bible Dictionary* was quick to point out that, "Many Bible scholars identify Michael with Christ."[223] Adventist apologists, pastors, authors, sources, and laymen alike constantly argue that there is *only one* archangel to defend that that archangel is Jesus Christ. They dismiss the majority of the English translations of Daniel 10:13 that says "one of the chief princes" (ESV, HCSB, KJV, etc.), and favor any translation that says "first of the chief princes" or "chief of the princes," so that they can pound their squared theology into a round hole.

In an article about the identity of Michael the Archangel, the famous Adventist pastor and televangelist Doug Batchelor considered the translation "one of the chief princes" to be "an unfortunate translation." He said, "It appears at first glance that Michael is only "one of" the chief princes. This is an unfortunate translation in the King James."[224] They must have *only one* archangel. I've read a lot of Adventist materials on this issue. I have had endless dialogues and debates with Adventists from just about every sector of Adventism, and they all unanimously defend and

---

[222] Don F. Neufeld, *Seventh-day Adventist Encyclopedia*, Second revised edition, Commentary Reference Series (Hagerstown, MD: Review and Herald Publishing Association, 1995), Michael, The Archangel.

[223] Siegfried H. Horn, *SDA Bible Dictionary* (Washington, DC: Review and Herald Publishing Association, 1979), p. 737.

[224] Doug Batchelor, *Who is Michael the Archangel?* https://www.amazingfacts.org/media-library/book/e/85/t/who-is-michael-the-archangel#Is-Michael-Only-One-of-Many- (Date accessed Dec. 17, 2020).

argue that Michael is *the only* Archangel. No other archangels can exist in their worldview and theology because for them Jesus *is* Michael the Archangel. If other archangels exist, they see the inextricable dilemma that they would be in regarding Jesus' deity and the obvious Arianism that they would naturally affirm.

Ellen White says there are many archangels!

Irrespective of all the spins, obfuscations, and redefinitions by Adventists to make Michael to be *the only* archangel, they cannot escape the fact that there are many archangels. Scripture reveals that there is more than one archangel (more on this later), so does Jewish apocryphal writings, Christian writings, and the Apostolic Fathers, as was already shown. The responses of Adventists to these will be the torturing of Scripture to gel with Adventist doctrines and the dismissal and rejection of all of those other writings that say that there are many archangels. This attitude of Adventists is never surprising. This is what they always do. But they cannot escape their fearful dilemma despite all of these attempts because their prophetess Ellen White says that there are many archangels. She states, "Cherubims and seraphims, angels and *archangels*, are watching the battle that is going on in this life"[225] (emphasis mine). She again stated, "Angels and *archangels* are looking upon God's chosen ones with the most earnest interest to see what influence the truth is having upon mind and character, to see how much they appreciate the One who was crucified for them, that they might have eternal life"[226] (emphasis mine). She stated that *archangels* are part of the "angelic host" when she said, "And the angelic host, angels and *archangels*, covering cherub and glorious seraph, echo back the refrain of that joyous, triumphant song saying, "Amen: Blessing, and glory, and wisdom, and thanksgiving, and honour, and power, and might, be unto our God for ever and ever (Revelation 7:12)"[227] (emphasis mine).

To further compound this Adventist dilemma and to additionally prove one of my earlier points that Ellen White conceptualized Satan

---

[225] White, *Sermons and Talks*, Vol. 1, p. 241, par. 1.

[226] White, *The Ellen G. White 1888 Materials*, p. 1036, par. 2.

[227] White, *In Heavenly Places*, p. 371, par. 4.

and Jesus as being created beings who were equals, and that Jesus was promoted to divinity, which then evoked the ire and jealousy of Satan because he thought that he should have been the one promoted, and this jealousy sparked this whole "Great Controversy Between Christ and Satan," Ellen White stated that even Satan was an archangel. For Ellen White and Adventists, not only is Jesus an archangel whose other name is Michael, not only do many archangels exist, but also Satan himself is an archangel! Note the cultic and demonic influence throughout this chapter. Jesus is diminished while the devil is elevated. Ellen White said:

> "Rebellion is as the sin of witchcraft, and stubbornness is as iniquity and idolatry." Rebellion originated with *Satan*. Notwithstanding the exalted position which he occupied among the heavenly host, he became dissatisfied because he was not accorded supreme honor. Hence he questioned God's purposes and impugned his justice. He bent all his powers to allure the angels from their allegiance. The fact that he was *an archangel*, glorious and powerful, enabled him to exert a mighty influence [emphasis mine].[228]

If these facts that you read do not show the Arianism of Ellen White and Adventists on their view of Jesus being Michael the Archangel, the inextricable dilemma that they are in, their warped and heretical Christology, and the untenability of their position, then I do not know what will be clearer for you.

---

[228] White, *The Signs of the Times*, September 14, 1882, par. 9.

Chapter Twelve

Jesus Is Not Michael The Archangel:
A Biblical Survey

"The facts scream vociferously, "Michael the Archangel *is not* our Lord and Saviour Jesus Christ!""

Hebrews 1: Jesus is not a created angel nor an archangel

Given the Jewish Old Testament and apocryphal writings[229] theology of Michael the Archangel, as well as the New Testament and the various literature that emerged within and after that time, and the writings of the Apostolic Fathers, it is extremely difficult to make Jesus and Michael to be one and the same person.

Hebrews 1 (also John 1:1) is clear that Jesus is not a created angel. Having expressed that Jesus is God's final prophetic voice to the world through whom God speaks to believers, that Jesus is one

---

[229] It is very characteristic of SDAs to dismiss and reject teachings of the Apocrypha, especially when they undermine their doctrines, assumptions, and views. They generally do not value what it says. But their prophetess says, "I saw that the Apocrypha was the hidden book, and that the wise of these last days should understand it."---White, *Manuscript Releases*, Vol. 16, p. 34, *Manuscript Releases*, No. 1190- "A Vision Received in Oswego, New York, January 26, 1850." Despite the fact that the Apocrypha is not authoritative Scripture, nonetheless, their prophetess says they should read and understand it. And if they do, they would understand what it teaches about Michael the Archangel, which would dismiss their making him to be Jesus Christ.

with God, that He is the transcript of God's character, and having made full atonement for sin He sat at the right hand of God in heaven, verse 4 says, "…having become as much superior to angels as the name he has inherited is more excellent than theirs." The inspired author lets us know two things from this text 1) Jesus is superior to angels and 2) He has inherited a name that is more excellent than theirs. What this automatically means for Michael the Archangel is that Jesus is superior to Him and has a name that is more excellent than his. This statement automatically dispels the idea that Michael is somehow equal to Jesus or just another name for Jesus. He is not. The Scriptures and the prevalent theology of Jews and Christians, and even Christian heretics, was that Michael was a created being, a chief, powerful angel, but a created angel nonetheless.

In verses 5-7, the author defends the fact that God has never called an angel a son that He has begotten, but instead when Jesus came into the world the angels were commanded to worship Him (vs. 6). Jesus is deserving of the worship of angels and archangels. Knowing what we now know about Michael the Archangel, can the same argument be made for him? Are Adventists, after perusing all of this information, willing to argue that Michael is deserving of worship? I hope that they would not, but it would not be surprising if they do. In verse 7, instead of the angels being unique sons who are deserving of worship, the author says they are "spirits" and "a flame of fire." The author then contrasts the supremacy of Jesus with the angels by quoting Psalm 45:5-6 and showing that Jesus is the unique Son of God. In verses 8-9 he says, "But of the Son he says, "Your throne, O God, is forever and ever, the scepter of uprightness is the scepter of your kingdom. You have loved righteousness and hated wickedness; therefore God, your God, has anointed you with the oil of gladness beyond your companions."" Here, the author explicitly calls Jesus God. God the Father calls the Son God. The kingdom does not belong to angels, but the author says it belongs to Jesus. Angels are not the Messiah but the author said that Jesus was "anointed with the oil gladness," which is messianic language. Angels cannot be God nor the Messiah, but the Son is both.

In verses 10-12 the author builds his argument even more to set Jesus apart from created angels. He says, "And, "You, Lord, laid the foundation of the earth in the beginning, and the heavens are the work of your hands; they will perish, but you remain; they will all wear out like a garment, like a robe you will roll them up, like a garment they will be changed. But you are the same, and your years will have no end." In these verses, the author calls Jesus Lord, meaning He is sovereign. Which Adventist is willing to argue for the sovereignty of Michael the Archangel? He says Jesus is the creator. He created the heavens and the earth. Can Michael the Archangel be called the creator of the heavens and earth? The author further expressed that the created order breaks down and changes but Jesus the Son and Sovereign Lord is constant, immutable, and eternal. This cannot be said of Michael nor of any other angel because the entire purpose of the contrast the author is drawing is to show that the Son is better than the angels. He is superior. He is God and sovereign, whereas the angels are created ministers who are tasked to do God's will and also minister to believers (vs. 13-14).

From what Scripture and Judeo-Christian historical writings tell us about Michael the Archangel, and what this passage reveals by contrasting Jesus and the angels, any thought or idea that would make Jesus and Michael to be one and the same should be instantly banished from the mind.

Michael the Archangel is presented in the Book of Daniel as being merely one among many chief princes (10:13). He is a guardian angel of the Jewish nation and considered to be the "great prince who has charge of your people" (10:21; 12:1). He may even be "the Prince of the host" that chapter 8:11 talks about. Commenting on these passages, *The International Standard Bible Encyclopedia* noted, "In all these passages Michael appears as the heavenly patron and champion of Israel; as the watchful guardian of the people of God against all foes earthly or devilish."[230] In their excellent commentary on the Old Testament, for Daniel 10:13 Keil and Delitzsch noted:

---

[230] James Orr, ed., *The International Standard Bible Encyclopedia: 1915 Edition*, (Albany, OR: Ages Software, 1999), Michael.

In the war against the hostile spirit of the kingdom of Persia, the archangel Michael came to the help of the Angel of the Lord. The name *Michael, who is as God*, comes into view, as does the name Gabriel, only according to the appellative signification of the word, and expresses, after the analogy of Exo. 15:11; Psa. 89:7, the idea of God's unparalleled helping power. *Michael* is thus the angel possessing the unparalleled power of God. He is here said to be "one of the chief princes," i.e., of the highest angel-princes, Dan. 10:21, "your prince," i.e., the prince who contends for Israel, who conducts the cause of Israel. The first title points undoubtedly to an arrangement of orders and degrees of angels, designating Michael as the most distinguished of the angel-princes... [Italics in original][231]

Revelation 12: Michael the Archangel and the war in heaven

Revelation 12 explicitly mentions Michael. Verses 7-9 says:

Now war arose in heaven, Michael and his angels fighting against the dragon. And the dragon and his angels fought back, [8]but he was defeated, and there was no longer any place for them in heaven. [9]And the great dragon was thrown down, that ancient serpent, who is called the devil and Satan, the deceiver of the whole world—he was thrown down to the earth, and his angels were thrown down with him.

In this passage, Michael is presented as the warrior-angel who went to battle with Satan and his angels, defeated them, and then kicked them out of heaven. Because the passage says "Michael and *his* angels" Adventists are quick to argue that this must be Jesus because of the personal possessive pronoun. They believe that only about Jesus can it be said that He personally owns angels who are

---

[231] Carl Friedrich Keil and Franz Delitzsch, *Keil and Delitzsch Commentary on the Old Testament*, Dan. 10:13.

part of His army, who stands in contrast to Satan, who also has his angels who are part of his army. But this is totally unwarranted and stretching the narrative without considering the historical context and battle imagery at play here. Recall that where Jewish angelology is concerned, Michael is a powerful angel who leads God's army. Recall that in any battle, God can lead the angels or He can delegate that to an archangel such as Michael. So, this by no means deifies Michael by referring to the angels as "his," nor does it make him and Jesus to be one and the same.

Jewish and Christian theology and thought were prevalent that archangels can lead God's army into battle. Specifically, with respect to the battle imagery, this is no different from a king delegating one of his generals to lead his army into battle. This was a common practice in the biblical world. The army of the king being led by the king's general was called the general's army, despite the fact that the army was not existentially his. In Judges 4:7 and 15 Sisera was the general of Jabin's army, but the army that Sisera was leading into battle was considered to be Sisera's army. 2 Samuel 11:1 bears a striking similarity with what we see in Revelation 12. The text says, "In the spring of the year, the time when kings go out to battle, David sent Joab, and his servants with him, and all Israel. And they ravaged the Ammonites and besieged Rabbah. But David remained at Jerusalem." David, as king, was supposed to have led the army into battle but instead of personally going to this battle, he delegated that to Joab, his commander. As commander of David's army, the army can be said to be Joab's as much as it was David's. This was very common in Scripture and the Ancient Near East.

2 Kings 18:17 says, "And the king of Assyria sent the Tartan, the Rabsaris, and the Rabshakeh with a great army from Lachish to King Hezekiah at Jerusalem." Here, we see again a king sending out his general and other important commanders with his army into battle. This is all that Revelation 12:7-9 is conveying. The text is not suggesting nor proving that Michael the Archangel is Jesus at all. As a matter of fact, this battle ensued after Jesus ascended to heaven (vs. 5). It is very plausible to conclude that at His ascension to heaven, Jesus then delegated Michael and the angelic army of heaven to fight Satan and the rebellious angels and they threw them out. This may

very well be what Jesus was referring to when He said to the disciples, "I saw Satan fall like lightning from heaven" (Luke 10:18). This statement seems to suggest that King Jesus did not personally throw Satan out of heaven, but may have had His archangel Michael and his army throw Satan and his angels out and He merely "saw" or watched it happen. Again, kings often sit back and watch their generals and armies fight all the time. This seems to be the most plausible thing that is happening in Revelation 12:7-9, rather than it proving that Michael the Archangel is Jesus Christ.

Jude 9: Michael the Archangel, the body of Moses, and Jesus Christ

Jude is a little epistle that undoubtedly shows that Michael the Archangel and our Lord Jesus Christ are not one and the same person. In vs. 1 Jude calls himself "a servant of Jesus Christ" and refers to believers as those who are "kept for Jesus Christ." It is inconceivable that he would have said this about Michael the Archangel. As a matter of fact, no biblical nor Apostolic Father ever referred to themselves as "a servant of Michael the Archangel" nor have they ever intimated that they were "kept for Michael the Archangel."

In vs. 4 Jude refers to Jesus Christ as "our only Master and Lord," titles which have never been used in reference to Michael nor can ever be used. In vs. 5 Jude says, "Jesus, who saved a people out of the land of Egypt, afterward destroyed those who did not believe." This is very similar to what Paul said in 1 Corinthians 10:4-5, 9. Jesus was the Sovereign Lord who delivered Israel from Egypt and punished the unbelievers. In verse 17 Jude refers to the apostles as "apostles of our Lord Jesus Christ." Scripture never refers to the apostles as "the apostles of our Lord Michael the Archangel." In verse 21 Jude says, "Keep yourselves in the love of God, waiting for the mercy of our Lord Jesus Christ that leads to eternal life."

In his profound doxology, Jude closes his epistle by saying only God receives "glory, majesty, dominion, and authority, before all time and now and forever" through Jesus Christ our Lord (24-25). These are things that Scripture never says nor reveals about Michael the Archangel. These are things that would be blasphemous to ascribe to Michael the Archangel. From the very beginning of this epistle, Jude elevates Jesus and says things about Him that cannot be said about nor attributed to Michael the Archangel. Throughout his letter, Jude purposefully presents Michael the Archangel and Jesus Christ as two separate and distinct persons. He did not give a shred of evidence nor made a statement that would indicate that they are one and the same.

In verses 6-7, Jude referred to angels and the cities of Sodom and Gomorrah who had committed sexual immorality and were subsequently punished for it. Then in verses 8-10, Jude contrasted the respect that angels have for authority with the lack of respect that false teachers have, even to the point of them rejecting authority and blaspheming glorious ones (vs. 8), something the angels who are more powerful than those false teachers would not venture to do. Verse 9 drives this point home by referring to an incident between Michael the Archangel and Satan, who disputed about the body of Moses. The text says, "But when the archangel Michael, contending with the devil, was disputing about the body of Moses, he did not presume to pronounce a blasphemous judgment, but said, "The Lord rebuke you." This verse is presenting Michael as the archangel who had no authority to pronounce judgement on Satan nor to rebuke him when they tussled over the body of Moses. Michael had to defer the rebuking of Satan to God, who had the authority to rebuke Satan. Jude used this as an anecdote to drive home his point about the brazen character of the false teachers in contrast to the subservience, deference, and respect that angels display, despite being more powerful than those false teachers. This is exactly what he says in the following verse, "But these people blaspheme all that they do not understand…" (vs. 10). This section of the Book of Jude mirrors closely what Peter wrote in 2 Peter 2. Peter says:

> And especially those who indulge in the lust of defiling passion and despise authority. Bold and willful, they do not tremble as they blaspheme the glorious ones, [11]whereas angels, though greater in might and power, do not pronounce a blasphemous

judgment against them before the Lord. [12]But these, like irrational animals, creatures of instinct, born to be caught and destroyed, blaspheming about matters of which they are ignorant, will also be destroyed in their destruction (vs. 10-12).

Jude and Peter are describing the same things and themes. Both of them are contrasting the blasphemous, impudent character of false teachers with the deferring, respectful, and humble character of angels. The only difference we can observe is that Peter refers to angels in a general way, while Jude uses Michael the Archangel specifically as an illustration of what he is talking about. This anecdotal story Jude used about Michael cannot be with the intention of making Jesus Christ to be the same person as Michael the Archangel for two reasons.

Firstly, whereas Michael deferred to God to rebuke Satan, Jesus rebuked Satan by *His own authority* throughout His ministry. He directly rebuked Satan without ever deferring to God to do so. We read in Matthew 4:10, "Then Jesus said to him, "Be gone, Satan! For it is written, ""You shall worship the Lord your God and him only shall you serve."" In Matthew 16:23 Jesus said, "Get behind me, Satan! You are a hindrance to me. For you are not setting your mind on the things of God, but on the things of man."

Secondly, Jude used this story from the apocryphal work the *Assumption of Moses*, as was already discussed. The fact that Jude used this story from that source to illustrate his point shows that, as a Jewish Christian, he was very familiar with Judeo-Christian angelology. He was familiar with what the Old Testament and the non-canonical works had said about Michael the Archangel. In verse 14-15, Jude even quoted from the Book of Enoch,[232] which is

---

[232] Scholars generally agree that Jude is quoting 1 Enoch. Compare the two for yourself. Jude 14-15 say, "It was also about these that Enoch, the seventh from Adam, prophesied, saying, "Behold, the Lord comes with ten thousands of his holy ones, 15 to execute judgment on all and to convict all the ungodly of all their deeds of ungodliness that they have committed in such an ungodly way, and of all the harsh things that ungodly sinners have spoken against him." 1 Enoch 1:9 says, "Behold, he comes with the myriads of his holy ones, to execute judgment on all, and to destroy all the wicked, and to convict all flesh

another apocryphal work that had a lot to say about Michael the Archangel and other angels, as was already discussed. Being aware of such angelology, Jude would have never conceptualized Michael to have been Yahweh nor his older brother and Lord Jesus Christ. Never. Jude specifically presents Michael as an archangel with limited authority, who had to defer to God to rebuke Satan, and also as an angel who respects authority and would not presume to pronounce judgement on Satan.

Despite these glaring and stubborn facts, Adventists torture Jude 9 in efforts to make Michael and Jesus Christ to be one and the same person. They often argue that the presence of the definite article that modifies archangel in the Greek text (Μιχαὴλ ὁ ἀρχάγγελος- Michael the Archangel) means that Michael is *the only* archangel. But this argument is very flawed and shows much desperation on their part. The presence of the definite article here serves to indicate specificity (Michael *the* archangel), rather than singularity (Michael the [only] archangel). The definite article modifies a number of things in Scripture and in the Book of Jude, of which a multiplicity of them exist, but they are definitized to show specificity. I believe that if Jude intended to say that Michael was the only archangel, he would have modified archangel with ‘ο μονος (ho monos- the only) as he does with Jesus Christ in vs. 4 to indicate that He is "the *only* Master and Lord" (τὸν μόνον δεσπότην καὶ κύριον- ton monon despoten kai kurion). I will go further to state that even if Jude did say that Michael was the only archangel, that still would not have automatically made Michael and Jesus to be the same person for the many reasons already expressed throughout these chapters, and also for the fact that some kings had only one general or captain of their army. But the singularity of that general or captain does not make them one and the same as the king they served. Their argument for the presence of the definite article indicating singularity further collapses when we consider the fact that in 1 Thessalonians 4:16, there is no definite article, in the Greek, that modifies archangel. It is indefinite and means "an archangel," which automatically assumes

for all the wicked deeds that they have done, and the proud and hard words that wicked sinners spoke against him."

the existence of many archangels. I will elaborate more on this when I expound on that text.

Adventists try to equate Michael's statement in Jude 9 "The Lord rebuke you" with Zechariah 3:2's statement,[233] "The LORD rebuke you, O Satan! The LORD who has chosen Jerusalem rebuke you!" to mean that Michael is the same LORD (Yahweh) in Zechariah 3 who rebuked Satan, thus making Michael to be Jesus (Yahweh) of Jude 9 who is doing the same in another incident. As I indicated before, this is cringe-worthy torturing of Scripture to make it agree with Ellen White's statements and Adventist beliefs. The contexts and uses of both statements reveal that they are not being used in the same way nor by the same person. As was demonstrated, in Jude 9 Michael the Archangel deferred to God to rebuke Satan. Despite being a powerful angel, he did not want to presume to cast a slanderous judgement on Satan, who was a glorious and powerful angel, so he *calls on* the Lord to rebuke Satan. He deferred judging and rebuking Satan to God. The situation in Zechariah is entirely different. Rather than making Michael the Archangel and Yahweh equal, as Adventists do, it actually sets them apart both in person and in authority.

Zechariah 3 informs us that Joshua the high priest was standing before the angel of Yahweh and Satan standing at Joshua's right hand to accuse him (vs. 1). The reason that Satan was standing there to accuse Joshua was because he was clothed with filthy garments (vs. 3). The text then informs us that it was not the angel of Yahweh that rebuked Satan but *Yahweh Himself*! Verse 2 says, "And the LORD said to Satan, "The LORD rebuke you, O Satan! The LORD who has chosen Jerusalem rebuke you! Is not this a brand plucked from the fire?"" It was *Yahweh Himself* who rebuked Satan, not the angel of Yahweh that was standing by. Yahweh has all authority to rebuke Satan: He rebuked him by His own authority. He did not defer rebuking Satan to anyone else as Michael did in Jude 9. So, far from Zechariah 3 and Jude 9 proving that Michael the Archangel is

---

[233] Francis D. Nichol's comment on this says, ""The Lord rebuke thee." Compare Zech. 3:2, where the Lord rebukes the devil. There can be no stronger condemnation than being rebuked by the Lord."--- *The Seventh-day Adventist Bible Commentary: The Holy Bible With Exegetical and Expository Comment.*, Commentary Reference Series, p. 706.

Jesus Christ and Yahweh, they are actually proving the opposite when carefully analysed.

1 Thessalonians 4:16: Michael the Archangel and the Parousia

Adventists always couple John 5:25-29 with 1 Thessalonians 4:16 to say that Jesus' voice is what is going to raise the dead at the Second Coming and it is Michael the Archangel's voice that will raise the dead at the Parousia, therefore Michael and Jesus are one and the same person. Neufeld says, "According to 1 Thess. 4:16, the voice of the archangel is heard when Christ descends and the righteous dead are raised, whereas in John 5:25-29 it is the voice of Christ, the Son of God, that summons the dead."[234] This forced equation and comparison of these two passages is shoddy and purposefully done to uphold their erroneous view. John 5:25-29 is very clear that it is the voice of Jesus that will raise the dead at the Last Day. Those who have done good will be resurrected to life and those who have done evil to the resurrection of judgement.

Unlike John 5, 1 Thessalonians 4:16 is not saying that it is the voice of the archangel Michael that will raise the dead to the resurrection life nor to the one of judgement. The text does not use Michael's name at all nor is the mention of the archangel suggesting that it is the archangel that will resurrect people. The critical Greek phrase in that text is "ἐν κελεύσματι, ἐν φωνῇ ἀρχαγγέλου καὶ ἐν σάλπιγγι θεοῦ" and should literally be translated as "with a cry of command, with a voice of an archangel, and with a trumpet of God." The preposition εν (en) that is modifying the three dative nouns is the dative of instrumentality and means "with." It is expressing accompaniment. The three nouns that the preposition is modifying are indefinite and so is archangel, hence my literal translation of the phrase. The indefiniteness of these nouns mean that there is more than one cry of command, more than one voice, more than one archangel, and more than one trumpet of God. This text is very compelling that Michael is not the only archangel.

---

[234] Don F. Neufeld, *Seventh-day Adventist Encyclopedia*, Second revised edition, Commentary Reference Series, Michael the Archangel.

Additionally, the text is actually describing the kingly procession and pageantry with which Jesus will return with His retinue of angels and the souls of the saints ("...God will bring *with him* those who have fallen asleep"- vs. 14). The text is not saying that Jesus will *personally* give the shout of command, *personally* blow the trumpet, nor that His voice *is* an archangel's voice. The preposition εν that is used before "a cry of command, a voice of an archangel, and a trumpet of God" means that He will be *accompanied with* these things going *before* Him in royal procession. He is not personally doing those things. In the biblical world, kings and royalty were escorted by royal processions and pageantry, and accompanied with much fanfare (2 Sam. 6; 1 Kings 8; Psa. 47:5-7; Psa. 68:25-27; Song of Sol. 3:6-11; John 12:12-19). It was customary that a herald would go before the king with either a shout to announce the arrival of the king or with the blowing of a trumpet (Psa. 47:5). This is why John was a herald that went before Jesus at His first coming, shouting and preparing the way for Him as he announced His arrival (Mark 1:2-3). Jesus' first coming was announced by a herald (John the Baptist). His triumphal entry into Jerusalem was with a procession (John 12:12-19). His Second Coming will be with pageantry and a procession. That is what 1 Thessalonians 4:16 is revealing with the "cry of command, with a voice of an archangel, and with a trumpet of God." He will not come alone the second time. He will "...descend from heaven with a cry of command, with a voice of an archangel, and with [a sound of] a trumpet of God" (author's translation). Our great King Jesus will descend in royal procession.

Several places in Scripture present Jesus' Parousia as something that will be accompanied with the retinue of angels in royal procession and pageantry. Matthew 24:30-31 says:

> Then will appear in heaven the sign of the Son of Man, and then all the tribes of the earth will mourn, and they will see the Son of Man coming on the clouds of heaven with power and great glory. [31]And he will send out his angels with a loud trumpet call, and they will gather his elect from the four winds, from one end of heaven to the other.

2 Thessalonians 1:7 says, "…when the Lord Jesus is revealed from heaven with his mighty angels." Jude 14 affirms, "It was also about these that Enoch, the seventh from Adam, prophesied, saying, "Behold, the Lord comes with ten thousands of his holy ones."

Another major flaw in the Adventist interpretation of 1 Thessalonians 4:16 is that they assume that it is the archangel's voice that will raise the dead at Jesus' Second Coming. This is a complete misreading of the text and eisegesis of the worst sort. The text does not say that it is the archangel's voice that will raise the dead. The text simply says, "And the dead in Christ will rise first." This is simply an affirmative statement—the dead in Christ will be resurrected first. The text does not say, "And the voice of the archangel Michael will raise the dead in Christ first." But unfortunately this is how Adventists subconsciously read this text. There is nothing in the passage, contextually and exegetically, that Adventists can point to that clearly shows that it is the voice of the archangel that will raise the dead in Christ at the Parousia. Absolutely nothing. What can be shown from the text is that at the Parousia there will be much fanfare and noise, and *subsequent to that* the dead in Christ will be resurrected and the living saints will be translated and raptured together with the resurrected saints to be with Christ (vs. 16-17). This is what we can exegete from the text. It cannot be shown from the text that it is the cry of command, the voice of an archangel, nor the trumpet of God that resurrects the dead in Christ. The text simply affirms that the dead will be resurrected but does not contextually say who or what will do the resurrecting.

However, we know that it is Jesus Himself who will resurrect the dead from what He had said in John 5:25-29, but the text itself does not say so. With respect to "a voice of an archangel" in the text, the only thing that can be exegetically shown about it is that it is a part of the fanfare and procession that will accompany Jesus. All of the things that Adventists read into this text in attempts to make Michael the Archangel to be our Lord Jesus Christ are done out of desperation in order to squeeze their Arianistic, false Christology into Scripture. But as you read through this chapter and carefully consider the overwhelming amount of biblical and historical facts presented, you can see clearly that all of their theories, obfuscations, eisegesis, and assumptions are a perforated basket that cannot hold water. The facts scream vociferously, "Michael the Archangel *is not* our Lord and Saviour Jesus Christ!"

Chapter Thirteen

Dem Goats: Who Is Our Scapegoat: Satan Or Jesus?

"If Satan is their scapegoat then he atones for their sins. It is impossible to have it otherwise. As long as they continue to hold onto this heretical doctrine, Satan will be the one who atones for their sins."

Satan: The Adventist scapegoat and sin-bearer

One of the most heretical doctrines of the Seventh-day Adventist Church is the teaching that Satan is the scapegoat and sin-bearer of Leviticus 16. Like many other doctrines of Adventists, one will not find where Scripture teaches this, but Adventists have tortured Leviticus 16 and countless other proof-texts for decades to make Satan the scapegoat and sin-bearer because Ellen White opined that he is. Their best attempts only prove how heretical and anti-Gospel the teaching is. In *The Great Controversy* she said:

It was seen, also, that while the sin offering pointed to Christ as a sacrifice, and the high priest represented Christ as a mediator, the scapegoat typified Satan, the author of sin, upon whom the sins of the truly penitent will finally be placed. When the high priest, by virtue of the blood of the sin offering, removed the sins from the sanctuary, he placed them upon the scapegoat. When Christ, by virtue of His own blood, removes the sins of His people from the heavenly sanctuary at the close of His ministration, He will place them upon Satan, who, in the execution of the judgment, must bear the final penalty. The scapegoat was sent away into a land not inhabited, never to come again into the congregation of Israel. So will Satan be forever banished from the presence of God and His people, and he will be blotted from existence in the final destruction of sin and sinners.[235]

The teaching that Satan is the sin-bearer was a consistent teaching of Ellen White. She again asserted:

As the priest, in removing the sins from the sanctuary, confessed them upon the head of the scapegoat, so Christ will place all these sins upon Satan, the originator and instigator of sin. The scapegoat, bearing the sins of Israel, was sent away "unto a land not inhabited;" so Satan, bearing the guilt of all the sins which he has caused God's people to commit, will be for a thousand years confined to the earth, which will then be desolate, without inhabitant, and he will at last suffer the full penalty of sin in the fires that shall destroy all the wicked.[236]

Once more Ellen White stated:

When the times of refreshing shall come from the

---

[235] White, *The Great Controversy*, p. 422, par. 2.

[236] White, *The Faith I Live By*, p. 213, par. 4.

presence of the Lord, then the sins of the repentant soul who received the grace of Christ and has overcome through the blood of the Lamb, will be removed from the records of heaven, and will be placed upon Satan, the scapegoat, the originator of sin, and be remembered no more against him forever. The sins of the overcomers will be blotted out of the books of record, but their names will be retained on the book of life.[237]

These statements by Ellen White are unequivocally clear. For Adventists, Satan is their scapegoat and sin-bearer. This is official, standard SDA teaching. It is unique to them. They teach this from the university level to the Sabbath School level. *Seventh-day Adventists Believe* states, "A careful examination of Leviticus 16 reveals that Azazel represents Satan, not Christ, as some have thought."[238] They then used three arguments that they believe support their interpretation: 1) the scapegoat wasn't slain as a sacrifice and therefore it could not bring forgiveness (Heb. 9:22), 2) that the sanctuary was cleansed by the blood of the Lord's goat before the scapegoat was introduced to the ritual, and 3) that Leviticus 16 treats the scapegoat as a personal being who is in opposition to God.[239] These arguments by Adventists are very weak and show a great deal of desperation to make Satan the scapegoat in order to justify Ellen White's heretical statements. After all, they can't disagree with her nor disavow her teachings. Sadly, they must believe whatever she says and defend them at all cost. As we proceed in this chapter, you will see why these arguments are very weak, dishonest, and heretical.

Let me briefly highlight that the scapegoat's purpose in the ritual was not to forgive sin by its death, but to *remove sin* from the community. The removal of sin was an equally necessary aspect of the *one sin offering* that both goats made. The second point tried to make the introduction of the scapegoat an issue that should prove that it must be Satan, but this is classical sneakiness on their part. The

---

[237] White, *The Signs of the Times*, May 16, 1895, par. 4.

[238] *Seventh-day Adventists Believe*, p. 353.

[239] Ibid, p. 353.

scapegoat was a part of the ritual from the very beginning. God told Moses, "And he shall take from the congregation of the people of Israel two male goats for a sin offering...." (Lev. 16:5). The time in which the scapegoat carries out its function is irrelevant. The fact is the goats were a pair that made *one sin offering*. After the first goat fulfilled its role (dying), the second one would have fulfilled its own as well (bearing away sin). The role of one goat and when it fulfilled that role was not more important than the role of the other goat and when it fulfilled its role. They were literally two opposite, equal, and absolutely necessary sides of the same coin.

The last argument that suggested that the scapegoat was a personal being in opposition to Yahweh is totally unsound. The untenability of this position will be seen in full as we examine Leviticus 16. On page 406 of *Seventh-day Adventists Believe,* Adventists basically regurgitated what Ellen White said about Satan being the scapegoat and why sins will be placed on him:

> ...He [Jesus] will place the sins of His people upon Satan, the originator and instigator of evil. In no way can it be said that Satan atones for the sins of believers—Christ has fully done that. But Satan must bear the responsibility of all the sin he has caused those who are saved to commit.[240]

There is nothing in the Bible that says nor suggests that God will place sins on Satan because he instigated sin. The Bible does not teach that Satan will bear responsibility for sins that he caused saved people to commit. In this statement, Adventists try to deny that Satan atones for the sins of believers and affirm that it is Jesus who did that. But the fact is if Satan is their scapegoat, then he definitely is the one who atones for their sins, as that is precisely what the scapegoat was for, that is what it did. Leviticus 16:10 says, "But the goat on which the lot fell for Azazel shall be presented alive before the LORD to *make atonement* over it...." (Italics mine). One simply cannot separate the scapegoat from atonement. Both goats were necessary for the ritual to make *one atonement* for the people. This is

---

[240] Ibid, p. 406.

exactly what vs. 29-30 says regarding the Day of Atonement, "And it shall be a statute to you forever that in the seventh month, on the tenth day of the month, you shall afflict yourselves and shall do no work, either the native or the stranger who sojourns among you. *For on this day shall atonement be made for you to cleanse you.* You shall be clean before the LORD from all your sins" (italics mine).

In the 1st century A.D., the Jewish historian Flavius Josephus made a statement that revealed the common understanding of all Jews that the scapegoat was for atonement. He said, "And besides these, they bring two kids of the goats; the one of which is sent alive out of the limits of the camp into the wilderness for the scapegoat, and to be an expiation for the sins of the whole multitude."[241] The *Jewish Virtual Library* concurs with Josephus by saying, "According to the sages, the goat dispatched to Azazel as part of the Temple ritual on the Day of Atonement atones for all transgressions (Shev. 1:6)...."[242] It is an axiomatic fact in Scripture and all of Jewish history that the scapegoat made atonement for sin. Adventists know this and this is precisely why they try to separate the scapegoat from its atoning work because they have erroneously made Satan their scapegoat. They are not comfortable with Satan atoning for their sins, but at the same time they cannot renounce what Ellen White said about Satan being the scapegoat. So, they go out of their way to extract the atonement symbolism from the scapegoat, but unfortunately that is not possible. The scapegoat atoned. If Satan is their scapegoat then he atones for their sins. It is impossible to have it otherwise. As long as they continue to hold onto this heretical doctrine, Satan will be the one who atones for their sins.

A plain reading of Leviticus 16 will never support the notion that Satan is the scapegoat and ultimate sin-bearer. Absolutely nothing! Because of these statements of Ellen White and their attempts at making the earthly sanctuary to be a one-to-one equivalent with the heavenly sanctuary, Adventists have hunted for proof-texts and invented bad arguments that would make it appear that Satan is the

---

[241] Flavius Josephus, *Antiquities of the Jews*, Book 3, 10:3.

[242] Jewish Virtual Library, "Day of Atonement," https://www.jewishvirtuallibrary.org/day-of-atonement (Date accessed Feb. 25, 2021).

scapegoat to be an airtight conclusion. A favourite text of theirs that they inject this idea into is Revelation 20:1-3. This will be explored later. Much has been presented by Adventists scholars, pastors, and laymen alike in attempts to justify that Satan is the scapegoat. I have no intention in engaging every single one of their arguments and assumptions in this chapter. I will simply show biblically that it is impossible for Satan to be the scapegoat, and logically if he is, then he is a co-redeemer with Jesus. The main passage that teaches about the scapegoat is Leviticus 16:5-26, the yearly Day of Atonement.

The scapegoat had to be perfect, spotless, and without blemish

Before we get into Leviticus 16 itself and see what it reveals about the goats on the Day of Atonement, it needs to be understood from the outset that animals that were used in the sanctuary services for sacrifices and rituals were to be perfect, spotless, and without blemish. From this fact alone we can already see that the scapegoat can only typify Jesus and not Satan.

In Leviticus 1, God told Moses to instruct the Israelites that when they bring an offering to Him, it must be from their herds and flocks, and the offering must be "without blemish" (1:2-3). If it was a burnt sacrifice, it had to be a male goat or sheep without blemish (vs. 10). A peace offering could have been a female or a male animal, without blemish (3:1, 6). If a priest sinned, he had to bring "a young bullock without blemish" for his sin offering (4:3). If a ruler sinned, his sin offering was a kid goat without blemish (4:23). If a commoner sinned, his or her sin offering was a female goat without blemish (vs. 27-28). If the person brought a lamb instead of a goat, it had to be a female without blemish (vs. 32). If a person committed a trespass against the holy things of God, their trespass offering was "a ram without blemish" (5:15, 18; 6:6).

When the sacrificial services were being inaugurated, Aaron had to offer a young calf for a sin offering and a ram for a burnt offering for himself, both had to be without blemish (9:2). For the offerings for the people, he had to use a kid from the goats for a sin offering, a calf and a lamb for a burnt offering. Both of them had to be 1 year old and without blemish (9:3). For the cleansing ceremony of lepers, God instructed, "...he shall take two male lambs without blemish, and one ewe lamb a year old without blemish...." (14:10). Every animal offering or sacrifice that one will read about concerning the sanctuary system of the Old Covenant had to be "without blemish." God was specifically clear that any animal that was imperfect, had any defect, or deficiency in it should not be offered. It would be rejected. Leviticus 22:20-25 says:

> You shall not offer anything that has a blemish, for it will not be acceptable for you. [21]And when anyone offers a sacrifice of peace offerings to the LORD to fulfill a vow or as a freewill offering from the herd or from the flock, to be accepted it must be perfect; there shall be no blemish in it. [22]Animals blind or disabled or mutilated or having a discharge or an itch or scabs you shall not offer to the LORD or give them to the LORD as a food offering on the altar. [23]You may present a bull or a lamb that has a part too long or too short for a freewill offering, but for a vow offering it cannot be accepted. [24]Any animal that has its testicles bruised or crushed or torn or cut you shall not offer to the LORD; you shall not do it within your land, [25]neither shall you offer as the bread of your God any such animals gotten from a foreigner. Since there is a blemish in them, because of their mutilation, they will not be accepted for you.

What this reveals is that even before we deliberate on the Day of Atonement and the goats involved, we can already see the impossibility of Satan being the scapegoat. When the offerings for the Day of Atonement were listed, God specifically instructed, "...see that they are without blemish" (Numbers 29:8). God was keen and meticulous about the perfection of these animals involved in the sanctuary service because they pointed forward to His perfect, spotless sacrifice—His Son Jesus Christ. He is the spotless sacrifice that the sanctuary services pointed to (1 Pet. 1:18-19). If any of the offerings represented Satan, there would not have been the need and meticulousness for them to be "without blemish," as Satan is imperfect, defective, and sinful. Any defective, deformed, or lacerated goat could have been used if Satan would be represented in one of the goats for the sin offering. But this was not the case, the goats had to be perfect. Now that this foundational fact is established, let us examine Leviticus 16 and see how impossible it is for Satan to be the scapegoat and sin-bearer.

The Day of Atonement and dem goats

Leviticus 16:5 says, "And he shall take from the congregation of the people of Israel two male goats for a sin offering, and one ram for a burnt offering." What this text shows is that both goats were for *one sin offering*, while the ram was for a burnt offering. The two goats on the Day of Atonement were not two separate offerings. Both goats represented *one sin offering*. They represented both aspects of Christ's *one atonement* for sin. One goat died while the other "bore away" sin. Christ is the one who died: He is also the one who bears away sin. *The Woman's Study Bible* puts it beautifully, "Both the goat sacrificed and the scapegoat sent away were part of the sin offering. The goat sacrificed symbolized propitiation for sins, and the scapegoat pictured the complete removal of the sins for which atonement had been made."[243] Charles L. Feinberg offered several arguments why Satan cannot be the scapegoat. In one of those arguments he powerfully observed:

> Another cogent argument against this interpretation is that the goat can have nothing whatever to do with Satan, for the Scriptures state clearly that the live goat, equally with the sacrificial goat, was a sin offering to the Lord. The first goat set forth the means of reconciliation with God, whereas the second goat represented the effect of the sacrifice in removing the sins from the presence of the holy God, thus illustrating Psalm 103:12 and Micah 7:19 in a striking manner.[244]

---

[243] Thomas Nelson, *The Woman's Study Bible* (Nashville: Thomas Nelson, 1995), Lev. 16:11.

[244] Charles L. Feinberg, "The Scapegoat of Leviticus Sixteen," in *Bibliotheca Sacra: A Quarterly Published by Dallas Theological Seminary,* Vol. 115, Issue 460, 1958 (Dallas, TX: Dallas Theological Seminary, 1955–1995).

Injecting Satan in this text as the scapegoat who bore the sins of Israel is not only impossible but heretical. Both goats were to be presented "before the Lord" at the tabernacle (vs. 7). Lots were cast to determine the fate of each goat (vs. 8). Now, by the very fact that lots were cast to determine the fate of each goat, it obviously shows that both goats had to be perfect and spotless, and either goat could have equally died for sin or be the goat of departure to bear away sins. If one of these goats represents Satan, this logically means that Satan is perfect and spotless, and he could have equally died for our sins. This also means that Christ could have been the live goat to bear away sin and be separated from the covenant community, never to return also. The thought of Satan being able to die for sin is heretical, but that is the logical conclusion if indeed Satan is the scapegoat who bore away sin.

The passage continues, "And Aaron shall present the goat on which the lot fell for the LORD and use it as a sin offering, [10]but the goat on which the lot fell for Azazel shall be presented alive before the LORD to make atonement over it, that it may be sent away into the wilderness to Azazel" (vs. 9-10). Again, both goats made *one sin offering* for the people before the Lord but because of the limitations of a singular goat to both die and also to be sent away to bear away sin and thus make atonement, two goats were needed for this *one sin offering, one atonement*. The singularity of the sin offering cannot be stressed too much. This needs to be understood. In both dying and being sent away, the two goats represented the *one atonement* of Jesus Christ in both dying and bearing away our sins. There is nothing in this ritual that can be referring to Satan. All of the sacrificial and purification services and rituals of the Old Covenant sanctuary represented Christ (John 2:19-22; 5:39). Colossians 2:16-17 is clear that the festivals, new moons, and Sabbaths of the Old Covenant are shadows of what were to come, but the substance is Jesus Christ. The Day of Atonement was a festival (Lev. 23:2, 26-32). Every aspect of the Day of Atonement festival was a shadow that pointed to Jesus Christ as the substance. All of the Law prophesied of Christ, and not Christ *and* Satan. This text leaves no room for part of the Day of Atonement to have foreshadowed Christ and part to have foreshadowed Satan. It is Jesus Christ who died. He is also the one who bore away our sins. It is Christ who makes atonement for us, who cleanses us. Scripture never talks about Satan doing any of those things. This is a stubborn, egregious, and heretical doctrine Adventists refuse to let go of and let common biblical sense and good hermeneutics prevail because they dare not accept that Ellen White was wrong on this issue.

Because the text says one goat "for Azazel," Adventists think that this proves that Azazel was Satan himself who a goat was being sent to in order to appease him and thus make atonement for Israel.[245] But this is a horrendous conclusion. There are better explanations and conclusions than that. *The International Standard Bible Encyclopedia* aptly notes:

> Both goats, according to Leviticus 16:5, are to be regarded as a single sin-sacrifice, even should we interpret Azazel as demon or Satan, and we are accordingly not at all to understand that a sacrifice was brought to these beings. This too is made impossible by the whole tenor of the Old Testament in general, as of Leviticus 16 in particular, so that in 16:8 the two members introduced by the preposition [*le-*] would not at all be beings of exactly the same importance. Both goats, so to say, represent two sides of the same thing. The second is necessary to make clear what the first one, which has been slain, can no longer represent, namely, the removal of the sin, and accordingly has quite often aptly been called the hircus redivivus. But what is to be represented finds its expression in the ceremony described in 16:20f.[246]

---

[245] Some Jews during the Intertestamental Period did conceptualize that Azazel was a demon dwelling in the wilderness, which was understood to be the abode of sin, outside of the Holy Land. But they did not see the scapegoat as a ransom being paid to Azazel, but more so that Azazel was getting what belonged to him and that was sin. And in that symbolism, sin was being removed from the covenant community. For a justification of this view see Michael S. Heiser, *The Unseen Realm: Recovering the Supernatural Worldview of the Bible* (Bellingham, WA: Lexham Press, 2015), p. 176-178.

[246] James Orr, ed., *The International Standard Bible Encyclopedia: 1915 Edition*, (Albany, OR: Ages Software, 1999), Azazel.

The author went on to justify that "for Azazel" should best be translated as "removal," "sending away," "releasing" or "dismissal."[247] Therefore, "for Azazel" should be understood as "for removal," "for sending away," "for releasing," or "for dismissal," and not "for Satan." Adventists insisting that the scapegoat symbolizes Satan makes absolutely no sense because if the scapegoat is already Satan, how can it be "sent to Satan" ("for Azazel") to bear away sin? Satan (the scapegoat) being sent away to Satan to atone for sin is ludicrous and heretical on many levels. But this is the logical end of the Adventist belief.

Two animals, one sin offering

Adventists assume that because two goats were involved in the ceremony on the Day of Atonement then that proves that one represents Christ and the other Satan. But this is not true at all. Having two animals for *one sin offering* to represent different aspects of that *one offering* is not a foreign practice in Scripture.

In Leviticus 5:6-10, we read that an individual should bring "…a female from the flock, a lamb or a kid of the goats, for *a sin offering*. And the priest shall make atonement for him for his sin" (italics mine). But if the individual could not have afforded to bring either animal that was stipulated, he or she could have brought two doves or two pigeons (which were cheaper) for the same, single sin offering and atonement.

In Leviticus 14:1-7, we see another beautiful ritual involving two animals for *one offering* that is very similar to the two goats of the Day of Atonement. At the cleansing ceremony of a leper, two living birds were to be presented for his cleansing. One bird was to be killed and the blood drained out and collected, while the other (live) bird was to be dipped in the blood of the slain bird, and then released into the open field. This ritual is no different from the Day of Atonement regarding the involvement of two animals that suffered two different fates, but were for *one offering*. This leper cleansing ritual represented the cleansing of one individual. One bird died for his sin and cleansing, while the other was released in the open field

---

[247] Ibid, Azazel.

to bear away his sin. In comparison to the Day of Atonement, it is the same ritual, same symbolism, the same *singular offering* with both animals doing different things because of their limitations, but those different roles they played actually represented two aspects of *a single offering*. The Day of Atonement ritual was collective for the entire nation, while the two birds for the leper were for the individual. That is the only difference between the two rituals.

Jesus is our scapegoat and sin-bearer

In Leviticus 16:20-22, we again see a beautiful picture of our Lord Jesus Christ as our sin-bearer. And nothing there can remotely be about Satan. It reads:

> And when he has made an end of atoning for the Holy Place and the tent of meeting and the altar, he shall present the live goat. [21] And Aaron shall lay both his hands on the head of the live goat, and confess over it all the iniquities of the people of Israel, and all their transgressions, all their sins. And he shall put them on the head of the goat and send it away into the wilderness by the hand of a man who is in readiness. [22] The goat shall bear all their iniquities on itself to a remote area, and he shall let the goat go free in the wilderness.

Scripture is unanimously clear that it was on Jesus our sins were laid, not on Satan. Isaiah 53 echoes this work of Jesus beautifully. We read there:

> Yet He Himself bore our sicknesses, and He carried our pains; but we in turn regarded Him stricken, struck down by God, and afflicted. [5] But He was pierced because of our transgressions, crushed because of our iniquities; punishment for our peace was on Him, and we are healed by His wounds. [6] We all went astray like sheep; we all have turned to our own way; and the LORD has punished Him for the iniquity of us all (vs. 4-6-HCSB).

Verse 8 says, "He was taken away because of oppression and judgment; and who considered His fate? For He was cut off from the land of the living; He was struck because of my people's rebellion" (HCSB). The latter part of verse 12 says, "...yet He bore the sin of many and interceded for the rebels" (HCSB).

The New Testament says, to the point of overkill, that it is Jesus who bore our sins. When John the Baptist saw Jesus coming towards him he exclaimed, "Behold, the Lamb of God, who takes away the sin of the world!" (John 1:29). 1 Peter 2:24 says, "He himself bore our sins in his body on the tree, that we might die to sin and live to righteousness. By his wounds you have been healed." Scripture cannot be clearer than this. Jesus Christ is the one who bore away our sins in His body while He hung on the Cross. It was on Him our rebellions, wrongdoings, sins, and immoralities were laid. He is the one who makes atonement for us and reconciles us to God (Rom. 5:11), not Satan. He was the one who was separated from God for us, just as the live goat was separated from the covenant community on the Day of Atonement (Matt. 27:46; Heb. 13:12-13).

On the Day of Atonement, when the high priest laid his hands on the live goat and confessed the sins of the people on that goat, it became the people's sin. The sins of the people were transferred to it. When the goat was sent away into the wilderness, it symbolized the sins of the people being removed from them. That symbolized their cleansing from sin. The New Testament shows Jesus fulfilling all of these too. He is the one who became sin for us. 2 Corinthians 5:21 says, "For our sake he made him to be sin who knew no sin, so that in him we might become the righteousness of God." He is the one who cleanses us from sin. 1 John 1:7 says, "...the blood of Jesus his Son cleanses us from all sin." These biblical facts are extremely clear about who our scapegoat is. It is Jesus and not Satan.

Even without the plethora of these biblical facts proving that Jesus is the scapegoat, Satan is still automatically disqualified from being a candidate based on the very concept of what a scapegoat is. The concept of a scapegoat, as derived from Leviticus 16, is an innocent person that is blamed or punished for the wrongdoings, mistakes, and faults of others. By this very definition and concept Satan is automatically disqualified from being a scapegoat. He is not an innocent victim who either takes, or is blamed for, the wrongdoings of others. Satan is guilty, evil, and deserves every blame or punishment he gets. Every human being is automatically disqualified from being the scapegoat too, by this concept, because we all have sinned and fallen short of God's glory (Rom. 3:23). We are all guilty before God (Rom. 3:19); and we deserve death for our sins and wrongdoings (Rom. 6:23). The concept of a scapegoat can only be epitomized by one person and that is Jesus. He is the only Innocent Person qualified to take the blame or be punished for sins, faults, and wrongdoings of others. Irrespective of the angle from which we analyse the scapegoat doctrine, everything points to Jesus as the only suitable candidate. He is our scapegoat.

Does Revelation 20 prove that Satan is the scapegoat?

Seventh-day Adventists have one major proof-text upon which they try to establish their position in an effort to justify Ellen White's heresy that Satan is the scapegoat. That proof-text is Revelation 20:1-3, 7-10. Ellen White alluded to this passage in her statements that were quoted in the beginning of this chapter and Adventists, to this day, continue to latch onto this proof-text as justification for their "Satan is the scapegoat" teaching. But despite all of the contortions and torturing they have done to this text, it still does not and cannot prove their scapegoat doctrine. Verse 1-3 reads:

> Then I saw an angel coming down from heaven, holding in his hand the key to the bottomless pit and a great chain. ²And he seized the dragon, that ancient serpent, who is the devil and Satan, and bound him for a thousand years, ³and threw him into the pit, and shut it and sealed it over him, so that he might not deceive the nations any longer, until the thousand years were ended. After that he must be released for a little while.

The scapegoat in Leviticus 16 had to be "without blemish," lots were cast for it, it was to be presented "before the Lord" in front of the sanctuary, the high priest laid his hands on its head confessing the sins of the people on it, it bore the iniquities of the people, it was then led into the wilderness by a strong man, and he "let the goat go free in the wilderness" (Lev. 16:22). All of this happened in the context of the Day of Atonement where the goat made "atonement" for the people. Adventists must have serious reading comprehension problems to read Revelation 20:1-3 and compare it with Leviticus 16 and conclude that Revelation 20 proves that Satan is the scapegoat! There is nothing in Revelation 20 that remotely resembles what occurred with the scapegoat in Leviticus 16. Nothing in Revelation 20 suggests that Satan is "without blemish." Nothing shows that lots are being cast for him or that he is presented "before the Lord" in front of the sanctuary. Nothing in this passage suggests that our High Priest Jesus laid His hands on Satan's head and placed our sins on him. Nothing suggests that Satan bears our sins.

Whereas the scapegoat was led into the wilderness and released to wander, in this passage the opposite happens to Satan. He is bound and thrown into the bottomless pit, after which the pit is shut and sealed so that he cannot have freedom to deceive the nations during that time. And whereas the goat most likely did not return to the covenant community nor had access to anyone after being released into the wilderness, Satan will experience the opposite according to this passage. After the millennium "...he must be released for a little while" (vs. 3). How can anyone analyse these two scenarios and conclude that they are the same? It is flabbergasting what false doctrines can do to people. Now, I am not vying for an exact one-to-one equivalent for the scapegoat type and its antitypical fulfilment. That is not how the symbols and their reality are meant to be correlated nor understood. Nevertheless, the major aspects and basic concept of the scapegoat and what happened to it do not remotely resemble what we see happening to Satan here. But despite the vast differences between the scapegoat and Satan's imprisonment here, unfortunately Adventists see them as being one and the same. That is insane. That is Adventism.

The first section of the Adventist proof-text (Rev. 20:1-3) totally dismisses their view that Satan is the scapegoat. The second part annihilates every shred of hope they had left that it would vindicate their heresy. Verses 7-10 says:

> And when the thousand years are ended, Satan will be
> released from his prison [8]and will come out to deceive

the nations that are at the four corners of the earth, Gog and Magog, to gather them for battle; their number is like the sand of the sea. [9]And they marched up over the broad plain of the earth and surrounded the camp of the saints and the beloved city, but fire came down from heaven and consumed them, [10]and the devil who had deceived them was thrown into the lake of fire and sulfur where the beast and the false prophet were, and they will be tormented day and night forever and ever.

This paragraph is crystal clear that Satan is not the scapegoat and neither will he be annihilated after bearing sins as Ellen White vehemently asserted. The passage says that he will be loosed from his prison and, immediately after that, he will go out among the nations of the world to deceive them and gather them to battle against the saints in the beloved city (New Jerusalem). He and his vast host of deceived people will surround the city attempting to seize it, but fire will come down from heaven and engulf them. The text then informs us that the Devil was thrown alive into the lake of fire and "will be tormented day and night forever and ever." None of what is examined here resembles anything that we saw with the scapegoat in Leviticus 16. Nothing.

And whereas Ellen White stated that Satan and sinners will be annihilated, the passage says that Satan, the beast, and the false prophet will be "tormented day and night forever and ever." The single, major proof-text that Adventists resort to in efforts to justify Ellen White's heretical pronouncement that Satan is the scapegoat totally rubbishes their assumptions and arguments.

Just in case Adventists will reject all that I have presented here proving beyond a shadow of doubt that Jesus is our scapegoat and not Satan, I will let Ellen White herself tell them that Jesus is the scapegoat and not Satan.

Contradicting herself on dem goats and classic Adventist doublethink

True to what she does on countless other issues and teachings, Ellen

White contradicted herself on this issue as well. She said that Jesus is the scapegoat and not Satan. Ellen White was plagiarizing so much that she seemed to have not been able to keep track of what she had stolen or said before, and constantly contradicted herself. She stated:

> Some apply the solemn type, the scapegoat, to Satan. This is not correct. He cannot bear his own sins. At the choosing of Barabbas, Pilate washed his hands. He cannot be represented as the scapegoat. The awful cry, uttered with a hasty awful recklessness, by the Satan inspired multitude, swelling louder and louder, reaches up to the throne of God, His blood be upon us and upon our children. Christ was the scapegoat, which the type represents. He alone can be represented by the goat borne into the wilderness. He alone, over whom death had no power, was able to bear our sins.[248]

You are probably in shock just as I was when I initially became aware of this statement. But given what I have demonstrated over and over, it should not be surprising to you that she contradicted Scripture and herself so much.

In 2013, Associate Director of the Ellen G. White Estate Dr Alberto R. Timm sought to explain away this contradiction of Ellen White. After stating that she repeatedly identified Satan as the scapegoat and her overarching view, he said:

> Regardless of how this questionable passage became part of Manuscript 112, 1897, the statement should be viewed as exceptional. It does not provide a reason for anyone to fall into the dangerous fallacy of "generalization," by which one or a few exceptions are generalized as the overall rule. Ellen White's writings provide enough evidence that, up to the end of her life, she continued to identify Satan as the eschatological scapegoat.[249]

---

[248] White, *Manuscript 112*, 1897, "Before Pilate and Herod."

[249] Dr Alberto R. Timm, *The Scapegoat in the Writings of Ellen G. White*, October 2013,

No doubt, this statement is indeed exceptional, and Ellen White did continue to identify Satan as the scapegoat. What this exception does though is that it proves that she contradicted herself, like she did on so many other matters and occasions. Ellen White just could not keep track of all the things that she was plagiarizing from the writings of others. So, this argument that it is an exception and that she continued to contradict even this statement does not give her a pass nor does it vindicate her. Dr Timm continued by saying:

> Yet, we are left with some obvious questions: Did Ellen White herself write that unusual paragraph? How did it become part of one of her manuscripts? And when was it cut from the fuller manuscript? We know only that the shortened copy is what was on file when the collection of her unpublished writings was microfilmed for safekeeping in 1951. But no additional information has been found to help answer those questions. Therefore, any attempt to answer those questions remains in the speculative realm.[250]

Dr Timm did much mental gymnastics just to avoid the obvious—Ellen White contradicted herself about the scapegoat. I don't know why he tried to pretend to be surprised at this when he has access to a lot more damning information than this that shows how false and heretical she was. But of course, he will not and cannot publicly admit this nor divulge much. Ellen White has to be defended and protected at all costs. She must be made to always be right no matter how absurd her pronouncements are or how many times she contradicts herself and Scripture. You have seen the evidence repeatedly.

But the fact remains, whether or not Ellen White contradicted herself, irrespective of the question marks they attempt to put on this statement of hers, whether or not she kept on teaching that Satan is the scapegoat even after this statement, it makes no material difference. The

---

https://www.ministrymagazine.org/archive/2013/10/the-scapegoat-in-the-writings-of-ellen-g.-white1 (Date accessed Feb. 24, 2021).
[250] Ibid.

biblical facts and analyses I presented are solidly clear that Jesus is our scapegoat and sin-bearer. It is not Satan. Adventists holding onto both contradictory statements of Ellen White is a classic case of Orwellian Doublethink. In his classic novel and film *1984*, George Orwell explains doublethink:

> To know and not to know, to be conscious of complete truthfulness while telling carefully constructed lies, to hold simultaneously two opinions which cancelled out, knowing them to be contradictory and believing in both of them, to use logic against logic, to repudiate morality while laying claim to it, to believe that democracy was impossible and that the Party was the guardian of democracy, to forget whatever it was necessary to forget, then to draw it back into memory again at the moment when it was needed, and then promptly to forget it again: and above all, to apply the same process to the process itself. That was the ultimate subtlety: consciously to induce unconsciousness, and then, once again, to become unconscious of the act of hypnosis you had just performed. Even to understand the word 'doublethink' involved the use of doublethink.[251]

This perfectly explains the SDA mindset and approach to their doctrines that not only contradict Scripture, but also when Ellen White contradicts herself. This will continue to be shown throughout these volumes.

---

[251] George Orwell, *1984* (London: Penguin Publishing Group, 1949), p.32

Part V

Sinless Perfectionism

Righteousness By Works

Perfecting the Flesh

Never Good Enough

False Hope

Chapter Fourteen

Will The Sinlessly Perfect Seventh-day Adventist Please Stand Up!

"In her writings, Ellen White made it abundantly clear that it is necessary to achieve sinless perfectionism before Jesus returns. If Adventists do not become sinlessly perfect by then, they will be lost."

Sinless perfectionism is a requirement for salvation

For Seventh-day Adventists, salvation is a combination of faith in Jesus plus their works of law-keeping, specifically the Ten

276

Commandments. Ellen White said, "Obedience to the law of Ten Commandments is the condition of salvation. This is God's positive requirement."[252] Ellen White impinged the Ten Commandments as a requirement for salvation for Adventists and developed a system of sinless perfectionism. Adventists try to harmonize this teaching of hers with Scripture by constantly proof-texting the KJV's references to persons in the Old Testament who were said to be "perfect," such as Noah (Gen. 6:9), Job (Job 1:1), etc. But the Hebrew word *tamim* that is translated as "perfect" in the KJV, when used in reference to humans does not mean sinless perfection, nor sinlessness. When used in a moral sense, it simply meant that they were pious, blameless, upright, or lived with integrity. None of those biblical characters were sinlessly perfect or achieved sinless perfection in their lifetimes. Anyone who reads their stories can quickly see this. In some of their actions, personal statements, or the inspired commentary of the biblical authors the imperfections, sins, mistakes, and wretchedness of those biblical characters are very apparent. None of them ever had or achieved flesh sinless perfection.

Sinless perfectionism for Adventists is striving to keep the Law and other requirements that Ellen White has laid down to the point that they reach a state where they cease to sin, perfect the flesh, and are "fit" for heaven. In her writings, Ellen White made it abundantly clear that it is necessary to achieve sinless perfectionism before Jesus returns. If Adventists do not become sinlessly perfect by then, they will be lost. Where Ellen White is concerned, before one can be justified and in order for one to retain one's justified status one must be continually obedient. While she does not say "obedient to the law," that is what she means when her other statements are considered, especially the one I quoted above. She says:

> While God can be just, and yet justify the sinner through the merits of Christ, no man can cover his soul with the garments of Christ's righteousness while practicing known sins, or neglecting known duties. God requires the entire surrender of the heart, before justification can take place; and in order for man to retain justification,

---

[252] White, *Review and Herald*, May 3, 1898, par. 13.

there must be a continual obedience, through active, living faith that works by love and purifies the soul. . . .[253]

The latter part of this statement seems biblically accurate, but it is misleading because Ellen White already revealed that she has a faulty premise on justification. Justification and salvation for her is achieved by obeying the Ten Commandments. They are also retained by the same. She made that abundantly clear. In Ellen White's Christology, Jesus came into the world to live a sinless life in order that through His power, we too may live sinlessly perfect. She said, "He [Christ] came to this world and lived a sinless life, that in His power His people might also live lives of sinlessness."[254] She stated that if anyone thinks it is not possible to live sinlessly perfect, then that person is impugning God with "injustice and untruth." For Ellen White, this sinless perfection will be achieved via "exact obedience." She says:

> "If ye be willing and obedient, ye shall eat the good of the land; but if ye refuse and rebel, ye shall be devoured with the sword." These words are true. Exact obedience is required, and those who say it is not possible to live a perfect life throw upon God the imputation of injustice and untruth.[255]

In Ellen White's mind, we are on "probation" and the time we are given now is for the purpose of perfecting ourselves for usefulness in this life and to possibly earn salvation in the next life. She says, "The precious hours of probation are granted that you may remove every defect from your character, and this you should seek to do, not only that you may obtain the future life, but that you may be useful in this life."[256]

Ellen White pushed sinless perfectionism so hard that she left no room for anyone to have a single "spot or stain" upon their characters. In order for anyone to ever receive the "seal of God" (the

---

[253] White, *Selected Messages*, Vol. 1, p. 366.

[254] White, *Review and Herald*, April 1, 1902.

[255] White, *The Southern Review*, December 5, 1899, par. 13.

[256] White, *Counsels to Parents, Teachers, and Students*, p. 226, par. 1.

Sabbath) and be saved, one must remedy the defects in one's character and cleanse one's self from "every defilement." Ellen White firmly asserted, "Not one of us will ever receive the seal of God while our characters have one spot or stain upon them. It is left with us to remedy the defects in our characters, to cleanse the soul temple of every defilement."[257] She reiterated this viewpoint and made it clear that we can "never see our Lord in peace" if we are not sinlessly perfect. In order to see Christ (be saved at the Second Coming), one must bear the "perfect image of Christ." Ellen White said, "We can never see our Lord in peace, unless our souls are spotless. We must bear the perfect image of Christ."[258] Not only won't we be able to "see Jesus in peace" if we do not achieve sinlessness in this life, Ellen White stated that we cannot inherit heaven either: "We must reach perfection of character, or we can never inherit the kingdom of heaven."[259]

Sinless perfectionism is something that Ellen White says that Adventists must work very hard, throughout their lifetime, to attain. She says, "It will require much painstaking effort to reach God's standard of true manhood....Perfection of character is a lifelong work, unattainable by those who are not willing to strive for it in God's appointed way, by slow and toilsome steps."[260] According to Ellen White, perfection of character must be *earned step by step* as Adventists strive to receive eternal life. She said, "Much patience is required in the striving for that life which is to come. We may all strive for perfection of character, but all who come into possession of it will earn it step by step, by the cultivation of the virtues which God commends."[261]

As a matter of fact, Ellen White suggested that the reason that Jesus has not returned is because Adventists are not sinlessly perfect yet. In other words, the whole world suffers because of Adventists delaying the return of Christ. Adventists must work much harder to

[257] White, *Testimonies for the Church*, Vol. 5, p. 214.

[258] White, *Review and Herald*, May 30, 1882.

[259] White, *Review and Herald*, June 11, 1889, par. 8.

[260] White, *Testimony for the Church*, Vol. 5, p. 500.

[261] White, *Notebook Leaflets from the Elmshaven Library*, Vol. 1, p. 90, par. 4.

perfect themselves and end the delay. She intimates that Jesus is waiting for Adventists to have His character "perfectly reproduced" in them before He can come to claim them. She said:

> Christ is waiting with longing desire for the manifestation of Himself in His church. When the character of the Saviour shall be perfectly reproduced in His people, then He will come to claim His own. It is the privilege of every Christian, not only to look for, but to hasten, the coming of our Lord. Were all who profess His name bearing fruit to His glory, how quickly the whole world would be sown with the seed of the gospel! Quickly the last great harvest would be ripened, and Christ would come.[262]

This statement is constantly used by Adventist pastors and leaders to guilt-trip their members for delaying the Second Coming. They often lambaste them for not becoming sinlessly perfect quick enough and for not being engaged in enough evangelism, as Ellen White intimated. This false theology used to place much burden on me when I was an Adventist. And I, in turn, used to place a lot of burdens on the people.

Not only are Adventists to be sinlessly perfect and spread their message in order for Jesus to return, but they also need to achieve sinlessness in order to be able to stand before God "without a mediator" when Jesus ceases His intercession in heaven and will be on His way to redeem the saved from earth. She says:

> Those who are living upon the earth when the intercession of Christ shall cease in the sanctuary above are to stand in the sight of a holy God without a mediator. Their robes must be spotless, their characters must be purified from sin by the blood of sprinkling. Through the grace of God and their own diligent efforts, they must be conquerors in the battle with evil. While the investigative judgment is going forward in heaven, while the sins of penitent believers are being removed

---

[262] White, *Counsels to Parents, Teachers, and Students*, p. 324.

from the sanctuary, there is to be a special work of purification, of putting away sin, among God's people on earth.[263]

This statement used to strike much fear and trepidation in me when I was an Adventist. Phew! I am not alone. Many of my former Adventist friends testified the same about their experiences. Many Adventists continue to be crippled with fear at the thought of standing before God without a mediator. They will be on their own with their worked-up sinless perfectionism while Jesus will be on His way. She says, "When He leaves the sanctuary, darkness covers the inhabitants of the earth. In that fearful time the righteous must live in the sight of a holy God without an intercessor."[264] Fear, agony, doubt, anxiety, misery, and turmoil will hound Adventists during this time. Ellen White described this in great detail in *The Great Controversy* chapter 39, "The Time of Trouble."[265]

Adventists must take these statements and injunctions very seriously and do their best to perfect their characters because a single spot, stain, or defect on their part will forever debar them from heaven. Ellen White said:

> Those who do not control their passions cannot appreciate the atonement, or place a right value upon the worth of the soul. Salvation to them is not experienced nor understood. The gratification of their animal passions is to them the highest ambition of their lives. But nothing but purity and holiness will God accept. One spot, one wrinkle, one defect in the character, will debar them from Heaven, with all its glories and treasures, forever.[266]

Despite this deeply held belief of Adventists that causes so much fear and agony among them, Scripture does not support the notion

---

[263] White, *Review and Herald*, January 17, 1907, par. 4.

[264] White, *The Great Controversy*, p. 614, par. 1.

[265] Ibid, 613-634.

[266] White, *A Solemn Appeal*, p. 145, par. 1.

that believers will have to stand before God without Jesus' intercession when He is coming again. Scripture teaches quite the opposite—that He will never leave nor forsake us. In Matthew 28:20, after Jesus gave the disciples the Great Commission, He assured them by saying, "...And behold, I am with you always, to the end of the age." He promised to never leave the original disciples and the disciples that they would make of "all nations" (vs. 19). This certainly includes us today and every single believer up to the Second Coming. Whereas in Adventist theology there will come a time when Jesus' intercession will cease for us and we will have to stand before God without His intercession, Hebrews 7:25 is emphatic that, "...he always lives to make intercession for them [us]." There will never come a time when Jesus will cease interceding for believers or that we will have to stand before God without Him as our mediator. Ellen White's assertion to the contrary is wrong. Hebrews 13:5-6 assures us that Jesus will never leave us nor forsake. Never. He is always there to help us. It says, "Keep your life free from love of money, and be content with what you have, for he has said, "I will never leave you nor forsake you." [6]So we can confidently say, "The Lord is my helper; I will not fear; what can man do to me?"" All Christians can have assurance of Jesus' eternal intercession on their behalf. There will never come a time when we will be left on our own to wallow in fear, agony, and mental anguish as Ellen White said.

To be perfect or not to be perfect: Ellen White can't decide

One would expect that because Ellen White thumped sinless perfectionism so much that she would have been consistent. But just like many other things, Ellen White contradicted herself on this matter as well. The main reason that I bring up this aspect of her theology on sinless perfectionism is to reveal how contradictory and unreliable Ellen White is on biblical and theological matters. In contradiction to herself, she said:

> Our earthly life, however long, honored, or useful it may be, is but childhood, frail, imperfect, and undeveloped. Manhood, with its full, perfect, glorious development,

will come, when, freed from the taint of sin, we stand among the redeemed throng. Then we shall enjoy a life which measures with the life of God, and through everlasting ages we shall go on increasing in wisdom and knowledge.[267]

This is very significant. Adventists continue to live in cognitive dissonance on Ellen White matters and her glaring contradictions. I have been in conversations and debates with them where they argue for the veracity of both of these contradictions. They vie for sinless perfectionism in this life as necessary to be saved, as she demands over and over. They also hold to the fact that we will never be perfect in this life, irrespective of how long we may live, just as she says.

May 16, 1876, Ellen White wrote a letter to her husband James and made this confession:

> I wish that self should be hid in Jesus. I wish self to be crucified. I do not claim infallibility, or even perfection of Christian character. I am not free from mistakes and errors in my life. Had I followed my Saviour more closely, I should not have to mourn so much my unlikeness to His dear image.[268]

What this reveals is that throughout those years that Ellen White was demanding and writing about sinless perfectionism, she herself could not follow her own counsels and achieve it. Ellen White died July 16, 1915. About 3 months before her death she said:

> I do not say that I am perfect, but I am trying to be perfect. I do not expect others to be perfect; and if I could not associate with my brothers and sisters who are not perfect, I do not know what I should do. I try to treat the matter the best that I can, and am thankful that I have a spirit of uplifting and not a spirit of crushing down. Yes, I am going to make that appear

---

[267] White, *Signs of the Times*, June 9, 1881, par. 21.

[268] White, *Daughters of God*, p. 272, par. 6.

just as much as possible. No one is perfect. If one were perfect, he would be prepared for heaven. As long as we are not perfect, we have a work to do to get ready to be perfect. We have a mighty Saviour.[269]

What you are reading here is a lot of bald-face lying and hypocrisy on the part of Ellen White. She claimed that she did not expect others to be perfect, when in fact she had preached and demanded sinless perfection as a requirement for salvation throughout her life and prophetic career to the Seventh-day Adventist Church. She also said that she is not perfect but that she is trying to be. This is revealing how absurd this Adventist theology and Ellen White demands are. Ellen White demanded sinless perfectionism all her life and yet she herself never attained sinless perfection. This is daunting and dismal for Adventists. If the most revered and authoritative figure in their church did not and could not have attained sinless perfectionism, where does that leave the rest of them? If their venerated prophetess, whose rules and doctrines they must follow, did not achieve sinlessness, how can anyone who is lower than her in Adventist ranking ever achieve such? Adventist sinless perfectionism is like a dog chasing its own uncatchable tail. By Ellen White's own statements and standards, both herself and every Seventh-day Adventist are incapable of being saved and therefore stand condemned. (You have read the plethora of her statements in this chapter and see the logical conclusions.)

In another shocking, but not surprising statement, Ellen White stated that Adventists should "never indulge the thought that they are sinless"! She said:

> Those who are truly seeking to perfect Christian character will never indulge the thought that they are sinless. The more their minds dwell upon the character of Christ, and the nearer they approach to his divine image, the more clearly will they discern its spotless perfection, and the more deeply will they feel

---

[269] White, *Pacific Union Recorder*, April 29, 1915, par. 7-8.

their own weakness and defects. Those who claim to be without sin, give evidence that they are far from holy. It is because they have no true knowledge of Christ that they can look upon themselves as reflecting his image. The greater the distance between them and their Saviour, the more righteous they appear in their own eyes.[270]

She again said:

There are many, especially among those who profess holiness, who compare themselves to Christ, as though they were equal with him in perfection of character. This is blasphemy. Could they obtain a view of Christ's righteousness, they would have a sense of their own sinfulness and imperfection. There is not a case recorded in the Bible, of prophet or apostle claiming, as do the "holiness" people of today, to be without sin.[271]

And again:

We cannot say, "I am sinless," till this vile body is changed and fashioned like unto His glorious body. But if we constantly seek to follow Jesus, the blessed hope is ours of standing before the throne of God without spot or wrinkle, or any such thing; complete in Christ, robed in His righteousness and perfection.[272]

And again:

So long as Satan reigns, we shall have self to subdue, besetting sins to overcome; so long as life shall last, there will be no stopping place, no point which we can reach and say, "I have fully attained." Sanctification is the result of lifelong obedience. None of the apostles and prophets ever claimed to be without sin. Men who

---

[270] White, *The Spirit of Prophecy*, Vol. 4, p. 302, par. 1.

[271] White, *Review and Herald*, March 15, 1887 "In What Shall We Glory?"

[272] White, *Signs of the Times*, March 23, 1888.

have lived the nearest to God, men who would sacrifice life itself rather than knowingly commit a wrong act, men whom God has honored with divine light and power, have confessed the sinfulness of their nature.[273]

And this last one:

No other science is equal to that which develops in the life of the student the character of God. Those who become followers of Christ find that new motives of action are supplied, new thoughts arise, and new actions must result. But they can make advancement only through conflict; for there is an enemy who ever contends against them, presenting temptations to cause the soul to doubt and sin. There are hereditary and cultivated tendencies to evil that must be overcome. Appetite and passion must be brought under the control of the Holy Spirit. There is no end to the warfare this side of eternity. But while there are constant battles to fight, there are also precious victories to gain; and the triumph over self and sin is of more value than the mind can estimate.[274]

The underlying crux of all of these statements of Ellen White is that sinless perfection is not possible in this life. It is unattainable; despite the "precious victories" that may continually be won. She admits the sinfulness of human nature, irrespective of our relationship with God.

It was noteworthy that I highlighted these glaring contradictions of Ellen White on the matter and her confession because to this day, Adventists continue to preach and demand sinless perfectionism as Ellen White taught. One would have hoped that they took the latter position that we will never be perfect in this life, as she said, but that is not the view they hold nor what they teach. This teaching of Adventists has produced a lot of delusional fanaticism, puritanical frigidity, stifling judgmentalism, and rigid legalism among them. The Adventist historian Dr George R. Knight, having recalled his personal

---

[273] White, *Acts of the Apostles*, p. 560-561.

[274] White, *Counsels to Parents, Teachers, and Students* (1913), p. 20.

experience and some Adventist's nit-picking, legalistic practices to achieve sinless perfection, candidly confessed, "Some Seventh-day Adventists have gone in strange directions in their quest for character perfection."[275] The amount of this that I experienced, perpetuated, and continue to encounter from Adventists is beyond my ability to pen here. It is extremely disheartening.

Chapter Fifteen

A Refutation Of The Adventist Myth Of Sinless Perfectionism

"The flesh cannot be perfected and made sinless in this life. However, by continuing to walk in the Spirit we can minimize the

---

[275] George R. Knight, *I Used To Be Perfect: A Study of Sin and Salvation 2nd Edition* (Berrien Springs, MI: Andrews University Press, 2001), p. 90.

power and control of the flesh in our lives and coerce it to walk in holiness and Christ-likeness."

The flesh can't become sinless or perfected in this life

Contrary to Ellen White's garrulous rants about sinless perfectionism, the fact is we will never attain sinless perfection in this life, neither through Christ's empowerment nor through our diligent, rigorous efforts. Scripture does not teach sinless perfectionism as something that we will achieve in this life nor as something that we need to achieve in order to be saved at the Second Coming of Jesus. Our justification, perfection, and sinlessness are things that we have by virtue of being in Christ (Rom. 4:23-25; Col. 2:10; 3:1-4), and Him imputing His righteousness and perfection to us (Rom. 5:18-19). They are not things that our flesh can ever achieve. We read in Galatians 5:16-17, "But I say, walk by the Spirit, and you will not gratify the desires of the flesh. [17]For the desires of the flesh are against the Spirit, and the desires of the Spirit are against the flesh, for these are opposed to each other, to keep you from doing the things you want to do." The flesh and the Spirit are gridlocked in a tug-o-war. They are opposed to each other in every way and have mutually exclusive desires. The only way we can avoid gratifying the desires of the flesh is by consistently walking by the Spirit. But should we ever decide to not walk by the Spirit, the flesh will not take over to assist us in godliness, holy living, sanctification, nor perfection. Instead, it will take over to have us fulfill its immoral desires (vs. 19-21).

We are urged by the apostle Peter in 1 Peter 2:11, "Beloved, I urge you as sojourners and exiles to abstain from the passions of the flesh, which wage war against your soul." The tug-o-war that exists between the Spirit and the flesh is a lifetime war. In this war, the passions of the flesh are constantly warring against our souls (or spirits). This war between the Spirit and the flesh will persist until the day we die. The flesh cannot be perfected and made sinless. No amount of Ten Commandment keeping, Sabbath-keeping, dietary restrictions, dress reforms, tithing, evangelistic outreaches, church attendance, praying, fasting, or any other religious activity can perfect the flesh and make it sinless. The flesh will be the flesh—sinful, degenerate, depraved, evil, wicked, at variance with God, undesirous of holy things, and wretched. The flesh cannot ever be perfected in this life, however, it can be subdued to prevent it from controlling us and having us live in habitual, inveterate sin. The flesh can be tamed, subdued, and forced to walk in holiness and the direction of the Spirit, but it can never be changed and perfected. In 1 Corinthians 9:24-27 Paul said:

> Do you not know that in a race all the runners run, but only one receives the prize? So run that you may obtain it. [25]Every athlete exercises self-control in all things. They do it to receive a perishable wreath, but we an imperishable. [26]So I do not run aimlessly; I do not box as one beating the air. [27]But I discipline my body and keep it under control, lest after preaching to others I myself should be disqualified.

In Matthew 26:41 Jesus said, "Watch and pray that you may not enter into temptation. The spirit indeed is willing, but the flesh is weak." Although Jesus was talking about prayer here, nonetheless His statement reveals a poignant truth about the flesh. It is weak. In Romans 8:3, Paul says that the Law is "weakened by the flesh." This means that the Law is emptied of sanctifying, moralizing power because the flesh is weak and sinful. In the previous chapter, Paul had expressed how sin that dwells in the flesh capitalizes on the Law to deceive him and have him do what he does not want to do, while preventing him from doing the good things that he wants to do (7:7-25). This dilemma exists because the Law empowers sin. 1 Corinthians 15:56 says, "...the power of sin is the law." Sin, which resides in the flesh, is empowered by the Law. Therefore, no amount of Law-keeping on the part of Adventists or anyone else can ever perfect their flesh and make them sinless in this life.

The very thing they attempt to use the Law to do, perfect the flesh and avoid sinning, will be thwarted because sin and the flesh will use the Law to arouse and produce all sorts of sin and immorality in them. The Law cannot be tortured to do what it was never designed to do, perfect the flesh. If the Law can ever perfect their flesh and make them sinlessly perfect, then they would have no need for Jesus. Paul said it best in Gal. 2:21 "…if righteousness were through the Law, then Christ died for no purpose." If sinless perfection can be achieved through Law-keeping, then Jesus' death was in vain. If there is any chance that righteousness and sinlessness can be achieved by Law-keeping, we would only need to try extremely hard until we achieve them. Jesus' sacrifice would be totally irrelevant. This is what Paul is saying. But this can never happen. With respect to the flesh, the only thing that can be done with the Law is to die to it so that we can become alive to Christ and to righteousness. Paul made this consistently and abundantly clear in the books of Romans and Galatians.

Christians will never be sinlessly perfect before Jesus returns

In Romans 15:1-2, Paul exhorted, "We who are strong have an obligation to bear with the failings of the weak, and not to please ourselves. ²Let each of us please his neighbor for his good, to build him up." What this essentially means is that we will always have weak, but saved, brothers and sisters among us who will fall into sins. Their weaknesses do not negate their saved, justified status in Christ. They are saints. They are believers. They are sanctified in Jesus. Nevertheless, for many reasons, they will still have weaknesses that will occasionally get the best of them. They will fall into sin. Paul recognized this fact and said that it is the obligation of the stronger, spiritually mature ones to bear with the failings of the weak and to build them up.

In Galatians 6:1-2 Paul said, "Brothers, if anyone is caught in any transgression, you who are spiritual should restore him in a spirit of gentleness. Keep watch on yourself, lest you too be tempted. ²Bear one another's burdens, and so fulfill the law of Christ." This exhortation is similar to the previous one he gave in Romans 15. But this one adds a few elements that expand on the previous one. Paul recognized that among believers, there will be those who will be caught in sin. Therefore, he advised, again, that the spiritual and mature ones act in a gentle, loving way towards the fallen and restore them.

The second exhortation that Paul gives in this text is humbling and shows that no matter how "spiritual" and strong we may be, we are still susceptible to temptations and falling into sin. Paul says the "spiritual" are to be circumspect and cautious about their own selves lest they too be tempted, that is, be caught in a sin just as the weaker one had. If Paul had believed in sinless perfectionism, he would have hardly issued these injunctions in Romans 15:1-2 and Galatians 6:1-2. What we can see in these injunctions is that despite being strong and spiritual, believers are still susceptible to "failings," weaknesses, transgressions, temptations, and sins. This is so because the flesh cannot be perfected and become sinless, irrespective of how strong and spiritual we may be. The flesh will be the flesh. The way Paul advised that we alleviate each other's burdens and help in the struggle against the flesh is to "bear one another's burdens and so fulfil the law of Christ." We bear each other's burdens by being compassionate, sympathetic, encouraging, and spiritually nurturing. We are not to be quick to condemn and lambaste fellow believers when they fall. We should build them up, strengthen them, reassure them of God's love, and their forgiveness in Jesus Christ. This task the Body of Christ will continue to do until the day that Jesus comes. There will never come a time in this life when the Body of Christ will be sinlessly perfect, incapable of erring and making mistakes, and therefore will not need any compassion, sympathy, encouragement, counselling, strengthening, etc. There will never come a time when no one in the Body of Christ will ever fail, fall into sin, or experience weaknesses. Until Jesus comes, as long as we are in this flesh, the struggle between the Spirit and the flesh will continue. Occasionally, we will fall into sin and therefore need restoration, strengthening, and uplifting.

In 2 Corinthians 12:5-10, the great apostle Paul revealed that he had a weakness that latched onto him. He could not shake it off. He asked God three times to remove it from him, but God taught him that His grace was sufficient for him and that His power was made perfect in his weaknesses. Having come to this realization, Paul said that he gloried in his weakness because when he was weak, he was strengthened by God's grace, and Christ's power rested on him. He became settled in this conviction, "For the sake of Christ, then, I am content with weaknesses, insults, hardships, persecutions, and calamities. For when I am weak, then I am strong" (vs. 10). What Paul reveals about his experience is astounding and refutes Adventist sinless perfectionism. Paul was a mature apostle, deep in the spiritual, travelling around preaching the Gospel, making disciples, planting churches, writing Scripture, expounding on the mysteries of God, and yet he had weaknesses. He was not sinlessly perfect! By his statements, over and over, it is obvious that he did not expect to be sinlessly perfect in this life. Instead of vainly expecting to achieve sinless perfection and perfecting the flesh, as Adventists do, Paul learned to trust in God's grace and power to keep him in his weaknesses.

We should be mature, humble, and circumspect because we sin in many ways

The apostle James also made a profound statement that shows that we will never achieve sinless perfection. In chapter 3:1-2 he says, "Not many of you should become teachers, my brothers, for you know that we who teach will be judged with greater strictness. ²For we all stumble in many ways. And if anyone does not stumble in what he says, he is a mature man, able also to bridle his whole body." James says we should not enter the preaching and teaching ministry flippantly because we will be judged with greater strictness. Entering pastoral ministry should be done with much reflection, caution, and a deep sense of God's call on one's life because pastor-teachers are judged with more severity. The reason James gives for this admonition is because "we all stumble in many ways." The Greek word for "stumble" is πταιω (ptaio) and it means "to trip, to err, to make a mistake, or to sin." James speaks in the first person, as a pastor-teacher, and says that we stumble in many ways. He is admitting that he falls into sin in many ways. In various ways, we all sin, make mistakes, and will continue to sin in this life, irrespective of our position and ministerial calling in the Body of Christ. In short, as a pastor-teacher, James is admitting that he is not sinlessly perfect and it does not seem that he is expecting to ever become sinlessly perfect either. What he advised is that pastor-teachers should have grit, self-control, and strength of character because when they fall into sin, they will be judged with greater severity.

James is not normalizing flagrant and habitual sin for believers and pastors here. He is merely stating the fact that we will sin, what the responses will be when we sin, and the need for maturity in speech and bodily self-control. Ministers and believers are not expected to make a practice of sinning (1 John 3:6). We are expected to be mature in Christ. As we mature, we will be able to lessen our incidences of sin as we learn to subdue the flesh. Contrary to what Ellen White and Adventists say, we will never attain sinless perfection by keeping the Ten Commandments, the Law, the Sabbath, dietary restrictions, nor by any other rule they have confected. It is impossible. 1 John 1:8-10 is very emphatic on the issue, "If we say we have no sin, we deceive ourselves, and the truth is not in us. ⁹If we confess our sins, he is faithful and just to forgive us our sins and to cleanse us from all unrighteousness. ¹⁰If we say we have not sinned, we make him a liar, and his word is not in us." No one can ever claim to be sinlessly perfect or have achieved sinless perfection. This is what John is saying. To claim sinless perfection is self-deception and a revelation that one does not have the truth in one. To claim to have never sinned is to impugn God with falsehood and reveal that His word does not abide in one. The Adventist sinless perfection teaching is psychological, emotional, and spiritual abuse and it is squarely unbiblical and wrong.

Sinless perfection is not required for salvation

Just because we cannot and will never achieve sinless perfection in this life, it does not mean that we are not saved now and will not be saved at the Second Coming of Jesus Christ. Both immediate and eschatological salvation are not things that we can earn by our hard efforts and striving to be sinless. Salvation is a free gift we receive from God. It is not something that we can ever earn by our strenuous efforts and religious practices.

In spite of our inability to achieve character perfection, Scripture consistently affirms that believers are currently saved. Acts 2:47 says, "…And the Lord added to their number day by day those who were being saved." Ephesians 2:8-9 emphatically says, "For by grace you have been saved through faith. And this is not your own doing; it is the gift of God, [9]not a result of works, so that no one may boast." God does not need us to achieve sinlessness in order to save us. He has already saved us in Jesus in spite of our sinfulness. Salvation is a present reality which all true believers currently enjoy. 2 Timothy 1:9 similarly repeats that God "…saved us and called us to a holy calling, not because of our works but because of his own purpose and grace, which he gave us in Christ Jesus before the ages began." Titus 3:4-7 beautifully says:

> But when the goodness and loving kindness of God our Savior appeared, [5]he saved us, not because of works done by us in righteousness, but according to his own mercy, by the washing of regeneration and renewal of the Holy Spirit, [6]whom he poured out on us richly through Jesus Christ our Savior, [7]so that being justified by his grace we might become heirs according to the hope of eternal life.

We are justified and saved in Jesus Christ right now. Despite this, we will continue to wrestle with the flesh. The flesh cannot be perfected and made sinless in this life. However, by continuing to walk in the Spirit we can minimize the power and control of the flesh in our lives and coerce it to walk in holiness and Christlikeness. This is what Scripture teaches. It does not teach the Adventist doctrine of sinless perfectionism.

Part VI

The Adventist Health Message

Salvation by Diet

Vegetarianism

Levitical Dietary Laws

New Covenant Liberty

Chapter Sixteen

What Is The Adventist

Health Message All About?

"...if Seventh-day Adventist health habits and dietary restrictions were only for cultural, peculiar, and personal reasons there would be no problem with their focus and practices at all. But as will be discovered, because they do them for moral, salvational, and spiritually-superior reasons, therein lies the problems."

The foundation and theology
of the Adventist Health Message

Seventh-day Adventists place a lot of emphasis on health, specifically diet. Throughout the world, they are known for their health seminars, hospitals, clinics, and even the fact that their health consciousness and practices have landed one of their communities, Loma Linda, California, USA, in the category of "Blue Zone,"[276] where people live a few years longer than the general population. Because Adventists in Loma Linda, California, are among persons who live to be 7-10 years longer than the average population, Adventists all over the world use this as proof that everyone should adopt their vegan/ vegetarian diet to achieve longevity. But of course, every Seventh-day Adventist all over the world does not achieve this longevity that many Adventists in Loma Linda achieve. There are many factors that contribute to longevity than just a strict vegan or vegetarian diet. Some of these factors include moderate consumption of alcohol and pork, which Adventists are completely against and say shortens life. The Ikarians of Greece consume alcohol as a regular part of their diet. The Okinawans of Japan consume pork as a part of their diet. They are both members of Blue Zone communities, who live the longest.[277]

Adventists usually attempt to sell their "Health Message" with a misrepresentation of facts, gross exaggerations, and an air of

---

[276] Ruairi Robertson, PhD, *Why People in "Blue Zones" Live Longer Than the Rest of the World?*, August 29, 2017, https://www.healthline.com/nutrition/blue-zones (Date accessed Jan. 18, 2021).
[277] Ibid.

superiority should one adopt their diet. But the fact is, the Adventist diet does not guarantee what they promise nor does it prevent one from getting sick, dying of cancers and diseases, developing bodily malfunctions, etc. Adventists contract and die of these things just like the rest of the population. Some of the most ardent, strict, and fanatical Adventist vegan leaders, pastors, and members that I knew contracted cancers, and sometimes rare ones, and died prematurely. The average SDA lifespan worldwide is no higher than the general population. Every SDA community across the world is not a Loma Linda, California, where following strict regimes of overall health, such as eating a lot of whole foods, having access to high-tech medical technology, a close-knit social and spiritual community, regular regimental exercise, getting enough sleep, etc., has caused them to become a Blue Zone.

Having said this, what is the Adventist Health Message really all about? Is it that they merely want to be healthy and live longer, and therefore practice health habits and diets that better foster this? What are the main reasons that they adhere to some aspects of the Old Covenant dietary distinctions and restrictions? Why do they discourage the eating of even "clean" meats? Why don't they drink wine, alcohol, coffee, and caffeinated drinks? Exactly why do they place so much emphasis on diet? Is it merely for physical health or is there more to it? Are they really following the Bible's teaching on diet or are they following something else? These questions will all be sufficiently answered in this chapter. I must hasten to say that if Seventh-day Adventist health habits and dietary restrictions were only for cultural, peculiar, and personal reasons there would be no problem with their focus and practices at all. But as will be revealed, because they do them for moral, salvational, and spiritually-superior reasons, therein lies the problems. Those reasons put them in the pale of biblical error, teaching doctrines of demons (1 Tim. 4:1-5), and treading down on Christian liberty (Rom. 14).

Seventh-day Adventists torture Scripture in gruesome ways in attempts to make their "Health Message" and dietary restrictions seem biblically sound. But the fact is, they are not. Their Health Message and dietary restrictions are not grounded in Scripture contextually exegeted, but on the writings of Ellen White. Without getting into the many complexities involved in the development of their Health Message, Ellen White's plagiarism of medical doctors of her day, the quack health beliefs and practices of her time that she parroted, and how they torture biblical teachings on diet to make them fit with Ellen White's statements and beliefs, I will simply show what they truly believe about diet and why their theology of diet should be rejected. Ellen White has written extensively on health reform, medical missionary work, dietary issues, etc. It is not my aim in this chapter to survey all of that. My main intention here is to show the underlying assumptions, the crux, and unbiblical theology and beliefs that undergird the Adventist Health Message while undermining Christianity.

The multifaceted teachings of Ellen White on dietary issues are keenly followed by Seventh-day Adventists. They are enshrined in their official beliefs.[278] The refusal of Adventists to drink tea, coffee, and caffeinated drinks is not something that is grounded in Scripture. This is something that Ellen White counselled against and considered to be sin to consume. Ellen White said, "Tea and coffee drinking is a sin, an injurious indulgence, which, like other evils, injures the soul."[279] She stated again, "The only safe course is to touch not, taste not, handle not, tea, coffee, wines, tobacco, opium, and alcoholic drinks."[280] She repeated this statement in a different way in another book by saying, "In relation to tea, coffee, tobacco, and alcoholic drinks, the only safe course is to touch not, taste not, handle not."[281] From these statements, we can see clearly that in Adventist theology, foods are things that they believe can affect the soul or defile one spiritually. But Jesus made it clear that foods cannot defile one's soul nor affect one's morals (Mark 7:14-23).

It is also interesting to note further that Ellen White quote-mined Colossians 2:21 which says, "Do not handle, Do not taste, Do not

---

[278] See *Seventh-day Adventists Believe*, Fundamental Belief 22, "Christian Behavior," p. 311-323.

[279] White, *Counsels on Diets and Foods*, p. 425, par. 3.

[280] White, *Counsels for the Church*, p. 105, par. 6.

[281] White, *The Faith I Live By*, p. 231, par. 7.

touch" to enforce her prohibitions on tea, coffee, wines, and other things, whereas the Bible text is actually discouraging her practice of dictating the diet of others in telling them "Do not handle, Do not taste, Do not touch." In other words, Ellen White extracted the statement and converted it to do exactly what the statement is condemning! If this is not egregious butchering of Scripture and blatant disregard for its teaching and context, I don't know what is.

In her book *Counsels on Health*, Ellen White said, "A diet of flesh meat tends to develop animalism. A development of animalism lessens spirituality, rendering the mind incapable of understanding truth."[282] This statement is self-explanatory. Eating meat will animalize one. When one is animalized by meat-eating, one's spirituality will be lessened and that will make one's mind incapable of understanding truth. The reference to "truth" here is the teachings, interpretations, and doctrines of Adventism, that is what Ellen White means. It does not mean objective, Christian truths.

Eating meat by Adventist pastors is setting an "evil example," according to Ellen White. She says eating meat will animalize them and their children: "Let not any of our ministers set an evil example in the eating of flesh meat. Let them and their families live up to the light of health reform. Let not our ministers animalize their own nature and the nature of their children."[283] If this statement is true, then the priests and the entire nation of Israel were "animalized" and had "set an evil example" because they ate meat. Meat was an integral part of their staple diet, sacrificial services, and holy festivals. Ellen White's statement would also mean that Jesus, the apostles, and the New Testament saints were all "animalized" and "set an evil example" because they all ate meat regularly.

Where Ellen White is concerned, eating meat, butter, cheese, pastries, spiced foods, and condiments are signs of intemperance that will enfeeble one's intellect and make it impossible for one "to attain to Christian perfection," which is the false doctrine of sinless perfectionism that was already discussed and refuted. She said:

It is impossible for those who give the reins to

---

[282] White, *Counsels on Health*, p. 575, par. 4.
[283] White, *Counsels on Diet and Foods*, p. 399, par. 3.

appetite to attain to Christian perfection. The moral sensibilities of your children cannot be easily aroused, unless you are careful in the selection of their food. Many a mother sets a table that is a snare to her family. Flesh meats, butter, cheese, rich pastry, spiced foods, and condiments are freely partaken of by both old and young. These things do their work in deranging the stomach, exciting the nerves, and enfeebling the intellect.[284]

Ellen White seemed to have been on an all-out legalistic war against enjoyable foods. Just about every category of tasty, palatable foods and delicacies are denigrated by her, and their consumption discouraged. As one can see in the quote, even cheese and butter were not spared of her anti-ambrosial vitriol. She was even more stringent about cheese by saying, "Cheese should never be introduced into the stomach. Butter is less harmful when eaten on cold bread than when used in cooking; but, as a rule, it is better to dispense with it altogether. Cheese is still more objectionable; it is wholly unfit for food."[285]

The Bible does not condemn dairy products

Like many other things that were proven thus far, Scripture does not take the position that Ellen White teaches on these matters. She condemns and forbids the use of cheese and butter altogether, but Scripture never does that. Cheese and butter were actually staple foods in biblical times. When David's brothers were about to go to war with the Philistines, their father Jesse knew that they would have needed food so he sent David to take some food to them. Cheese was among the food items that he sent for them (1 Sam. 17:18-19). When King David was ousted by his son Absalom and was in hiding, along with his faithful entourage, some of his loyal friends brought him and the people food to eat. Cheese was among those items that were taken to them (2 Sam. 17:27-29). When Abraham was visited by the heavenly

---

[284] Ibid, p. 236, par. 2.
[285] Ibid, p. 368, par. 5.

300

messengers, among whom was God Himself, he prepared for them a meal which consisted of meat, cheese, and milk (Gen. 18:7-8). God Himself, along with the heavenly angels in human form, ate those articles of food. All of these items were condemned by Ellen White. One really has to wonder if she ever read these passages or what she assumed about God and these angelic messengers, given that she speaks ill of these food items.

Scripture has a very positive attitude towards cheese and dairy products (Prov. 27:27). Having an abundance of food supplies, including dairy products, was a sign and condition of God's blessings upon Israel for covenant faithfulness when they inherited the Land of Canaan (Deut. 6:3; 32:14). The prophet Isaiah prophesied that the Messiah Himself, Jesus Christ, would eat dairy products (Isa. 7:14-15). Scripture has a lot more to say about dairy products. It endorses their use for nutrition and sustenance. Scripture does not condemn their temperate use. But Ellen White forbids them completely.

It must be kept in mind that just because Scripture endorses the eating of those things, it does not mean that one must automatically consume them. One may decide to abstain from dairy products for allergy, sinus, and other personal or health reasons. That is perfectly fine. But when one disavows their use on moral, spiritual, and salvific grounds as Ellen White and Adventists do, that is where the problem lies. Scripture condemns such misguided views and dietary legalism.

The Adventist Health Message is salvation by diet

Not only does Ellen White place strict restrictions on eating meat, cheese, dairy products, pastries, drinking tea and coffee, caffeinated beverages, and alcoholic beverages, she also is very clear in her assessment that Adventists must be gradually reforming in dietary intake and practices as they anticipate Christ's Second Coming. Any Adventist who is not converted to Ellen White's "health reform" will be among those who will apostatize from Adventism and thus will not be saved. She said:

Greater reforms should be seen among the people who

claim to be looking for the soon appearing of Christ. Health reform is to do among our people a work which it has not yet done. There are those who ought to be awake to the danger of meat eating, who are still eating the flesh of animals, thus endangering the physical, mental, and spiritual health. Many who are now only half converted on the question of meat eating will go from God's people, to walk no more with them.[286]

If you ever wonder why Adventists are generally vegetarians, strict vegans, or why new converts to Adventism adopt vegetarianism rather quickly when they join the Adventist Church as they adjust to its culture, it is because vegetarianism is something that they all must strive towards in preparation for heaven and to be saved. If they do not give up meat and gradually become vegetarians, especially when they become aware via Ellen White's writings that they must do so, they will become apostates and salvation will not be possible for them. Ellen White said, "Among those who are waiting for the coming of the Lord meat eating will eventually be done away; flesh will cease to form a part of their diet. We should ever keep this end in view and endeavour to work steadily toward it."[287]

Ellen White made it absolutely clear that Adventists must discard meats, adopt her form of vegetarianism as they seek to become "pure, refined, and holy" that they "may have the companionship of heavenly angels." She states:

> Is it not time that all should aim to dispense with flesh foods? How can those who are seeking to become pure, refined, and holy, that they may have the companionship of heavenly angels, continue to use as food anything that has so harmful an effect on soul and body? How can they take the life of God's creatures that they may consume the flesh as a luxury? Let them, rather, return

---

[286] White, *Review and Herald*, May 27, 1902, par. 2.
[287] White, *Last Day Events*, p. 81, par. 5.

to the wholesome and delicious food given to man in the beginning.[288]

The general accusations that Adventists like to throw at me is that I am taking these statements out of context or that I am just incapable of understanding them. Dear reader, the contexts of these statements are clear and were properly perused before I used the relevant sections to reveal what SDAs believe and teach about diet. With respect to my intellectual capability and perspicacity, if you have read this book this far, you have read enough to be able to accurately determine my acumen. These statements are clear, direct, and understandable by anyone who is capable of reading them.

I have read the majority of Ellen White's works on dietary matters, health reform, counsels, etc. I can assure you that I am not taking any of these statements out of context in efforts to misrepresent Ellen White and Adventist teachings. These quotes are saying exactly what they say. Any of her books cited by me can be checked over and over and one will see that this is exactly what she said and meant. There is no other way of interpreting and understanding her statements. If my testimony and expositions of them is still not sufficient to explain what they are truly saying, then I urge you to watch or read any Adventist evangelist, leader, pastor, medical missionary, or layperson's teachings on these issues, whether official or unofficial, and you will quickly see that they have the same understanding of them that I am explaining here. Do a quick internet or YouTube search and this will be readily apparent.

What I have presented so far from Ellen White is unequivocally lucid that Adventist dietary issues are considered spiritual, moral, and salvational. If one is still unconvinced that they are, or think that I am misinterpreting them, allow me to let Ellen White herself to tell us that they are salvational. She said:

> The light God has given on health reform [diet issues] is for our salvation and the salvation of the world. . . . [ellipsis in original] The Lord has been sending us

---

[288] White, *Child Guidance*, p. 383, par. 1.

line upon line, and if we reject these principles, we are not rejecting the messenger who teaches them, but the One who has given us the principles. Reform, continual reform, must be kept before the people, and by our example we must enforce our teaching.[289]

Ellen White could not be more clear and forthright regarding how she conceptualized and understood her "health reform" (dietary restrictions and injunctions). She says that they are for the salvation of Adventists ("our salvation") and for the salvation of the entire world.

The Adventist Health Message is "another gospel"

She again asserts that it is the "right arm" of the third angel's message, which, as was already discussed, is essentially their gospel, and this gospel is to be preached to everyone. She says:

> The medical missionary work[290] is as the right arm to the third angel's message which must be proclaimed to a fallen world; and physicians, managers, and workers in any line, in acting faithfully their part, are doing the work of the message. Thus the sound of the truth will go forth to every nation and kindred and tongue and people.[291]

---

[289] White, *Testimonies for the Church*, Vol. 9, p. 112-113.

[290] Medical Missionaries in Adventism are usually naturopaths who have dedicated themselves to spreading the Advent Message by using medical means and dietary education. Ellen White advised that persons should be trained to be medical missionaries because they can use that as an "entering wedge" to gain people's confidence, remove prejudice, etc., in the medical services they provide to them. When the prejudices have been removed, Adventists can eventually teach them and win them over to the Advent Message. She says, "I can see in the Lord's providence that the medical missionary work is to be a great entering wedge, whereby the diseased soul may be reached. Medical missionary work is the pioneer work of the gospel, the door through which the truth for this time is to find entrance to many homes. . . . [ellipsis in original] A demonstration of the principles of health reform will do much toward removing prejudice against our evangelical work. The Great Physician, the originator of medical missionary work, will bless all who thus seek to impart the truth for this time."— White, *Evangelism*, p. 513, par. 4-5.

Ellen White considered her health and dietary restrictions and injunctions to be a gospel. She calls it "the gospel of health" that should be linked with the ministry of the word. She says, "The principles of health reform are found in the word of God. The gospel of health is to be firmly linked with the ministry of the word. It is the Lord's design that the restoring influence of health reform shall be a part of the last great effort to proclaim the gospel message."[292] She again asserts that this "gospel of health" is a "ray of light God has given" that Adventists should practice, be blessed by it, and then anxiously present it to people who do not know it. She states:

> The time has come when each soul must be staunch and true to every ray of light God has given, and begin in earnest to give this gospel of health to the people. We shall have strength and power to do this if we practice these truths in our own lives. If we all followed the light we have received, the blessing of God would rest on us, and we should be anxious to place these truths before those who know them not.[293]

What was presented should leave no doubt in your mind why Adventists place so much emphasis on diet and health, and what are the underlying motivations and theology behind it. Their emphasis on health, dietary rules, and practices are for moral, spiritual, and salvational reasons. They believe that their salvation and the salvation of the world is hinged on it. As a matter of fact, Adventists constantly proof-text Isaiah 66:17 and 1 Corinthians 3:17 to support their belief that God will destroy believers at the Second Coming of Jesus for eating pork, unclean foods, and shellfish, and for drinking wine and alcohol, tea, coffee, caffeinated drinks, etc., but He will save them for abstaining from these things and for becoming vegetarians.

Additionally, Adventists reject the plain reading of all the pivotal

---

[291] White, *Testimonies for the Church*, Vol. 6, p. 229.

[292] White, *Medical Missionary*, p. 259.

[293] White, *Review and Herald*, November 12, 1901, par. 15.

New Testament passages that abolish the Old Covenant dietary restrictions and reinterpret them in ways that uphold their belief that the dietary rules are mandatory and salvational. Ellen White, several times, called their Health Message "the gospel of health." She was adamant that rejecting it tantamounts to rejecting God Himself: "God gave the light on health reform, and those who rejected it rejected God."[294] This is literally another gospel. Scripture is very clear that any other gospel that distorts the Gospel of Jesus Christ, or that is preached other than the Gospel of Christ should be accursed. Paul said:

> I am astonished that you are so quickly deserting him who called you in the grace of Christ and are turning to a different gospel—[7]not that there is another one, but there are some who trouble you and want to distort the gospel of Christ. [8]But even if we or an angel from heaven should preach to you a gospel contrary to the one we preached to you, let him be accursed. [9]As we have said before, so now I say again: If anyone is preaching to you a gospel contrary to the one you received, let him be accursed (Gal. 1:6-9).

The Adventist Health Message is "another gospel" that opposes the Gospel of Jesus Christ and Christian dietary liberty. It is a false gospel that should be rejected by every Bible-reading, Bible-believing Christian.

---

[294] White, *General Conference Bulletin*, April 6, 1903, par. 24.

Chapter Seventeen

A Biblical Survey Of The Levitical Dietary Laws And Refutations Of The Adventist Assumptions And Arguments

"Defilement is internally generated and not externally induced."

The diet of humans before sin and after the Flood

After God created the world and gave humans dominion over everything, Genesis 1:29 says, "And God said, "Behold, I have given you every plant yielding seed that is on the face of all the earth, and every tree with seed in its fruit. You shall have them for food." Plants that yielded seed were given to man as food. Concerning the animals, the following verse says, ""And to every beast of the earth and to every bird of the heavens and to everything that creeps on the earth, everything that has the breath of life, I have given every green plant for food." And it was so." After Adam and Eve sinned, the ground was cursed. The human pair would painfully and laboriously eat from it. We read in Genesis 3:17-19:

> And to Adam he said, "Because you have listened to the voice of your wife and have eaten of the tree of which I commanded you, 'You shall not eat of it,' cursed is the ground because of you; in pain you shall eat of it all the days of your life; [18] thorns and thistles it shall bring forth for you; and you shall eat the plants of the field. [19] By the sweat of your face you shall eat bread, till you return to the ground, for out of it you were taken; for you are dust, and to dust you shall return."

After the Flood, God told Noah, "Every moving thing that lives shall be food for you. And as I gave you the green plants, I give you everything. [4]But you shall not eat flesh with its life, that is, its blood" (Gen. 9:3-4). God gave Noah permission to eat "every moving thing" (animals). They were to ensure that they did not eat the flesh of the animals with blood. This seems to be saying that they should not eat raw meat containing blood. Because Genesis 7:2 says that Noah had to take 7 pairs of clean animals and birds but only 2 pairs of unclean animals and birds, Adventists maintain that only the clean animals God gave Noah permission to eat in Genesis 9 and not the unclean ones.[295] They further argue that had Noah eaten any of the unclean animals, whether the male or the female, then that species would not have existed today because it would not have been able to reproduce. But these assumptions and arguments are not grounded in what Scripture says.

The Bible does not tell us that the reason that God told Noah to take 7 pairs of clean animals into the Ark was for dietary purposes. The main purpose that Scripture gives for the instruction on how many animals to take into the Ark was "to keep their offspring alive on the face of all the earth" (7:3b). After the flood waters subsided and Noah exited the Ark, Genesis 8:20 says, "Then Noah built an altar to the LORD and took some of every clean animal and some of every clean bird and offered burnt offerings on the altar." Noah sacrificed some of every clean animal and bird to the LORD. This may be another reason that more unclean animals were taken into the Ark than unclean ones.

The argument that Noah could not have eaten any unclean animal because that species would have become extinct is not grounded in the biblical narrative. In their haste to prop up their assumptions and arguments, Adventists completely gloss over and misunderstand what the text says. When we look at the text carefully, we will realize that there were more than one pair of unclean birds and animals taken into the Ark. When one examines the text, the clean animals were to be taken by sevens making them 14 in total, and the unclean were to be taken by twos making them 4 in total. The translators of the LXX even recognized this and translated the Hebrew into Greek as ἑπτὰ ἑπτὰ ἄρσεν καὶ θῆλυ (hepta hepta arsen

---

[295] *Seventh-day Adventists Believe*, p. 318, par. 5.

kai thelu- "seven seven male and female"- seven males and seven females) in reference to the clean animals. They also translate the reference to the unclean ones as δύο δύο ἄρσεν καὶ θῆλυ (duo duo arsen kai thelu- "two two male and female"- two males and two females).

Regarding the birds, 7 pairs of every one of them were to be taken into the Ark, irrespective of its clean or unclean designation (7:3). That would make 14 unclean birds, the same number as the clean birds, for every species. Even if we reject this interpretation, we would still be left with more than two unclean birds. We would still have them in pairs of two (4 in total) as we have the unclean animals, because in reference to them the LXX also reads δυο δυο αρσεν και θηλυ (duo duo arsen kai thelu- "two two male and female"- two males and two females). Whether we prefer the reading of seven pairs or two pairs, we still end up with much more unclean birds than Adventists grant us. So, to argue that an unclean species would become extinct if one was eaten is not a good argument. That is not grounded in the facts. If one animal was eaten, at least three more would still be available to procreate.

A plausible reason for which much less unclean animals were taken into the Ark may be because many unclean animals have a shorter gestational period and also bigger litters when they reproduce. But either way we look at it, Noah was told to eat "every moving thing" in the animal world without exception. Of course, wisdom, preference, and bodily reactions to certain animals would determine what he ate and what he didn't. From this point on, Noah and his family had full liberty to eat any animal. And the peoples that descended from his sons to populate the earth ate anything thereafter, as the historical diets of nations, tribal groups, and peoples inform us.

The context and purpose of the Levitical dietary laws

Leviticus 11 and Deuteronomy 14:3-21 are the major Bible passages that discuss diet in the Old Testament. But the dietary instructions and laws we read in them were not for "all humanity" but for the nation of Israel, exclusively. This section is a part of the "holiness code" that God gave to Israel. And one of the main purposes of the holiness code was to separate Israel from the rest of the nations around them. They were to be distinguished even by their diets. After God gave them the dietary instructions, He specifically told them the reason He had done so. We read in Leviticus 11:44-45, "For I am the LORD your God. Consecrate yourselves therefore, and be holy, for I am holy. You shall not defile yourselves with any swarming thing that crawls on the ground. 45 For I am the LORD who brought you up out of the land of Egypt to be your God. You shall therefore be holy, for I am holy." God had separated Israel to be "holy" because He Himself is holy. The holiness of God is existential. The holiness of Israel was conferred and observable, to demonstrate their separateness in culture, lifestyles, worship, ethics, practices, and diet (Lev. 20:22-26).

Among the land animals, Israelites could have eaten whatever parted the hoof, is cloven-footed, and chewed the cud (Lev. 11:3). Animals that met only one or two of these criteria could not be eaten. These included pigs, camels, rock badgers, and hares (vs. 4-8). These animals were "unclean" to the Israelites. They were not to touch their carcasses nor eat their meat. Sea and river creatures had to have fins and scales to be clean for the Israelites. Anything that did not meet both criteria was to be regarded as "detestable" (vs. 9-12). Birds to be considered unclean were specifically named. We read in vs. 13-19:

> And these you shall detest among the birds; they shall not be eaten; they are detestable: the eagle, the bearded vulture, the black vulture, 14the kite, the falcon of any kind, 15every raven of any kind, 16the ostrich, the nighthawk, the sea gull, the hawk of any kind, 17the little owl, the cormorant, the short-eared owl, 18the barn owl, the tawny owl, the carrion vulture, 19the stork, the heron of any kind, the hoopoe, and the bat.

With the exception of the locust family, the bald locust family, the cricket family, and the grasshopper family, every other family of winged insects were unclean to them (vs. 20-23). All four-footed, pawed animals were unclean to them (vs. 27). Among the terrestrial swarming animals, they could not eat mole rats, mice, great lizards, geckos, lizards, sand lizards, and chameleons. The carcasses of these animals made the person who touched them unclean. Their carcasses also made unclean any "article of wood or a garment or a skin or a sack, any article that is used for any purpose" that they fell on or touched (vs. 29-32). Their carcasses defiled earthenware, foods and drinks, potable water, ovens, and stoves (vs. 33-35). Earthenware vessels, ovens, and stoves were to be broken. But their carcasses did not defile cisterns and springs of water (vs. 36). Reptiles were unclean to them. Verse 42 says, "Whatever goes on its belly, and whatever goes on all fours, or whatever has many feet, any swarming thing that swarms on the ground, you shall not eat, for they are detestable."

Adventists are defiant in incessantly arguing that these laws are "health laws" and timeless. Some of them go so far as to argue that these animals are "non-food" foods. But the reality is that these laws have nothing to do with health, as a primary focus and reason for being given. These laws were purely for ceremonial, separating purposes. I already proved that unclean does not mean "unhealthy or unfit for human consumption" as they argue, so there is no need to repeat that here.

When one observes what is said about defilement by these animals as well as the rituals performed, one can see clearly that the laws were not about health. The carcasses of unclean animals did not make the Israelites "unhealthy." Instead, it made them "unclean until the evening." We read, "And by these you shall become unclean. Whoever touches their carcass shall be unclean until the evening, [25]and whoever carries any part of their carcass shall wash his clothes and be unclean until the evening" (vs. 24-25). Being "unclean until the evening" meant that unclean Israelites were to be separated from the "clean" covenant community for the entire day, then at sunset they could have returned, taken a ritual bath, and then returned to the community. This ritual could have been repeated every day. If these food rules were about health, the remedy that God gave to restore their health and participation in the covenant community would have been patently absurd. There is no way one can become "healthy" after eating "unhealthy" animals by simply being separated from people for several hours, and then taking a bath after sunset. No way. Were this true, we would have had the automatic cure to every diet-related disease, disorder, and disability. The ritual was purely ceremonial.

Additional proof that these food laws were purely ceremonial is the fact that even clean animals that the Israelites could have eaten could have made them unclean. We read in vs. 39-40, "And if any animal which you may eat dies, whoever touches its carcass shall be unclean until the evening, [40]and whoever eats of its carcass shall wash his clothes and be unclean until the evening. And whoever carries the carcass shall wash his clothes and be unclean until the evening." What is further telling about this rule is that clean animals that died naturally could have made an Israelite unclean and they should not have eaten it, but they could have given that same animal to Gentiles living among them to eat or they could have sold the animal to not suffer loss. Deuteronomy 14:21 says, "You shall not eat anything that has died naturally. You may give it to the sojourner who is within your towns, that he may eat it, or you may sell it to a foreigner. For you are a people holy to the LORD your God...." If this rule was about the health of the Israelite, the negative implications on God's character would have been astronomical for instructing Israelites to give or sell the dead animal to Gentiles living among them to eat it. But on the contrary, this rule reveals what I have been showing thus far, that these dietary distinctions and rules were purely ceremonial. They applied only to the Israelites as a means of separating them from the nations around them. These dietary rules are not about morality and health, and neither were they universal laws and principles to be followed by every nation.

The Israelites ate unclean foods under certain conditions

Despite the fact that the Israelites were not permitted to eat certain animals, under certain conditions, they still ate them, such as in times of apostasy, rebellion, and famine. In 1 Samuel 14:24 King Saul had made a rash vow by placing a curse on anyone who would eat any food before he was avenged on his Philistine enemies. Because of this, the soldiers were starving all day and were faint (vs. 28). After Saul's son, Jonathan, persuaded them against the oath, the narrative says, "The people pounced on the spoil and took sheep and oxen and calves and slaughtered them on the ground. And the people ate them with the blood" (vs. 32). This was a violation of the Noahide Law (Gen. 9:4) and the Mosaic Law that forbade the eating of blood (Deut. 12:23). When Saul became aware of this though, he did correct it and urged them to slaughter the animals and prepare them properly for consumption (1 Sam. 14:33-34).

2 Kings 6 records a great famine in Samaria that was caused by the Syrian siege (vs. 24). The famine was great "until a donkey's head was sold for eighty shekels of silver, and the fourth part of a kab of dove's dung for five shekels of silver" (vs. 25). Donkeys were unclean animals for the Israelites. Dove's faeces were definitely unclean as well. But because they were in dire straits and starving, they were forced to eat whatever they could get their hands on. The famine was so gruelling and the starvation excruciating that persons were even eating their children (vs. 28-29). Interestingly, God had told them that famines, sieges by their enemies, and eating their children and objectionable things would come upon them for their covenant violations (Deut. 28:52-58).

Isaiah 65:1-7 describes the nation of Israel in rebellion and apostasy against God. They were stubborn, provoking God with their idolatries, involved in occult practices, eating "pig's flesh, and broth of tainted meat is in their vessels" (vs. 4). Isaiah presents the eating of pork and other unclean creatures as part of Israel's idolatrous and occult practices. They specifically went to gardens and graves at night to do this (vs. 3-4). Chapter 66:17 reiterates, "Those who sanctify and purify themselves to go into the gardens, following one in the midst, eating pig's flesh and the abomination and mice, shall come to an end together, declares the LORD." Despite their immoral and rebellious state, they were still thinking that they were more righteous and holier than others (65:5). These acts irritated God, so He promised to punish them (65:6-7), although He would not destroy every one of them (vs. 8).

Chapter 66 continues with the same trajectory. God will come to judge and destroy the disobedient and rebellious ones in Israel (vs. 15-17, 24), but He will spare the righteous ones and restore proper, continuous worship (vs. 18-23). Adventists love to use these two passages as proof-texts to prove that God will destroy Christians for eating pork and unclean foods over laws they themselves claim were ceremonial and thus done away at the Cross. But that is shoddy proof-texting on their part. These passages are about the nation of

Israel under the Old Covenant, who were forbidden to eat those things. In these passages, not only were they eating these unclean creatures but they were also eating them as part of occult rites and worship. Because these practices violated the covenant stipulations, God threatened to judge and punish them (which did happen on a number of occasions). These passages are not talking about believers under the New Covenant.

As we proceed, we will see clearly that the New Testament abolished these clean and unclean dietary distinctions and restrictions. Additionally, we will never observe in Scripture where God judged, punished or destroyed Gentile nations for eating unclean creatures, despite the fact that they ate those things indiscriminately. Gentile nations were not under the Levitical dietary rules and restrictions, and therefore they were never judged nor punished by God over those issues.

The New Testament abolishes the
Old Testament dietary distinctions

Jesus declared all foods clean

Mark 7:14-23 is a passage that undergoes a great amount of distortion by Adventists because it causes their entire salvational Health Message to crumble. The context of this section starts with vs. 1 where the Pharisees and Scribes took issue with Jesus because His disciples were eating with unwashed hands. The Pharisees and Scribes performed elaborate washings before they ate (vs. 3-4). When they saw Jesus' disciples not following their tradition they asked Him, "Why do your disciples not walk according to the tradition of the elders, but eat with defiled hands?" (vs. 5). Jesus responded to them with a rebuke revealing how they were worshiping God in vain by setting aside God's commandments in order to keep their own traditions, the traditions of men (vs. 6-8). He gave an example of how they were doing this by diverting offspring's personal responsibility to honor their parents by taking care of them, instead the Pharisees took such needed support and declared them to be Korban, dedicated to God's service (vs. 9-13). In doing this, they rejected the Word of God and made it void.

314

Jesus springboarded from this to teach the people that nothing they physically ate can defile them. Verses 14-15 say, "And he called the people to him again and said to them, 'Hear me, all of you, and understand: ¹⁵There is nothing outside a person that by going into him can defile him, but the things that come out of a person are what defile him.'" This statement by Jesus was revolutionary. It singlehandedly dismantled the entire dietary ceremonies of the Old Covenant. As was seen already, countless animals and improper food preparations could have defiled an Israelite. But now Jesus overthrows that and says "nothing outside a person that by going into him can defile him." His disciples completely missed the thrust of what He said, like they usually did with many other things, so when they were secluded in the house with Him they asked Him to explain what He meant (vs. 17). His response in vs. 18-19 was even more forthright than the previous statement. He said, ""Then are you also without understanding? Do you not see that whatever goes into a person from outside cannot defile him, ¹⁹since it enters not his heart but his stomach, and is expelled?" (Thus he declared all foods clean.)"" Jesus was adamant and straightforward that nothing a person eats can defile them. What is eaten is digested then expelled. That process cannot produce defilement. It cannot affect the morals of individuals.

Even clearer in this text is Mark's parenthetical commentary about Jesus' statement. Jesus did not say "all foods are clean," rather it was Mark who was inspired by the Holy Spirit to say that this is what Jesus meant by His statement. R. T. France noted:

> The syntax clearly marks out καθαρίζων πάντα τὰ βρώματα as a parenthetical editorial comment, since there is no masculine singular subject within the reported speech to which it can relate (hence the emendations found in some MSS, representing attempts to 'correct' the syntax by those who failed to recognize the nature of the clause....) The subject therefore is Jesus (the subject of λέγει, v. 18a), whom Mark thus interprets as 'cleansing all food' in the sense of declaring that it is no longer to be regarded as ritually 'unclean'.[296]

315

After this statement, Jesus proceeded to explain that it is the things that come out of a person that defiles them or makes them unclean. These things are moral, ethical issues, not dietary. We read in vs. 20-23:

> And he said, "What comes out of a person is what defiles him. ²¹For from within, out of the heart of man, come evil thoughts, sexual immorality, theft, murder, adultery, ²²coveting, wickedness, deceit, sensuality, envy, slander, pride, foolishness. ²³All these evil things come from within, and they defile a person."

Despite the clarity of this paragraph, the *Seventh-day Adventist Bible Commentary*²⁹⁷ and all their other literature that I have read on this, including my personal interactions with many of them, have resorted to endless obfuscations to deny the thrust of this paragraph. All their fruitless contortions of the text land us back at the same conclusion—Jesus declared all foods clean. There are several things in the text that prove this.

Although the contention began with the issue of hand washing, Jesus widened it to include any external thing that is ingestible. In vs. 15, He said "nothing" (Gk. οὐδέν [ouden]- "not one thing, not even one [thing]") externally that one ingests can "defile" one. The Greek word οὐδέν is an all-inclusive adjective that is being used as a negation here. It literally means nothing at all that one eats can defile one, irrespective of what that thing is. Of course this does not mean that we should eat everything because it won't defile us. We should not eat everything because some things are poisonous, toxic, deadly, and indigestible. So of course wisdom, dietary needs, and health professionals and organizations, cultural norms and expectations will advise that we do not literally eat everything that exists. God has given us a sound mind, common sense, and self-control to navigate through life. Nevertheless, even if one ingests toxic, poisonous, and deadly things they *still will not defile* one. They still will not affect

---

²⁹⁶ R. T. France, *The Gospel of Mark: A Commentary on the Greek Text* (Grand Rapids, MI: Eerdmans, 2002), p. 291.

²⁹⁷ Francis D. Nichol, *The Seventh-day Adventist Bible Commentary: The Holy Bible With Exegetical and Expository Comment.*, Commentary Reference Series, p. 625.

one's morals nor spirit. This is what Jesus is saying. This includes all of the previously unclean foods under the Old Covenant that Adventists argue still render believers defiled or unclean, and which will jeopardize our salvation.

In vs. 18-19, Jesus said "…whatever goes into a person from outside cannot defile him, since it enters not his heart but his stomach, and is expelled?" The Greek word πας (pas) that is translated as "whatever" is an all-inclusive adjective and means "anything, everything, and all." The unclean foods of Leviticus 11 and Deuteronomy 14 are included in this all-inclusive "whatever." Jesus' conclusion is that they cannot defile a person because they do not enter into his heart but the stomach, and is expelled. In other words, you are not what you eat. What you eat cannot affect your morals: they cannot transmogrify you. Anything that one eats goes through the digestive tract and is eliminated. It does not get into one's soul and determine or affect one's moral behaviour.

Lastly, in vs. 20-23 Jesus was very clear that defilement comes from within a person. Defilement is internally generated and not externally induced. Conclusively, even if we throw out Mark's parenthetical interpretation and commentary in vs. 19, we are still left with the same conclusion, and that is Jesus declared all foods clean. No food that one ingests can defile one.

"Rise, Peter; Kill and Eat"

Another major passage in the New Testament that refutes the Adventist Health Message is Acts 10. In that passage we ascertain that Cornelius was a Gentile God-fearer, along with his family and friends, who heard the Gospel from the apostle Peter and was saved. This was very significant because, as a Jew, Peter did not come into contact with Gentiles nor was he preaching the Gospel to them. God broke down this barrier by means of a vision of a great sheet from heaven let down to earth containing many unclean animals, reptiles, and birds, and instructed Peter to eat them. We read in vs. 13-15, "And there came a voice to him: "Rise, Peter; kill and eat." [14]But Peter said, "By no means, Lord; for I have never eaten anything that is common or unclean." [15]And the voice came to him again a second time, "What God has made clean, do not call common." Both the

317

instructions and conclusion are clear. God was instructing Peter to eat unclean animals. Peter declined, but God let him know that He had cleansed everything and Peter ought not to call them common nor unclean.

Adventists attempt to have a field day with this passage by means of verse 28, which says, "And he said to them, "You yourselves know how unlawful it is for a Jew to associate with or to visit anyone of another nation, but God has shown me that I should not call any person common or unclean."" They argue that this passage has absolutely nothing to do with food because it is about Cornelius and his Gentile associates. They argue that Peter ought not to call humans "common or unclean," and that the Levitical dietary distinctions are still in force. But this assumptive conclusion is wrong when we consider the facts. I have given this section a proper linguistic and contextual treatment in my first book, so I will not be doing that here.[298] What I will prove though is that when we consider the historical facts, we will see that God had abolished the dietary distinctions and He is informing Peter of that.

Jews considered Gentiles to be dogs and unclean beasts

The question that must be asked is, why did God use unclean animals, reptiles, and birds to represent Gentiles? The answer is simply this: Jews had considered Gentiles to be those unclean creatures because Gentiles indiscriminately ate them. Eating those creatures made Gentiles unclean. Because they ate them continuously, where a Jew was concerned, they were permanently "common or unclean." In Peter's 1st century Jewish culture, Gentiles were dogs and unclean creatures. Even Jesus was in sync with this cultural norm. In His dialogue with the Syrophoenician woman, He obliquely referred to her as a "dog." She accepted that designation and exhibited great faith which resulted in her daughter's healing (Mark 7:24-30). The culture and Jewish Talmud were absolutely clear about how they saw Gentiles. In Baba Mezia 114b we read,

---

[298] Elce-Junior "Thunder" Lauriston, *All Foods are Clean and Every Day is the Sabbath: A Response to Dr Samuele Bacchiocchi and Seventh-day Adventism on Romans 14* (Camp Verde, AZ: LAM Publications, LLC, 2017), p. 49-51.

"The 'goyim' are not humans. They are beasts." Tosapoth, Jebamoth 94b says, "If you eat with a 'goy'[299] it is the same as eating with a dog." Sanhedrin 74b says, "Sexual intercourse between the 'goyim' is like intercourse between animals." Yebamoth 98a is forthright, "All children of the 'goyim' are animals." This is the reason why Jews did not associate with Gentiles nor eat with them. They were perpetually unclean. They were animals to the Jews. All Gentiles living among the Jews would know this. Peter even said to Cornelius that he should know that this is the case when he said, "You yourselves know how unlawful it is for a Jew to associate with or to visit anyone of another nation…" (vs. 28).

The vision that God gave to Peter refers to the unclean foods of Leviticus 11 that were forbidden to be eaten by Jews, but they were permissible for Gentiles to eat. The diet distinctions of Jews and Gentiles created a great chasm between them and their relations. God removed the dietary distinctions ("what God has cleansed"), therefore Gentiles were no longer to be considered "unclean" because of what they eat. Given that now their food is no longer considered "unclean," they themselves are no longer "common or unclean," and to continuously be shunned by Jewish Christians. They were now "clean" brothers with whom Jewish Christians can associate and eat with, without being contaminated. This is what Acts 10 means. Peter understood this and that is why he was able to stay with Cornelius, in his house, for "some days" (vs. 48). For the very first time, Peter clearly understood Jesus' instructions and applied them. Jesus had told them:

> Whatever house you enter, first say, 'Peace be to this house!' [6]And if a son of peace is there, your peace will rest upon him. But if not, it will return to you. [7]And remain in the same house, eating and drinking what they provide, for the laborer deserves his wages. Do not go from house to house. [8]Whenever you enter a town and they receive you, eat what is set before you (Luke 10:5-8).

---

[299] The words "goy" and "goyim" in these statements mean "a Gentile" and "Gentiles." These were Jewish terms for non-Jewish nations and peoples.

Peter did this. This is why, from this point on, he was able to eat with all Gentiles (Gal. 2:11-14).

Upon his return to Jerusalem, the Jewish Christians had heard what he had done and were criticizing him for it. We read in Acts 11:2-3, "So when Peter went up to Jerusalem, the circumcision party criticized him, saying, "You went to uncircumcised men and ate with them.""" Peter then proceeded to defend his actions on account of what God had revealed to him—that Gentiles were no longer unclean; that they ought not to be shunned because of their diets, and that he himself as a Jew can now eat what they eat (vs. 4-17). After hearing this, the response of the Jewish Christians was phenomenal and in step with God's new order. Verse 18 says, "When they heard these things they fell silent. And they glorified God, saying, "Then to the Gentiles also God has granted repentance that leads to life.""" Acts 10 completely demolishes the Adventist Health Message and their continuous advocacy of the Levitical food distinctions for Christians today.

Gentiles do not have to keep the dietary laws to be saved

Acts 15 is a central passage in the New Testament regarding Gentile Christians and their relation to the Mosaic Law. The Jewish Christians were adamant that in order for Gentiles to be saved, they had to be circumcised and keep the Law. They said, "Unless you are circumcised according to the custom of Moses, you cannot be saved" (vs. 1). Recall that circumcision was the entry sign into the Old Covenant. Before one could have kept the Law and become a part of Judaism, one had to be circumcised. Circumcision was so important and non-negotiable for Jews that it eventually represented the entire covenant. When the Jewish Christians attempted to make this requirement for Gentiles, Paul and Barnabas had a contentious debate with them that could only be settled by the Jerusalem Council (vs. 3). When the Council was convened, the believers from among the Pharisees stood their ground saying, "It is necessary to circumcise them and to order them to keep the Law of Moses" (vs. 5). After some deliberations by the apostles, the conclusion was that Gentiles had received the Holy Spirit in the same way that the Jewish Christians did, by faith (vs. 8), they will be saved by grace through Jesus Christ as well (vs. 11), and therefore they did not have to be circumcised nor needed to keep the Law in order to be saved. Gentiles did not have to become Jews first in order to become Christians second.

Regarding dietary issues, they were given few things to adhere to so as to facilitate table fellowship with Jewish Christians in order to avoid causing offenses (vs. 19-21). The things they were to avoid were eating blood, eating meat sacrificed to idols, and meats that had been strangled (vs. 20, 29). Abstention from blood was enjoined by the Noahide Law (Gen. 9:4) and the Mosaic Law (Lev. 17:14), so this wasn't a new prohibition. It was reinforced because Gentiles were not under the Mosaic Law, they were lapse on the Noahide Law and did not generally follow that principle. Eating meat sacrificed to idols, at face value, would have been showing homage to that idol, so the apostles enjoined that as well because this would have caused great offense for the Jewish Christian whose conscience would have been very sensitive to those things. (We will look at this in 1 Corinthians chapters 8 and 10 and see how Paul dealt with this matter.) Eating strangled meat would have caused offense to Jewish Christians too because it was the same as eating blood. Blood was a delicacy among Gentiles. They would strangulate the animal to retain all of its blood instead of draining the blood out as the kosher law for the Jews require (Deut. 12:23-24).[300]

Sexual immorality was forbidden because seeing that Gentiles were not required to keep the Jewish Law regarding fornication, they may have thought that Christian liberty included being allowed to indulge the flesh. Paul explicitly talks about this in Romans 8. This prohibition against sexual immorality also prohibited idolatrous prostitution. Temple prostitution was prevalent and accepted among

---

[300] *The Wycliffe Bible Commentary* notes, "**Things strangled**. Meats from which the blood had not been properly removed. Such meat was considered a delicacy by many pagans. **Blood** refers to the pagan custom of using blood as a food. The last two requirements involved the same offense, for the Jew who believed that "the life is in the blood" (Lev 17:11) regarded the eating of any blood particularly offensive. This decree was issued to the Gentile churches not as a means of salvation but as a basis for fellowship, in the spirit of Paul's exhortation that those who were strong in faith should be willing to restrict their liberty in such matters rather than offend the weaker brother (Rom. 14:1-23; I Cor. 8:1-13)."---*The Wycliffe Bible Commentary: New Testament*, ed. Charles F. Pfeiffer and Everett Falconer Harrison (Chicago: Moody Press, 1962), Acts 15:20.

Gentiles. It was a form of idolatry that was very offensive to the Jews. The dietary prohibitions were necessary to facilitate fellowship among Jews and Gentile Christians because the Jews were ubiquitous and were still adhering to the Mosaic Law (vs. 21). But outside of these minimal prohibitions to facilitate fellowship, Gentile Christians were not expected to adhere to the Mosaic Law, especially the dietary laws, as part of their faith in Christ and salvation. It was also concluded that teaching points of law to the Gentiles was to subvert their souls. Here's the Adventists, doing just that. It is very sad that Adventists have rejected and overruled this apostolic injunction and have made the dietary laws a necessary part of initial faith in Christ and a test of fellowship. Before one can become a baptized member of the SDA Church, one must agree to adhere to their doctrines, teachings, and practices. A set of 13 vows are used to ascertain this. Vow number 10 is specifically about the Old Covenant dietary laws, and other food-related issues, and asks:

> Do you believe that your body is the temple of the Holy Spirit; and will you honor God by caring for it, avoiding the use of that which is harmful, and *abstaining from all unclean foods*; from the use, manufacture, or sale of *alcoholic beverages*; from the use, manufacture, or sale of *tobacco in any of its forms for human consumption*; and from the misuse of or trafficking in narcotics or other drugs?[301] [Italics mine]

Adventists also make the dietary laws absolutely necessary for eschatological salvation. This was already proven at length in the previous chapter.

No food is existentially unclean

One of my favourite New Testament passages that deals with dietary issues is Romans 14. My first book was on it, so you can appreciate that I will not be dealing with it thoroughly here, as I have already done so. I will keep it very basic and show how this passage dismisses the Adventist Health Message.

Romans 14 is dealing with dietary issues and the holy days of

---

[301] *Seventh-day Adventist Church Manual*, Revised 2005, p. 33.

Judaism that were constant bones of contention between Jews and Gentiles. The church at Rome was made up of Jewish and Gentile Christians. We can imagine that there was constant friction among them over these issues. Paul seems to have been aware of this and expounded at length on this issue to foster better relations among them, and also to explain to them how to maintain Christian liberty. The passage expresses many things but I will only focus on the specific portions that reveal how untenable the Adventist dietary view is.

Paul begins with a call to receive one who is weak in faith and not to quarrel about opinions (vs. 1). Without letting us guess what these opinions were, over which there should be no quarrels but reception, Paul says, "One person believes he may eat anything, while the weak person eats only vegetables" (vs. 2). The issue was about food. One person had faith that would allow him to eat everything (this would be the Gentile), while the weaker person only ate vegetables (this would be the Jew).[302] Ironically, Adventists always portray themselves as being biblically stronger for their vegetarian views and diet but Paul says here that vegetarianism, especially the Adventist version, is a demonstration of weak faith.

In a church setting where some persons were eating anything indiscriminately, while others were abstaining on the grounds of weak faith and scruples, of course there would be tensions and a lot of judging. So Paul says, "Let not the one who eats despise the one who abstains, and let not the one who abstains pass judgment on the one who eats, for God has welcomed him" (vs. 3). He does not present either group as being wrong for being omnivorous or for being vegetarian. He accepts both groups and their convictions as valid. But he does caution against despising and judging by either party because God has welcomed both of them. In vs. 6, Paul was clear in his deliberations that in either eating everything or being a vegetarian, both groups did so in honor of the Lord. He says, "...The one who eats, eats in honor of the Lord, since he gives thanks to God, while the

---

[302] Jews ate meat as part of their staple diet and in their religious ceremonies. However, in contexts, especially among Gentiles, where meats were offered to idols before being sold in meat markets and were not prepared in a kosher way, conscientious Jews often opt for vegetarianism (Dan. 1:8-13).

one who abstains, abstains in honor of the Lord and gives thanks to God." Given how clear this passage is on dietary issues, I am flabbergasted how Adventists read this passage and still promote their Health Message. It is the antithesis of the principles expressed here. But as was shown, they have an inflexible commitment to Ellen White and what she says, and they do a lot of doublethink. They must do whatever mental tricks and biblical distortion of passages such as this to uphold and promote what she said.

In vs. 14 Paul says, "I know and am persuaded in the Lord Jesus that nothing is unclean in itself, but it is unclean for anyone who thinks it unclean." Whereas the Old Covenant Law had designated certain animals as clean and unclean for Jews, Paul is saying here that New Covenant faith in Jesus completely changes that setup. He says that he is persuaded "in the Lord Jesus" that nothing is existentially unclean and that considering something unclean is personal and subjective. He repeated this same thing in a different way in vs. 20 by saying "everything indeed is clean." These verses are completely overhauling the Old Testament clean and unclean designations.

Verse 17 says, "For the kingdom of God is not a matter of eating and drinking but of righteousness and peace and joy in the Holy Spirit." The Adventist Health Message has made the kingdom of God to be a matter of eating and drinking. But Paul says that diet is not the focus of the kingdom, which in actuality means that it does not matter what one chooses to eat and drink as a believer. However, one ought to be cautious not to cause offense to a brother or sister by what one eats in their presence (vs. 15). But what one eats does not matter. What matters is living a life of righteousness, peace, and joy in the Holy Spirit.

Eat whatever is sold in the meat market

1 Corinthians 8 is another major passage that deals with foods. This specific passage is about meat offered to idols, eating that meat in that idol's temple, and how the weak Corinthians brother's conscience could have been wounded if he saw a mature believer eating in an idol's temple. Paul explains that despite that idols have no real existence (vs. 4), yet a mature believer should avoid flippantly eating in their temple because that can give the impression

of showing deference and allegiance to that idol. Doing so will affect weaker believers and cause them to stumble. A very significant verse in this chapter is verse 8. It says, "Food will not commend us to God. We are no worse off if we do not eat, and no better off if we do." This statement dismisses the Adventist idea that foods somehow commend us to God and that we are better off or worse off spiritually, as believers, depending on what we eat. This is a major aspect of their Health Message, but Scripture debunks that view.

1 Corinthians 10:23-33 is another great pericope that challenges the Adventist Health Message. Paul laid down some other great principles regarding how we should fellowship with believers and unbelievers alike on the matter of diet. You can read the entire paragraph in your spare time, but for the purpose of this chapter I will only offer a few comments on vs. 25-27. Paul says:

> Eat whatever is sold in the meat market without raising any question on the ground of conscience. 26For "the earth is the Lord's, and the fullness thereof." 27If one of the unbelievers invites you to dinner and you are disposed to go, eat whatever is set before you without raising any question on the ground of conscience.

Paul says they should eat "whatever" (all-inclusive adjective) that is sold in the meat market without raising any questions because the earth is the Lord's and everything in it. If an unbeliever invites a believer to dinner at their house, they should eat "whatever" (all-inclusive adjective again) that is set before them without asking questions.

The principle that Paul is enjoining is very similar to what Jesus had told His disciples in Luke 10:5-8. This passage and chapter 8 are closely related. They are talking about idolatry and how believers should conduct themselves before believers and unbelievers alike, without causing unnecessary offenses and stumbling by what they ate and when they ate. However, Paul was not restricting their liberty to eat anything they so desire, nor was he binding the Old Covenant food rules on them. He completely overhauled those as we see so far.

Gentiles sacrificed clean and unclean animals to their gods

Because Romans 14, 1 Corinthians 8, and 10:23-33 are so clear on food issues and also because they refute the Adventist Health Message, Adventists argue that they are not dealing with the dietary distinctions nor abolishing them. They claim that all three of these passages are dealing with clean foods that Gentiles sacrificed to their idols and that Paul was telling them that it was okay to eat those clean foods despite their being sacrificed to idols. By now, you can see that Romans 14 refutes this assumption of theirs. But there is something else that they don't seem to be aware of that also dismantles their warped argument and precipitous conclusion, and that is Gentiles in Corinth were not conscientious Jews who only offered clean foods as sacrifices to their idols, as the Jews did to Yahweh. In the biblical world, and specifically Corinth, Gentiles offered a variety of both clean and unclean animals to their deities.

After offering the animal sacrifice to their idol, they would take the rest of the meat to the meat market, which was usually close to the idol's temple, and then sell it for general consumption.[303] This is the same meat that Paul instructed believers to buy and eat, whatever that meat may have been! Andrew Brookes noted:

> More importantly, clean animals are those that can be offered to God in ritual worship, i.e. as animal sacrifices. Unclean ones cannot be so offered, and this was commonly because neighbouring peoples offered them to their own gods. The Hittites were known to sacrifice pigs to their gods. Such use of pigs lay at the heart of the infamous Abomination of Desolation and the persecution of the Jews linked to it as narrated in the Books of the Maccabees, around 165 BC. Antiochus IV Epiphanes, the (Greek) Seleucid king of the area sought to impose pagan worship on the Jews: he erected a statue of Zeus in the temple on the Jewish

---

[303] R. P. Martin notes, "The sacrifice was followed by a cultic meal, when the remainder of the consecrated food was eaten either in the precincts of the temple or at home. Sometimes the remaining food was sent to the market to be sold (1 Cor. 10:25)."---R. P. Martin, "Meats Offered To Idols," in *New Bible Dictionary*, ed. D. R. W. Wood, I. H. Marshall, A. R. Millard et al., 3rd ed. (Leicester, England; Downers Grove, IL: InterVarsity Press, 1996), p. 497.

altar and offered sacrifices of pigs to it (1 Macc. 1:47). Jews were then made to eat the flesh of pigs–and most probably of such sacrificed pigs–or lose their lives.[304]

Pigs were a favoured ambrosia—food of the gods. Whereas for Jews they were considered unclean, this was not the case for Gentiles, specifically the Greeks. Austin Cline observes, "In contrast to Jewish tradition, the ancient Greeks did not regard the pig as unclean. It was, in fact, the preferred animal for making sacrifices at rituals of purification."[305] This is very significant because Corinth was a Greek city littered with temples and idols. Pigs were the most common animal sacrificed to them on a daily basis, after which the meat was taken to the meat market to be sold for consumption. Pork would have been the most accessible meat in a Corinthian meat market. It is this same meat that Paul said to eat without asking questions. Patricia Donovan explains:

> In Greece…the pig served as a sacrificial animal, a votive offering to gods, especially those who preferred swine to a chicken or a hecatomb of oxen. Since protein was an important food group but less available than grains and vegetables, it was the rare pig whose entire self was consumed in the sacrificial flame. Instead, since that meat went bad quickly, it was important that freshly killed animals be distributed for food as efficiently as possible.[306]

Certain animals used for sacrifices were associated with certain gods. Dogs were sacrificed to Hecate, one of the goddesses of Hades. Among the other animals offered to their gods included sheep, goats, pigs, cattle, fish, and even birds.[307] Similar to the Greeks, the

---

[304] Andrew Brookes, *Biblical Beasts: Pig*, Sept. 5, 2011, https://www.english.op.org/godzdogz/biblical-beasts-pig (Date accessed Jan. 30, 2021).

[305] Austin Cline, *Methods of Sacrifice in Ancient Greece*, June 11, 2018, https://www.learnreligions.com/method-of-sacrifice-in-ancient-greece-4079925 (Date accessed Jan. 30, 2021).

[306] Patricia Donovan, *Hog Wild in Athens B.C.E.! Role of Pigs in Social and Religious Life Provides Insights into Ancient Greece,* August 16, 2000, http://www.buffalo.edu/news/releases/2000/08/4837.html (Date accessed Jan. 30, 2021).

Romans offered dogs to Robigus, usually a red one, along with other red things, during the feast of Robigalia to avert disasters from their crops.[308] As I pointed out earlier, Gentiles were not scrupulous Jews. They did not offer only clean animals to their gods. They offered a variety of clean and unclean animals, which were then sold in the meat markets afterwards. The underlying fact in all of this is that even if it is true that those passages were only talking about foods sacrificed to idols, that still would not change what they say and mean regarding clean foods and unclean foods, and our ability to eat them because Gentiles offered unclean animals to their idols before selling them in the meat market.

Dot not let Adventists judge you over what you eat and drink

Colossians 2 deals a definitive and major blow to the Adventist Health Message. Paul says in vs. 16 that no one is to "…pass judgment on you in questions of food and drink…." This negates exactly what Adventists do about food and drink. They pass a lot of judgements on believers on those matters. But Paul says it ought not to be done. He says judgements ought not to be passed on them because "These are a shadow of the things to come, but the substance belongs to Christ." Food and drink distinctions and regulations are shadows that have Christ as their reality. The believer who has Christ does not need to be hung up on shadows.

In vs. 20-22, Paul asked a profound rhetorical question. He asked, "If with Christ you died to the elemental spirits of the world, why, as if you were still alive in the world, do you submit to regulations— [21]"Do not handle, Do not taste, Do not touch" [22](referring to things that all perish as they are used)—according to human precepts and teachings?" Given the fact that believers died with Christ to the elemental spirits of the world, they ought not to submit to regulations about foods and drinks that will perish as they are used. Being commanded to not handle, taste, nor touch certain

---

[307]https://erenow.net/ancient/ancient-greece-and-rome-an-encyclopedia-for-students-4-volume-set/390.php (Date accessed Jan. 30, 2021).

[308]https://penelope.uchicago.edu/~grout/encyclopaedia_romana/calendar/robigalia.html (Date accessed Jan. 30, 2021).

foods and drinks are human precepts and teachings that have no bearing nor authority in New Covenant faith. Adventists subscribing to "do not handle, do not taste, do not touch" are not following what the New Testament teaches. They are following the precepts and teachings of Ellen White on these things. This Scripture refutes that and presents that practice to be a bad thing, especially given that they are doing that for moral, spiritual, and salvational reasons.

Verse 23 is definitive on the emptiness of abstention from foods and drinks for moral and spiritual purposes. It says, "These have indeed an appearance of wisdom in promoting self-made religion and asceticism and severity to the body, but they are of no value in stopping the indulgence of the flesh." This conclusion perfectly diagnoses what Adventists do regarding food and drinks. They only appear to be wise, but are only promoting "self-made religion, asceticism, and severity to the body." They centre a major part of their religion on foods and drinks. They promote asceticism and severe treatment of their body by demanding total abstention from many types of foods and drinks. Some Adventists develop many vitamin and mineral deficiencies because they are brainwashed to not eat certain animals and animal products. Some are so extreme, based on what they read from Ellen White, that they often claim that they prefer to die before they eat or drink certain things, even if they were a last resort to save themselves and their families. I recall my days of being that extreme. I am so glad I know better now and I am disabused of such a mentality.

Despite the abstention and asceticism on their part, Paul concludes that "...they are of no value in stopping the indulgence of the flesh." Abstaining from certain foods and drinks do not prevent indulgences of the flesh as Adventists would want them to. Abstention does not stop them from overeating, being obese, swearing, committing adultery, lying, stealing, breaking the Sabbath, fornicating, nor from committing hordes of other "works of the flesh" (Gal. 5:19). There is no existential power in foods and drinks to curb sinful desires. But the way Ellen White and Adventists talk on these matters, one would think that becoming vegan or vegetarian means an automatic ticket to stop sinning. This passage says foods and drinks cannot stop self-indulgence. If only Adventists would stop mangling this passage in order to promote their false Ellen White-made religion and follow its injunction to not judge believers on their dietary choices. I doubt this will happen any time soon though.

The Adventist Health Message is a teaching of demons

1 Timothy 4:1-6 is another major passage that puts dietary issues in proper perspective and shows us what are the deep-seated issues and influences behind demands for believers to abstain from certain foods. In vs. 1 Paul says, "Now the Spirit expressly says that in later times some will depart from the faith by devoting themselves to deceitful spirits and teachings of demons." Before we are exposed to what this departure from the Faith looks like, the Holy Spirit warns that it is a devotion to deceitful spirits and teachings of demons. It is a deeply spiritual issue. In the Last Days, people will depart from the historical Christian faith by devoting themselves to lying spirits and teachings of demons.

We are told in vs. 2-3, "through the insincerity of liars whose consciences are seared, who forbid marriage and require abstinence from foods that God created to be received with thanksgiving by those who believe and know the truth." What these verses are revealing is that these demonic teachings will be propagated through hardened, insincere liars. These callous, insincere liars will forbid marriage (a great gift from God) and require abstinence from foods that God created. It is not my aim to discuss Ellen White and marital issues, although she did discourage marriages for a time.[309] I will only deal with what is pertinent to the subject at hand, which is abstinence from foods.

Teaching believers to abstain from certain foods is demonically influenced because God created all foods "to be received with thanksgiving by those who believe and know the truth." Through much wrangling of Leviticus 11 and other parts of Scripture, both Ellen White and her Adventist Church command persons to abstain from certain foods as part of their religious faith and salvation. As was shown, one of the Baptismal Vows of the Adventist Church

---

[309] See Dirk Anderson, *Forbidding Marriage*, https://www.nonsda.org/egw/egw78.shtml (Date accessed June 5, 2021).

requires any and all prospective church members to pledge to "…abstain from all unclean foods; from the use, manufacture, or sale of alcoholic beverages…" before they can become baptized members of the SDA Church.[310] Where this passage is concerned, this is a departure from the Christian faith, a devotion to deceitful spirits, and a teaching of demons.

The passage continues, "For everything created by God is good, and nothing is to be rejected if it is received with thanksgiving, for it is made holy by the word of God and prayer" (vs. 4-5). This is reaffirming what we have seen from previous passages already. There is no animal creature that is existentially bad or "unclean" (Rom. 14:14, 20) and therefore should not be eaten. They are all good for food and should not be rejected. They should be received with gratitude to God because they have been made holy by God's Word and our prayers. We have already seen that Mark 7, Acts 10, Romans 14, and 1 Corinthians 8 and 10 sanctify all foods for believers to eat. This passage is reaffirming this truth and warning us that teachings to the contrary are demonic and are a departure from the liberty that the Christian faith gives us on these matters.

After explaining this, Paul said to[311] Timothy, "If you put these things before the brothers, you will be a good servant of Christ Jesus, being trained in the words of the faith and of the good doctrine that you have followed" (vs. 6). In teaching and reminding the church about these things, Paul said that Timothy would be a good servant of Jesus who was being trained in the truths of the Christian faith and of its sound doctrines that he had been following. It is the responsibility of faithful pastor-teachers of the Gospel to instruct believers on these matters and warn them that any teaching that demands them to abstain from certain foods on moral and spiritual grounds is demonic and a departure from the Christian faith. Hebrews 13:9 similarly states, "Do not be led away by diverse and strange teachings, for it is good for the heart to be strengthened by grace, not by foods, which have not benefited those devoted to them." All of these New Testament passages clearly demolish the Adventist Health Message and put the Old Covenant food rules and

---

[310] *Seventh-day Adventist Church Manual*, Revised 2005, p. 33.
[311]

restrictions in proper perspective.

Flawed Adventist arguments and interpretations refuted

True to who they are, Adventists grasp at every straw in attempts to desperately reinterpret certain texts in order to uphold the false dietary teachings of Ellen White. They do this with three pivotal New Testament texts. The first is 2 Corinthians 6:17-18 which says, "Therefore go out from their midst, and be separate from them, says the Lord, and touch no unclean thing; then I will welcome you, [18]and I will be a father to you, and you shall be sons and daughters to me, says the Lord Almighty." At face value, this text seems to be a very strong text that supports the Adventist Health Message and the need to abstain from unclean things. The text does say "touch no unclean thing," and calls for believers to "be separate from them" as a condition for God to welcome us into His family. But as airtight as this text seems to be in supporting the Adventist Health Message and the promotion of dietary distinctions for believers under the New Covenant, it is not doing that at all. This is nothing but another readily available proof-text where Adventists ignore its context and use it to prop up their false doctrine. But as usual, context always dismantles their false assumptions and conclusions.

This text is not reinforcing the Old Covenant dietary restrictions and distinctions for Christians under the New Covenant. Nor is it making adherence to them a precondition for God to accept us into His family. The context of those two verses begins with vs. 14 and the underlying message of that verse that controls the rest of the paragraph is, "Do not be unequally yoked with unbelievers." Paul's concern and prohibition is over unequally yoked relationships between a believer and an unbeliever. The specific nature of these relationships is not explicitly given in the paragraph, but the principle is broad enough to apply to a variety of relationships in which believers can be intimately tied with unbelievers.

To further underscore the point, Paul asked several rhetorical questions to show that believers have no legitimate right to be united in intimate relationships and partnerships with unbelievers. He asked, "For what partnership has righteousness with lawlessness? Or what fellowship has light with darkness? What accord has Christ with Belial? Or what portion does a believer share with an unbeliever?

What agreement has the temple of God with idols? (vs. 14b-16a)."
Again, Paul's concern and admonition is about intimate relationships
between a believer and an unbeliever. He is issuing a strong
exhortation that those relationships should not be deliberately entered
into because of the great spiritual chasm that separates a believer
from an unbeliever. Paul is not concerned about foods at all in this
passage. He is not writing about dietary issues. He had already
spoken clearly about dietary issues in 1 Corinthians 8 and 10,
respectively, and abolished the Old Covenant clean and unclean
distinctions and prohibitions. I already proved this beyond a shadow
of a doubt in my brief expositions of those chapters.

In this passage, Paul is not contradicting the principles and
theology he had expounded on in 1 Corinthians 8 and 10. His main
focus in this paragraph is intimate relationships and partnerships
between the saved and the unsaved. The fundamental premise of his
rhetorical questions is that they are unwise, divergent, and they
essentially will not work out well, and therefore they should be
avoided. Paul then undergirds his strong exhortation against
unequally-yoked relationships by fusing several Old Testament
statements together into one, as one main quotation. He says:

> …as God said, "I will make my dwelling among them
> and walk among them, and I will be their God, and
> they shall be my people. Therefore go out from their
> midst, and be separate from them, says the Lord, and
> touch no unclean thing; then I will welcome you, and
> I will be a father to you, and you shall be sons and
> daughters to me, says the Lord Almighty" (cf. Exo.
> 29:45; Lev. 26:12; Eze. 11:20; Isa. 52:11; 2 Sam.
> 7:14; Isa. 43:6).

Where Paul is concerned, the "unclean thing" that must not be
touched is not pork, shrimp, crabs, lobsters, snakes, snails, vultures,
and all other previously unclean animals. Paul was very clear that
these animals are not existentially unclean, and therefore should not be
rejected (Rom. 14:14, 20; 1 Tim. 4:4-5). The "unclean thing" that
should not be touched that Paul is talking about is the unbeliever with
whom the believer should not be yoked and intimately paired. No
animal is ontologically unclean under the New Covenant. But

unconverted, unregenerate, and ungodly people are (Mark 7:20-23; Gal. 5:19-21; Rev. 21:27; 22:15), therefore intimate relationships and partnerships with them should be avoided at all costs. Paul then closed this exhortation by saying, "Since we have these promises, beloved, let us cleanse ourselves from every defilement of body and spirit, bringing holiness to completion in the fear of God" (2 Cor. 7:1).

The second one is 3 John 2 which says, "Beloved, I pray that all may go well with you and that you may be in good health, as it goes well with your soul." Adventists read this and conclude that God wants us to be healthy and we will achieve this by following the Old Testament food distinctions and rules as part of our health regime. But this interpretation is so wild and foreign to the text. This text is not reinforcing the dietary rules of the Old Covenant. There is absolutely nothing in this text, nor the entire passage, that gives the remotest idea that John is discussing dietary rules as a means of achieving health. John is not discussing food rules at all. This text is a greeting! John greets Gaius (vs. 1) cordially expressing his desire that Gaius be holistically well and be in good health, in the same way that it is going well with his soul. That is all we see in this passage, a cordial greeting, nothing more.

The last text that I have seen some Adventists use to push the Old Covenant food rules is Revelation 18:2. The text reads, "And he called out with a mighty voice, "Fallen, fallen is Babylon the great! She has become a dwelling place for demons, a haunt for every unclean spirit, a haunt for every unclean bird, a haunt for every unclean and detestable beast." They argue that because Revelation is the last book of the Protestant Christian Bible and the fact that it mentions "unclean bird" and "unclean and detestable beast," then this justifies the continued food distinctions and dietary restrictions. By now you should easily see that this is very bad hermeneutics and a very poor argument on their part.

The mention of unclean birds and beasts is not in a dietary context. These animals are not mentioned as things to avoid eating. They are mentioned as symbols that represent demons and unclean spirits. John is using unclean birds and beasts to symbolize demons in this apocalyptic book. Doing so is not far-fetched, revolutionary, nor is it intended to reinforce the Old Testament dietary rules and distinctions. John equally uses unclean animals to represent Jesus and holy beings in Revelation. They are not in a dietary context nor is it his intention to present Jesus and those holy beings as being repulsive.

In Revelation 4:6-7, John saw four living, holy creatures around the throne of God. They worship Him ceaselessly. Interestingly, the semblance of two of those four holy, living creatures is that of two unclean animals, a lion and an eagle (Lev. 11:13, 27). In Revelation 5:5-6, John sees Jesus as both a lion and a lamb, an unclean and a clean creature. Lions were not to be eaten by Jews under the Old Covenant food rules. It is a feline and walks on its paws and is therefore unclean (Lev. 11:27). Yet Jesus is represented as an unclean lion. Does this fact mean that we should not eat Jesus' flesh and drink His blood (John 6:53-56)? Does this mean that we are eating an unclean lion when we eat the flesh and imbibe the blood of Jesus? By using unclean beasts and birds to represent demons, does it mean that when we eat those animals we are eating demons or being demon possessed? "Absolutely not!" is the answer to these three questions. Revelation is a highly symbolic book. It uses unclean animals to represent both holy and unholy beings, without any reference nor implication to diet. The New Testament removes the Old Covenant dietary distinctions and restrictions for Christians. Every major passage that I expounded on in this chapter singularly, and collectively, destroys the Adventist Health Message.

Conclusion

In this volume, I showed what Adventists believe and teach about the respective doctrines covered and why they believe the way they do. In addition to showing what they believe, I refuted those beliefs and their arguments and showed them to be unbiblical, unorthodox, and some heretical. In Chapter One, I have shown the sketchy roots and theological system of Adventism. In Chapter Two, I explained who Ellen G. White was and what she means to Adventists. She is their authoritative prophetess whose role and function in their denominational life and doctrines is sacrosanct. They believe that she is on par with Scripture and even above Scripture. Their doctrines, interpretations of Scripture, and peculiar views are grounded in her writings and not Scripture contextually exegeted. She was a false prophet.

In Chapter Three, we looked into their Investigative Judgement doctrine. It is heretical, contradictory to the Gospel, undermines it, and fraught with crippling psychological fear and salvational uncertainty. Chapter Four contrasted the difference between the biblical Gospel and the Investigative Judgement. We saw clearly that Jesus went into the Most Holy Place at His ascension and not on October 22, 1844 as Adventists believe and teach. In Chapter Five, *Let's Move God's Throne!*, I had shown the false vision and theory of Ellen White that gave God two thrones in the sanctuary and had Him and Jesus moving from the one in the Holy Place to the one in the Most Holy Place in 1844. This vision, by her own admission, proceeded from Satan because it not only contradicts Scripture but also it has Jesus functioning as a Levitical priest in heaven. And in addition to this, it has Satan occupying God's vacant throne in the Holy Place. Her heretical views are not taught in Scripture.

In Chapter Six, we looked at the fact that Scripture does not support the idea that God began investigating the lives of all believers, beginning with Adam, to determine if they are worthy of salvation after the Investigative Judgement is concluded. The saints were saved, worthy of salvation, and commended by God way before Adventists concocted this doctrine. The saints are in heaven right now and will not be evicted and processed through the Investigative Judgement to determine their destiny. In the Investigative Judgement, God has the sins of every believer recorded and stored in heaven to be held against us and to condemn some of us. But Chapter Seven dispelled that notion and proved that God has forgiven us, blotted out our sins, and does not hold them against us, nor even remembers them. Chapter Eight asked the question," Can believers know that they are saved right now?" And the answer was a resounding "Yes!" We know that we are saved by Jesus right now. In the Investigative Judgement, the assurance of salvation is not possible, but in the biblical Gospel we are currently saved. In Chapter Nine, I explored "11 Faulty Hermeneutical Principles and Assumptions of Seventh-day Adventists and How to Refute Them."

I switched gears in Chapter Ten and looked into an aspect of Adventist Christology. They believe that Jesus is Michael the Archangel, but the biblical and historical facts say that He is not. In Chapter Eleven, I demonstrated that Jesus is Michael the Archangel for Adventists because of their Arian roots and views about Jesus. Their Arianism is condemned by Scripture and orthodox Christianity. In Chapter Twelve, I surveyed the biblical facts and proved beyond a shadow of a doubt that our Lord Jesus Christ is not Michael the Archangel. Chapter Thirteen: *Dem Goats: Who Is Our Scapegoat, Satan Or Jesus?* concluded that Jesus is our scapegoat and not Satan as SDAs believe and teach. The concept of Satan being the scapegoat is heretical. In Chapter Fourteen, I showed the heart of

Adventist works-driven theology of sinless perfectionism. This doctrine is not taught in Scripture. In Chapter Fifteen, I refuted their sinless perfectionism theology. If you did not really know what the Adventist Health Message is all about, Chapter Sixteen explained it and showed the foundation and purpose of it. Adventists stress health and vegetarianism for moral, spiritual, and salvational reasons, and that is unbiblical. Chapter Seventeen closed this volume with a biblical survey of the Levitical dietary rules and refutations to Adventist arguments and assumptions.

As you studied this first volume of **Hiding in Plain Sight: The False Doctrines of Seventh-day Adventism**, I hope that you would have concluded that Adventist doctrines have been truly hiding in plain sight and that they are false, dangerously false, and Christians should stay away from their doctrines, pray for them, and seek to preach the biblical Gospel to them as the opportunities avail themselves.

But this volume, dear reader, is not all there is to Adventist false doctrines. We are just beginning the trek down this rabbit hole. This rabbit hole runs deep. In volume two, I will systematically explore and refute Adventist doctrines on ornaments, fashion, and cosmetics; tithing; the Ten Commandments and the Sabbath; Colossians 2:16-17 and the Weekly Sabbath; the Seal of God; the Mark of the Beast; Sunday Laws; the Remnant Church; how Adventists view Protestant churches; and their sneaky evangelistic tactics. Be sure to anticipate volume two. It will be just as exciting, revelatory, thorough, engaging, and equipping as this one.

Made in United States
North Haven, CT
20 September 2023

41766837R00187